SPIRITUAL DISCIPLINES FOR EVERYDAY LIVING

with

Leader's Guide

Ronald V. Wells

Originally published by Character Research Press, Schenectady, New York.

Third printing R. D. C. Books, June 1987
Library of Congress Catalog Card Number: 87-90606
ISBN: 0-9618701-0-9
Printed in the United States of America
Fourth Printing

ACKNOWLEDGMENTS

The author wishes to thank the following publishers, agents and authors for permission to reproduce quotations used from copyrighted material. All possible care has been taken to trace the ownership of every item quoted and to make full acknowledgment for its use. If any errors have accidently occurred, they will be corrected with full apology in subsequent editions, provided notification is sent to the author at Box 255, Kelly Road, East Chatham, New York 12060.

A & W Publishers, Inc., from *How to Help Your Child Have a Spiritual Life,* by Annette Hollander, M.D. Copyright © 1980 by Annette Hollander.

Curtis Brown Ltd. from *The World In Tune,* by Elizabeth Gray Vining, Copyright © 1954 by Elizabeth Gray Vining.

Corinth Books from *The Journal of John Woolman,* Introduction by Frederick B. Tolles. Copyright © 1961.

• Crossroad Publishing Co., from *Christian Maturity,* by Bernard Häring, translated by Arlene Swidler. Copyright © 1967.

J. M. Dent & Sons Ltd., from *Essays and Addresses on the Philosophy of Religion*, Vol. II (1926), from *Selected Letters 1896-1924* (1927), from *Letters of Baron Friedrich von Hugel to a Niece* (1929).

• Dimension Books, Inc., by Adrian van Kaam and Susan Muto, from: *Spirituality and the Gentle Life,* Adrian van Kaam, Copyright © 1974.

On Being Involved, Adrian van Kaam, Copyright © 1970.
On Being Yourself, Adrian van Kaam, Copyright © 1972.
Steps Along the Way, Susan Muto, Copyright © 1975.
Approaching the Sacred, Susan Muto, Copyright © 1973.

• Doubleday and Company, Inc., from *Reaching Out* by Henri J. M. Nouwen, Copyright © 1975 by Henri J. M. Nouwen.

• E. P. Dutton Publishers, from *Touchstones of Reality,* by Maurice Friedman, Copyright © 1972, by Maurice Friedman. From *Concerning the Inner Life with The House of the Soul,* by Evelyn Underhill, Copyright, E. P. Dutton, 1926.

• Fortress Press, from *The Valley of the Shadow,* by Hanns Lilje, Copyright © 1950, Fortress Press.

• Gyldendal Publishers, from *With the Door Open,* by Johannes

Anker Larsen, Copyright, 1931, published in the U.S.A. by Macmillan Publishing Co., Inc., 1931. Originally published in Denmark under the title *For Aaben Dor* (1926).

- Harper and Row Publishers, Inc. (approx. 1300 words, passim) from *Meister Eckhart: A Modern Translation,* by Raymond Bernard Blakney, Copyright, 1941, by Harper and Row, Publishers, Inc.

(approx. 2400 words, passim) from *A Testament of Devotion,* by Thomas R. Kelly. Copyright, 1941, by Harper and Row, Publishers, Inc. (approx 2200 words, passim) from *The Eternal Promise,* by Thomas Kelly. Copyright © 1966, by Richard M. Kelly.

(approx. 3000 words, passim) from *Letters of the Scattered Brotherhood,* edited by Mary Strong. Copyright, 1948, by Harper and Row, Publishers, Inc.

(approx. 1100 words, passim) from *Work and Contemplation* by Douglas V. Steere, Copyright © 1957 by Douglas V. Steere.

(approx. 200 words) from *Soul Friend: The Practice of Christian Spirituality* by Kenneth Leech, Copyright © 1977, by Kenneth Leech.

(approx. 900 words) from *A Place for You* by Paul Tournier, Copyright © 1968, by Paul Tournier.

(approx. 80 words) from *Purity of Heart* by Søren Kierkegaard, translated by Douglas V. Steere. Copyright 1938, 1948 by Harper and Row, Publishers, Inc.

(approx. 250 words) from *Christian Perfection,* by François Fénelon, Edited by Charles F. Whiston, Translated by Mildred Whitman Stillman. Copyright, 1947, by Harper and Row, Publishers, Inc.

- Jay Michael Barrie, Executor Estate of Gerald Heard, from *Training for a Life of Growth*, by Gerald Heard. Copyright © 1959, by Gerald Heard.
- Cornelia Brunner, from "Betty, a Way of Individuation," *Inward Light*, Number 37, Fall 1950, pp. 20-25. Used by permission of Charles Perry, Co-editor.

Verlag Josef Knecht, from *The Prison Meditations of Father Alfred Delp*, by Alfred Delp. Taken from "Im Angesicht de Todes" © 1965 by Verlag Josef Knecht, 6000 Frankfurt am Main.

Alfred A. Knopf, from *Men Who Have Walked With God,* by Sheldon Cheney, Copyright © 1946, Sheldon Cheney.

Markings, Dag Hammarskjöld, translated by Leif Sjoberg and W. H. Auden, Copyright © 1964, Alfred A. Knopf Inc., and Faber and Faber, Ltd.

- Longman Group Limited, from *Personal Religion and the Life of Devotion*, by W. R. Inge, Copyright © 1924, from *The School of Charity*, by Evelyn Underhill. Copyright © 1934 by Evelyn Underhill.

Macmillan Publishing Co., Inc., from *Mysticism East and West,* by Rudolph Otto, Copyright © 1932, by Macmillan Publishing Co., Inc., renewed 1960 by Margaret Ottmer, from *Letters and Papers from Prison,* Revised and Enlarged Edition by Dietrich Bonhoeffer, Copyright © 1953, 1967, 1971 by SCM Press Ltd.

- New Directions, from *New Seeds of Contemplation,* by Thomas Merton, Copyright © 1961, by The Abbey of Gethsemani Inc.
- W. W. Norton and Co., Inc., Publishers, from *Love and Will,* by Rollo May, Copyright © 1969, by W. W. Norton and Co., Inc.
- Penguin Books Ltd. (approx. 1000 words) from *The Cloud of Unknowing,* translated by Clifton Wolters. (Penguin Classics 1961), pp. 53, 53-54, 59-60, 61, 83-84, 85. Copyright © Clifton Wolters 1961.
- Priory Press, Inc. Thomas C. Donlan for the Priory Press, from *The Exemplar: Life and Writings of Blessed Henry Suso, OP,* Copyright © 1962, The Priory Press.

Charles Scribner's Sons, Publishers, from: *The New Being,* Paul Tillich, Copyright © 1955, Paul Tillich; copyright renewed, 1983 Hannah Tillich.

Dag Hammarskjöld: A Spiritual Portrait, by Sven Stolpe, Copyright © 1966. Sven Stolpe.

I and Thou, by Martin Buber, translated by Walter Kaufmann, Copyright © 1970. Charles Scribner's Sons.

A Diary of Readings, by John Baillie, Copyright © 1955 by John Baillie; copyright renewed 1983 Ian Fowler Baillie.

SCM Press, from *The School of Prayer,* Olive Wyon, Copyright © 1943 SCM Press. Published by Westminster Press 1944.

- Search Press, Ltd., from *Meditations on the Love of God,* Jean Nicholas Grou, S. J., London: Published 1928, 1938, 1948 by Burns, Oates and Washbourne, Ltd.
- Douglas V. Steere, from *On Beginning from Within*. Published by Harper and Row Publishers, Inc. Copyright © 1942 assigned to Douglas V. Steere, from a letter by Friedrich von Hugel supplied by Emelia Fogelklou Norlind.
- Mrs. Howard Thurman, from *Deep Is the Hunger,* Howard Thurman, Copyright © 1951, Mrs. Howard Thurman.
- Viking Penguin, Inc., Excerpts from *The Medium, the Mystic and the Physicist: Toward a General Theory of the Paranormal*, by Lawrence LeShan, Copyright © 1966, 1973, 1974 by Lawrence LeShan. An Esalen Book.
- Editorial Atlantida S.A. from *The Fallow Land,* by Constancio C. Vigil. Copyright, Editorial Atlantida S.A., Buenos Aires, Argentina. Published in the U.S.A. by Harper and Brothers, Publishers n.d.
- Westminster Press, from *Prayer and Personal Religion,* by John Coburn, Copyright © MCMLVII, by W. L. Jenkins.
- Whiston, Charles F., from *Teach Us to Pray,* by Charles F. Whiston. Copyright © 1948, by Charles Whiston.
- Tessa Sayle, Agent for Evelyn Underhill: Copyright © 1933 by Evelyn Underhill from *Mixed Pasture.* Copyright © 1926 by Evelyn Underhill, from *Concerning the Inner Life with The House of the Soul*. Copyright © 1953, by Evelyn Underhill, from *An Anthology of the Love of God.*

- Permission has also been granted by publishers to amend the masculine language in the selections quoted. These amendations are shown in bold face type. A number of publishers refused permission to amend quotations on the ground that authors must be quoted exactly as they wrote. In some instances, selections were eliminated entirely. In others, the selections were important to the discipline being considered and were included. Individual readers may read in appropriate amendations as they wish in these selections.

DEDICATION

To Kiersten Anne, Ian Woodburne, Lisa Marie and Vanessa Lynn Wells and all grandchildren everywhere, this book is dedicated in "faith, hope and love."

PERMISSION

I am indebted to my friend David Finn for permission to use his beautiful painting for the cover of this fourth printing of my book.

This splendid painting represents David Finn's own deep spiritual insight which came from reading T. S. Eliot's *Four Quartets* and being inspired by certain lines such as these which resulted in this painting:

"Time past and time future. Point to one end which is always present."

Thank you David Finn for showing us how poetry and painting reveal the life of the spirit.

How the Cover of This Book Speaks To Its Content

These Spiritual Disciplines for Everyday Living are for you to discover realistic and workable spiritual truths from some of the great religious leaders and thinkers from the **past**. These disciplines will also be valid for our spiritual maturing in the **future**.

But most important of all they provide insight and inspiration for all those who wish to live creatively in the **present**.

RONALD V. WELLS

Ronald V. Wells was graduated from:
East High School, Cleveland, Ohio January 1931
Denison University, A.B. 1935
Crozer Theological Seminary, B.D. 1938
Columbia University, Ph.D. in Philosophy, 1942

From 1938 - 1952 he served as senior minister of the First Baptist Church, Somerville, New Jersey, First Baptist Church, Bridgeport, Connecticut and the First Baptist Church, Ames, Iowa. This was followed by ten years as Executive Secretary of the Division of Christian Higher Education for the American Baptist Churches, U.S.A.

From 1962-70 Dr. Wells was President of Crozer Theological Seminary, then President of Sioux Falls College 1970 - 1974. From 1974-76 Dr. Wells was Vice President for Educational Affairs at the Crozer-Chester Medical Center, Chester, Pennsylvania, and then served for the next three and one half years as the Director of the Major Mission Fund of the United Presbyterian Church, U.S.A.

Over the years, the author taught courses in Philosophy and Religion at the University of Bridgeport and Iowa State University. At his own graduate school Crozer Theological Seminary he taught Homiletics, The Pastoral Office, and first offered the seminar in Spiritual Disciplines for Everyday Living. Since then he had directed these seminars at Princeton Theological Seminary, Pittsburgh Theological Seminary, Andover Newton Theological School and Sioux Falls College. Concurrently Dr. Wells has directed these seminars for church groups at Shadyside Presbyterian Church and St. Andrew's Episcopal Church in Pittsburgh, Pennsylvania, at Second Baptist Church in Wilmington, Delaware, First Baptist Church in Sioux Falls, South Dakota, First Baptist Church in Pittsfield, Massachusetts and First Baptist Church in Bridgeport, Connecticut.

He was senior consultant for Marts and Lundy, Financial Development Consultants. Dr. Wells is also available to conduct seminars at Seminaries for Master of Divinity, Doctor of the Ministry or Continuing Education classes, and with interested church groups. For availability and scheduling write the author at 3030 Park Ave., Suite 9W9, Bridgeport, CT 06604 or call (203) 373-6661.

TABLE OF CONTENTS

TABLE OF CONTENTS

INTRODUCTION

This entire volume is your invitation to become an authentic, God-centered person. Such an invitation is possible for it is rooted and grounded in the stunning fact that faith and theology can be translated into creative, mature Christian living. If this sounds like a firm conviction, it is; for all of this has been validated for me in forty years of following the disciplines of the life of the spirit.

This volume assumes that each reader has his or her own theological perspective within the broad spectrum of the Judeo-Christian tradition. Therefore this work does not argue a particular theology, nor seek to convert persons to that theological position. Its chief purpose is to provide insight and enrichment for one's own personal growth in spiritual experience and such theological understanding as may evolve under the guidance of God. The single theological grounding upon which this entire volume rests is the understanding that the living God is graciously available to any and all who seek in these disciplined ways to be related to God.

My pilgrimage began in the early 1940's when another minister and I discovered that our preaching was too academic. When we talked of God, our insights were theological arguments "about" rather than personal experience with God. In search of experience, in addition to continually living with the Bible, we turned to the writings of the saints and spiritual counselors whose testimonies and personal experience with God's presence offered insights as to how the presence may be found.

Johannes Anker Larsen, a Danish literary critic and novelist, in writing of his own spiritual pilgrimage, refers to these devotional classics as "family documents" to signify a collection of like-minded writings with verified experiences that testify to our oneness in the life of prayer, and the discovery of the presence of the living God.[1]

As my colleague and I read these "family documents," we found that the basic truths of our religious heritage emerged in

[1]Johannes Anker Larsen, *With the Door Open,* translated by Erwin and Pleasaunce von Gaisberg, with a Foreword by V. Grönbech (New York: Macmillan Co., 1931).

these readings as disciplines and characteristics of the spiritual life; first, to be understood as truth; then to be practiced; and finally, to become part and parcel of our essential selves.

At this same time, and because of this enriching and maturing process, I suggested to our college-age young adult group in our church the formation of a small disciplined group who would meet one night each week with one objective: to reflect, pray and act upon Paul's command, "overcome evil with good."[2]

For eight months, nine of us came together Monday nights for three hours. We read from the "family documents" and shared insights in our search for the meaning of Paul's clear-cut admonition to overcome evil with good. We learned the discipline of prolonged silence and of corporate prayer.

Out of our reflective discourse, reading, and prayer, there came action. We spent an unhurried time discovering and defining "evil" as experienced where each individual worked. A dental technician, for example, was up against the incessant, emotional demands of people who were hurting, irritated, and anxious. A dietitian in one of our hospitals was confronted with the stealing of food and supplies by kitchen employees--all under the complacent acquiescence of a weak administrator. A draughtsman worked under a departmental manager who, threatened by the bright inventive thrust of younger men under him, became a little dictator who operated a rigid, unimaginative department. In confronting these and other such realities, our definition of evil became clearer and more inclusive; we saw all of this as human action in need of being overcome with good, and we decided upon those initial steps which could be tried in beginning such transformation.

Each week we explored the next steps in overcoming the evil each individual experienced; we reviewed the success or failure of our previous decisions as to methodology which had been tried; and we charted the specific actions we agreed were worth trying in the new week's work. Slowly and yet with some degree of consistency, this alternation between reflection, prayer and meditation in the group and action by individuals at work proved that evil could be overcome with good. The departmental manager was provided with new ways of working positively with

[2]Romans 12:21.

the bright young men under him, and anxious, hurting dental patients experienced a more sensitive, caring receptionist.

For myself these experiences set the direction for the rest of my life. Exploring the "family documents" led me to make the acquaintance of many more of the writers in this field. I haunted the secondhand book stores and gradually built a working library of these "family documents" many of which were then out of print.

I discovered that the entire mystical tradition of a disciplined spiritual life is the one common factor in most of the great religions of the world. Because there is so much available in the writings of Eastern religions and since Protestants have generally ignored this tradition, I focused on the "family documents" in the Judeo-Christian tradition.

In the midst of all my reading, I became aware of the recurrence of certain ideas: the practice of the presence of God, humility, love, joy, attachment and detachment, peace, gentleness, and courage. I selected passages according to some of these themes and compiled a concentration of ideas which are the foundation for living a disciplined spiritual life that is centered in God.

Over the years, I have carefully expanded and edited my collection of ideas to become a source-text for use by individuals alone or in seminars in graduate theological seminaries and in churches. The focus is on eight ideas or disciplines: interrelatedness, creative solitude, the practice of the presence of God, humility, love, attachment and detachment, joy, and how then we hasten unto God and into the world. Since nearly three hundred persons have lived with this book, either individually or in a seminar experience, the following guidelines have emerged as helpful ways of approaching these spiritual disciplines.

Design of the Book

The Introduction, Chapters I and II provide the essential orientation and tools for preparing each individual for what has proven to be a rich and rewarding experience in spiritual growth.

Chapters III through X each present one of these disciplines of the spirit, for reflection, understanding and action. Each chapter has three sub-headings and under each heading is the following: first, my own writing which attempts to put the spotlight on the central idea at hand; second, a series of selections from the "family documents"; and third, questions and suggestions for reflection and action.

Chapter XI provides an additional rich treasury of selections from the "family documents" for personal reflection. These selections conform to the threefold division of each chapter: III through X.

The Bibliography is a selected listing of many of the standard works referred to in this book as well as others which are basic to the subject of the Spiritual Life, Mysticism, and Prayer. Those using this bibliography may want to discover new editions of some of these older works which are now available, and also be aware that there are many new and important works on this subject that are being published by many of the religious presses in America.

The Appendix: A Leader's Guide provides suggestions for professors, ministers and lay persons who wish to conduct a seminar on this subject and who plan to use this book as the basic source-text for study. It also offers suggestions for individual use by persons who wish to undertake a personal pilgrimage in exploring these disciplines of the life of the Spirit.

It is important to know that it is not wise to read this volume through as one reads a novel only to end up by saying, "I have finished that book." With this volume, it is best to take a chapter at a time and live with it long enough in a steady, unhurried pace, to experience enrichment through understanding and practice. This is like the difference between surface swimming from point to point and deep-sea diving.

Especially in church groups there are individuals whose time for reading this kind of "religious writing" has been limited. At first their reaction is that this is too difficult, or too dry. However, it is the testimony from a number of such persons that once they decided to stick with it, they were immersed in new insights and expanding vision.

How To Read and Use the Contents of Each Chapter

There is a quiet progression in each of the divisions. First, regard my own writing as an attempt to begin the enrichment process, for this writing is designed to stretch our minds and imagination into a fuller grasp of the meaning of each of these disciplines. Let this be a springboard into the reading of the selections from the "family documents" which come next.

Second, read through the selections noting the ones that impress you the most. Then begin the much slower process of taking those that appeal to you, and live with them reflectively until they come alive for you. Do not feel under any pressure to have every quotation be of supreme importance to you after the first reading. As you continue to re-read these selections, some which at first reading made no impression may come alive, and you will wonder how you could have missed it the first time around.

Here is an illustration of how to probe the depths of meaning from any one of the quotations. Turn to Chapter XI in **More Selections for Chapter V,** Selection #11. Read it through, and ask, what is the central idea in this quotation from Evelyn Underhill? Then rewrite the entire quotation in your own words. Here is how it came out in my re-write:

> Our entire spiritual life must be centered in God's reality. God's living presence is available to us. How? Perpetual turning, losing ourselves (even that is part of life in God), setting aside our most pressing work or practical problems--even our sins and failures (and our achievements) in order to be free to live with God. All this enables us to keep an awed, adoring sense of divine mysteries, in order to begin to recognize and be properly overwhelmed by this beginning knowledge.
>
> This disciplined inner life of the spirit, we then realize, can and does transmit and supernaturalize our lives in all ways and at all times. This is possible because the loving sense of God--so far beyond us--yet so close to us, keeps us truly humble and thus can

move us into trust and loyal love expressed in our life of prayer.

After you complete your paraphrase, then reflect about its meaning. Let the original selection and your rewrite lead you to ask, "when and where have I experienced this loving presence?" If never, "how do I imagine the dawn breaking in upon me? Where have I caught glimpses of the Divine presence in other persons' lives or experienced it in great art, music or literature, novels, plays, poetry? How could I begin my own turning; letting go of my possessive hold? How can I set aside for temporary periods practical problems or pressing work, long enough to let the loving presence of God fill one of the locks in the river of my life? How can I offer up my sin and failure to be freed of their burden of guilt in the loving forgiveness of God?"

Third, this kind of meditative grappling with these selections brings deeper insight and understanding which can provide a broader foundation for beginning the kind of reflection that leads to action. Hence, the third part of each sub-heading is entitled Reflection and Action. This section is designed to move each of us to an application and practice of spiritual disciplines. Persons involved in seminars are encouraged to share with the group the results of their attempts to apply these insights in the practice of everyday living. Persons working at this alone will want to take time to reflect about what happened when they attempted to put into practice some of these new insights.

Whether you are alone or in a seminar, this threefold approach will enrich your understanding of each of these disciplines, and through experimentation will further demonstrate their validity and viability.

As individual persons have completed the first intensive study of the entire book, many have discovered for themselves the deep interconnection between each of these disciplines, how in a very real sense they are dependent upon each other. Some have also caught the first glimpse of what these disciplines could contribute to an emerging creative and more mature lifestyle. Little wonder some have said "yes" to all of this as a lifetime adventure for themselves.

How To Begin a Lifetime Adventure

As you work with the material in this book, decide to take each discipline with you into your daily routine, attempting to live under the new insights that have come to you, being open to the evidence in your own life and in the lives of others as to how the discipline or lack of it, affects all human contacts each day. Then come back to further reading, reflection, and meditation to seek further enlightenment about the true meaning and function of this particular discipline.

As you make your way through the entire volume, you will find that each one of the disciplines will continue to be an available resource for your action and reaction in many phases of your everyday living. Take them out into your world with you; then bring them back with all you have learned, and reflectively expand your understanding and your next plan of action, until discipline becomes lifestyle for you.

Many persons have found themselves operating on this out and back principle, and in so doing have found themselves turning again and again to this resource for further insight, clarification, reinforcement and validation.

For this reason, Chapter XI has been included to provide more selections from the "family documents." It should be said that in no way are these second choice--there were simply too many to include in the main body of the text. They were of equal importance to the others, and should be so regarded as you discover them in subsequent reading.

It is recommended that each participant consider keeping a "Personal Journal" to supplement the reading. Write about your own spiritual experiences, past or present. Add appropriate selections garnered from other reading you may be doing. Respond to the suggestions and questions that appealed to you in the reflection and action sections.

Two Ground Rules

Throughout the years, two ground rules have been basic to using this source-text individually or in a seminar group. The *first* rule to be adopted and practiced is to *refrain from being judgmental of all spoken and written word.* Our tendency is to reject or belittle any idea, especially if it is new and unfamiliar. If we are threatened by a new idea, we frequently withdraw in arrogance to the safe accepted dogmas of our past.

So deeply ingrained in us is this judgmental attitude, we found that in the seminars we had to shift consciously and with considerable effort to becoming non-judgmental if we were to become open and trusting.

If, for example, a comment by another is radically different from my prevailing viewpoint, my immediate reaction is to say "that's ridiculous." If another's observation is outside my own experience, it is very easy to dismiss it as "far out." Being non-judgmental requires a quick determined throttling of these usual reactions, and a turning to ask what is really being said by this other person?

Often when the non-judgmental spirit finally prevails, an individual will preface the sharing of an especially choice and cherished insight or experience with a statement spoken hesitatingly, "I want to tell you about--maybe I shouldn't--well yes, I guess I can trust you enough now to talk about it."

In our own private reflection it requires strong measures to curb this tendency toward immediate judgment against ourselves. If, for example, we have walked the long road of utter loneliness, our immediate reaction to considering the discipline of creative solitude, which would take us beyond the trauma of loneliness, is to reject the whole section as being meaningless. What we really mean is that we are afraid it will be too painful to consider this new idea. When dealing with ourselves it is essential that we set aside all those judgments and assumptions we carry within ourselves.

An adventure in truth speaking is the *second* ground rule. All written or spoken word is to be understood as being an individual's best attempt to state truth as he or she sees it. This puts us all under the discipline of thinking at least twice before we speak. It also creates the spirit in which the truth of any idea can begin to be discovered as having many facets and dimensions far beyond my limited and self-universalizing approach.

When we begin by accepting another person's statement as

having validity and truth in it, we then begin to turn it over in relationship to our own understanding without prejudice toward rejection. In so doing we may well discover surprising similarities and just as surely we will come upon fresh insight to enrich our modest holdings. We may also come to the point where we cannot honestly see the truth of the other person's views. If this be so, then we are content to remain open and we refuse to be judgmental or exclusionist in attitude.

Keep these two rules in the foreground of your thinking and acting both in your personal reading and reflection and as you participate in any seminar experience.

ACKNOWLEDGEMENTS

Since this book has been in process over more than a decade, and has been through at least five revisions, many persons have been involved in its creation.

To Elinor Harris, Mary Pettilo, and Alice Bayley at Crozer Theological Seminary; Joan Barnette and Evelyn Olson Martin; Lydia Conklin, Carol Rivotti, Beth Knabel and Linda Smith at Pittsburgh Seminary for their careful and excellent typing, often under pressure to have another section done in time for seminars, I gratefully acknowledge their important contributions in the preparation of the manuscript.

My thanks go to Alfred Mann of the St. Andrews seminar, and Beth Knabel for many long hours in the tedious task of proofreading the entire fourth revision.

To my daughter Cathie Wells I am deeply indebted for her helpful insights concerning the content of the material and for typing the manuscript in its final form.

I wish to give special thanks to Larry Bowden, Harmon Bro, Karen Davis, Gordon Jackson, Douglas Steere, Edward Thornton, Lynn Leavenworth, Velma Carter, Joan Thatcher, Charles and Mary Flory, John Taylor, Lorne Gayles, Burr Gibson, and Lucia Beth Robinson for their constructive criticism and thoughtful insights given to me in time to be most helpful in this revision. Their friendships and support have sustained me in the arduous task of reworking the material.

For the privilege of having Penelope Morgan Colman edit this manuscript I am profoundly grateful. From her early pre-editing days of encouragement, through to this final reworking, she has provided serious and thoughtful analysis and has gently but firmly insisted on clarification, deletion as well as expansion. She has demonstrated great skill in being both open and creatively judgmental in forcing me to do my own careful rewriting. For her sustained and thorough work as well as her own personal involvement with the work itself, I offer my deep appreciation and thanks.

Without the quiet, loving support of my wife over a decade of involvement in the entire process, I would not have been able to complete this book. Attending seminars, discussing these seminars, and the content of the work, typing many parts and long hours of proofreading--for her part in all of this I am most especially grateful.

To all seminar participants in the five seminars at Crozer Theological Seminary, the one at Princeton Theological Seminary, one at Andover Newton Theological School, and the three at Pittsburgh Theological Seminary, and to those in the seminars at Second Baptist Church, Wilmington, Delaware, the Shadyside Presbyterian Church and the St. Andrews Episcopal Church of Pittsburgh, Pennsylvania, First Baptist Church of Pittsfield, Massachusetts and the First Baptist Church of Bridgeport, Connecticut, I am indebted for the many insights which have come from so many open and seeking persons. I am particularly grateful to them for their genuine involvement in demonstrating the many ways in which this pilgrimage with God can be very real within the groups and for each individual in personal practice.

Richard Gorsuch, president and administrative head of a Christian advertising agency in Sioux Falls, South Dakota, is a personal friend of the author, and was one of the participants of the Monday evening seminars growing out of the January interim seminar at Sioux Fall College.

Knowing of Richard's twenty-five years of creative, innovative experience in the field of advertising, marketing and graphic arts, and remembering his deep sensitivity to these disciplines we considered in the seminar, it was in a moment of inspiration I picked up the phone to see if he would be willing and would have the time to create the cover for this book. His answer was an enthusiastic *yes,* and by the grace of God we were able to meet within a few days in Philadelphia to begin thinking about the design and layout. Within three weeks Richard produced the cover for this book--another evidence of his creative talent and his sensitivity to living in full response to the leading of the Holy Spirit. It is in grateful acknowledgement of his response in love and friendship that I thank him for this cover for my book.

CHAPTER

I

SPIRITUAL DISCIPLINES FOR EVERYDAY LIVING

Susan Annette Muto
1942--

Courtesy: Susan Muto   Photo by Hans Jonas

Professor and Director of the Institute of Formative Spirituality, Duquesne University, Pittsburgh, PA. For eighteen years, Susan Muto has been teacher, writer and administrator, sharing with Adrian van Kaam in the development of the Institute, first as assistant director and now as director. As a single lay person, her teaching and writing give clear evidence of her own deep spiritual experience. Her specialty has been in the art and discipline of formative reading and in deepening the life of prayer in the practice of the presence of God. Author of seven books and co-author with Adrian van Kaam, Susan Muto is in every sense one of the writers of the "family documents."

Chapter I

WANTED:

A NEW KIND OF READING

Why and how do you read? Do you read for entertainment (best sellers)? Do you read to be informed in order to increase the quantity of factual knowledge? Do you read "defensively" in order to bolster your own rigidly held theories of religion and salvation?

A RADICAL APPROACH

Reading for spiritual growth and discipline is of another order and requires a radically different approach.

Johannes Anker Larsen tells how he came to choose the title for his book *With the Door Open.* A scholar friend of his said to him, "Leave the door open; it may be that one or another will feel inclined to linger and listen." "This," Anker Larsen says, "explains the external causes which have led to my confidential talk--with the door open."[1]

Just so with all the "family documents;" they are written "with the door open," not only for you to "linger and listen," but for you to live your way into the very presence of God who is the center and source of all our lives.

When we approach a particular writing in scriptures or in the "family documents" as windows letting in light and fresh air, then we ask, what does this passage or text say to me at this particular time in my life? What light does it shed on the ways in which I will react to the various experiences of this day? Michael De Wilde describes what it meant to him to read with humility Anker Larsen's book.

"... I approach the book "empty" or something close

[1]*With The Door Open*, p. 17

> to that which means that I am not so full of other "important things" or so full of myself that I cannot hear what he is saying. It means carrying the book around like a love letter . . . It means reading it as if the author had something to say or teach, and then *not* being surprised when in fact I learn something from it.[2]

As each of us works with the "family documents," it is essential to be patient and unhurried. I knew a freshman football player who was the fastest runner ever to attend my college. Yet he failed to make the team because he could never wait for the line to open up the hole for him to run through. So every time he carried the ball, he ran with tremendous speed right into the line for no gain. Just so with thinking that speed in spiritual reading will give you a victory.

When undertaking spiritual reading, the first reading is only the beginning, for as Susan Muto suggests there are many layers of meaning to these ideas and insights.[3]

Furthermore, we as readers have many previous layers of experience, or we may have new experiences which influence our understanding of all that we read. For example, if you have just read for the first time Brother Lawrence's statement that the love of God so filled his mind and heart that it didn't matter whether he was washing the pots and pans in the kitchen or on his knees in prayer in the chapel, he was never outside the presence. You may have brought to this first reading a high degree of frustration over the vast number of details that force themselves upon you--many of which seem totally irrelevant. So the idea of God's presence being available for dishwashing seems so ridiculous, you might easily conclude, "this man has nothing to say to me."[4]

[2]Michael De Wilde, unpublished paper, Spring, 1982

[3]Susan Muto, *Approaching the Sacred* (Denville, N.J.: Dimension Books, 1973), p. 39. For a fuller treatment of this, see pp. 35-40. Also she has splendid insight concerning the importance of living in wonder as preparation for spiritual reading--see pp. 30-31.

[4]Brother Lawrence of the Resurrection, *The Practice of the Presence of God* (London: SCM Press; Old Tappan, N.J.: Fleming Revell, 1950). See also David Winter, *Brother Lawrence for the 70's: Closer Than a Brother* (Wheaton, Illinois: Harold Shaw Publisher, 1971). This reinterpretation of the great devotional classic will be of interest to some after having read the quotations in this manuscript.

Or, you may have brought to the first reading a long time of dryness in worship when all prayers and preaching have been as a barren desert to you, so that you have a hard time bringing yourself to believe that God might be present to you in church.

Yet from that first reading this idea of the permanently abiding presence keeps haunting you. So you turn and read reflectively the same passage now with a simple turn of openness--how could this happen to me? Here is a different layer of you--no longer the preoccupied, skeptical you of the first reading, but a wistful, tentatively seeking person who is willing to begin a pilgrimage.

In subsequent readings you may come to accept the idea that God can be present when you are dealing with trivial detail, even when washing dishes! Then you may come to feel you are not alone, however trivial the detail.

Here's how it worked for one seminary student. Beverly Karr wrote:

> In my readings of Brother Lawrence's statements I was reminded of the campus job I have here at the Seminary which entails daily washing the blackboards in the classrooms, emptying the waste baskets and putting the chairs in order. Brother Lawrence affirms that "we ought not to be weary of doing little things for the love of God, who regards not the greatness of the work, but the love with which it is performed." Although at times this job seems to be menial, I have come to the realization that in doing it for the love of God this becomes the perfect time to spend in intercession--praying for the professors who write on the boards as well as for the students who sit in the chairs.[5]

Selections from the "Family Documents"

When I do spiritual, as distinct from informational, reading I approach the text as a life message. I want to enter into dialogue with God's word in Holy Scripture and as speaking in history through . . . the spiritual masters. Through reading and

[5]Beverly Karr, unpublished paper, Fall, 1980

reflection, I hope to meet God more personally. The text reveals a spiritual way or road I can follow. As a living mode of communication, it becomes master to me as disciple. I want the power of the word to permeate my life. A shift has to take place from myself as master of the word to myself as servant of the word. It is now I who am the disciple; the text is master. The truth contained in the text is the standard against which I am judged. It is not I who judge the text but the text that judges me.

What concerns us, then, in spiritual reading is not only what the text means in itself but what it means for me. What do those words on the page tell me about my actual situation here and now? About my relation to self, others, God?

[1]*Susan Muto*

I need to catch myself when I become defensive, when I begin to build systems of rationalization against a text that does not slide neatly into my way of thinking.

[2]*Susan Muto*

Other fears may emerge as I read further in St. John. Spiritual living calls for childlike faith in Christ; I fear the risk. Loving God demands uncompromising surrender; I fear the consequences. I must give all to God; yet how I fear an unconditional yes to **God's** will. All these fears of mine are really "ego" fears, that is, fears rooted in my self-centeredness. They are not related to the healthy fear of the Lord that is the beginning of wisdom, the sense of **God's** awesome power and my nothingness. Ego fears emerge because I may have to give up my old ways. I wanted to tell God what to do. Now I have to stop talking and try to listen.

[3]*Susan Muto.*

CLEARING OUT THE UNDERBRUSH

Often when reading the "family documents" we wish we could ask the author, "What do you mean?" Our present definitions and assumptions can cloud our understanding, as for example in any discussion of humility.

For many persons, humility is thought of as weakness, abject deference and a willingness to be walked over or pushed around. All this has to be set aside before we can even begin to approach an understanding of the meaning of humility.

In one seminar the early comments and reaction to the discipline of joy seemed superficial until one of the students said very simply, "We must differentiate joy from cheerfulness, pollyanna goodwill, and bonhomie!" For the next half-hour we separated out those similar but not precise ideas which were confused with the word joy. Then we were able to begin to think our way into the meaning of joy as these authors wrote about it.

My daughter, Cathie, reading this material for the first time, commented on the necessity of taking time to work through this process of expanding the meaning of words. Often this means backing away from our stereotyped and uncritical usage of words. She also discovered that it didn't help to jump to first impression conclusions. Her first reaction to the section *Hasten Unto God and Hasten Into the World* was "this is only for ministers and professionals." But upon further thought she came to the insight, "this is for everyone!"

Our past experiences can also be road-blocks to reflective understanding. One student's negative reaction to Anker Larsen's description of his experience with Reality dismissed this and all other such experiences as sheer romantic emotionalism and totally untrustworthy. In the discussion that followed, the student's explanation helped us to see why she reacted so vehemently. She had grown up in a tradition of extreme religious emotionalism; she had given credence and complete confidence to what she thought was a genuine religious experience, only to be let down in utter despair. Little wonder she reacted as she did!

As you approach the "family documents" reflect on these ideas about the way we should read:

Let go of the sedimented past.
Read in a "vacation mood."
Read in solitude.
Diminish the power of distraction--this may be done by choosing the right place in which to read.
Read with care and trust. Refrain from problem-

solving or analysis--rather to develop a ruminative, abiding style.[6]

Selections from the "Family Documents"

We should read very slowly, seeking to learn of God, in a spirit of prayer, letting the words sink down into our minds, tasting and savouring those which "speak" to us, till they become part of our life. For the aim of such reading is "to feed the heart, to fortify the will--to put these in contact with God."

[4]*Olive Wyon*

Of course *such "reading" is hardly reading in the ordinary sense at all.* As well could you call the letting a very slowly dissolving lozenge melt imperceptibly in your mouth, eating. Such reading is, of course, meant as directly as possible to feed the heart, to fortify the will,--to put these into contact with God--thus, by the book, to get away from the book, to the realities it suggests . . . . And, above all, perhaps it excludes, by its very object, all criticism, all going off on one's own thoughts as in any way antagonistic to the book's thoughts; and this not by any unreal (and most dangerous) forcing of oneself to swallow, or to "like" what does not attract one's simply humble self, but (on the contrary) by a gentle passing by, by an instinctive ignoring of what does not suit one's soul. This passing by should be without a trace of would-be objective judging; during such reading, we are out simply and solely to feed our own poor soul, such as it is here and now. What repels or confuses us now, may be the food of angels; it may even still become the light to our own poor soul's dimness. We must exclude none of such possibilities, "the infant crying for the light" has nothing to do with more than just humbly finding, and then using the little light that *it* requires. I need not say that I would not restrict you to only one quarter of an hour a day. You might find two such helpful. But I would not exceed fifteen minutes at *any one time;* you would sink to ordinary reading if you did.

[5]*Baron von Hügel*

[6]*Approaching the Sacred.* These ideas are interpreted more fully in Part I, The Art and Discipline of Spiritual Reading, pp. 15-78.

Selection Footnotes

1. Susan Muto, *Steps Along the Way* (Denville N.J.: Dimension Books, 1975), pp. 28-29.
2. *Approaching the Sacred,* p. 38.
3. *Approaching the Sacred,* p. 37. Dr. Susan Muto has written three excellent books which provide us with the most complete description of the methods of spiritual reading: *Approaching the Sacred (An Introduction to Spiritual Reading); Steps Along the Way (The Path of Spiritual Reading);* and *The Journey Homeward* (Denville, N.J.: Dimension Books, Inc.).
4. Olive Wyon, *The School of Prayer* (Philadelphia: Westminster Press, 1944), p. 108.
5. *Spiritual Counsel and Letters of Baron Friedrich von Hügel,* edited with an Introductory Essay by Douglas V. Steere (New York and Evanston: Harper and Row, 1964), pp. 24-25.

CHAPTER

II

SPIRITUAL DISCIPLINES FOR EVERYDAY LIVING

Baron Friedrich von Hügel
1852-1925

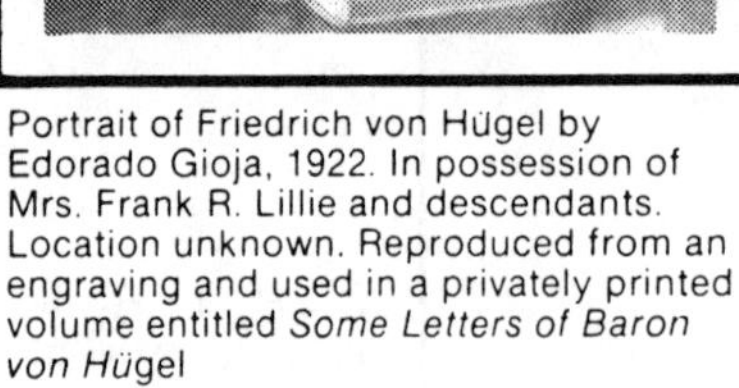

Portrait of Friedrich von Hügel by Edorado Gioja, 1922. In possession of Mrs. Frank R. Lillie and descendants. Location unknown. Reproduced from an engraving and used in a privately printed volume entitled *Some Letters of Baron von Hügel*

The son of an Austrian diplomat, Baron von Hügel lived most of his adult life in England. This Roman catholic layman, a private scholar, had a profound impact upon the theological and religious thinkers of his time through comprehensive works such The Mystical Element of Religion and many lectures.

In addition to his scholarly works, von Hügel touched countless lives in his role as a spiritual director. One who sought his guidance was Evelyn Underhill.

His essays and letters of spiritual counsel reveal a profound awareness of the workings of God in human life, and of the depth and fullness of spiritual life which is in tune with the living God.

Baron von Hügel was described by the London Times in this manner: "In him the man of religious fervour was combined in a rare way with the philosopher." A personal friend, the Reverend Eric Coleman, O.D.C., upon hearing of the death of von Hügel, wrote: "He was a very holy old man and a perfect type of Christian humility."

Chapter II

NEW DIMENSIONS FOR THOUGHT AND ACTION

Those who have grown in the life of the spirit have done so because they have shifted to another way of looking at and understanding themselves and the universe. They have discovered how to *see* life and to *live* life from a different angle.

SEEING LIFE FROM A DIFFERENT ANGLE

In this chapter we shall look at some of these different ways of seeing and living as being the means of preparing ourselves for undertaking the disciplines of the spiritual life.

Shifting from Argument to Hypothesis.

In making such a shift we put the spotlight on the fact that the universe and God are discoverable. Therefore, we do not begin by debating about either the existence or the nature of God, nor do we come to the search with an intellectual formulation or a categorical statement to be tested and strengthened by persuasive argument. We begin with the basic hypothesis: I will live as though God is real and it is possible for persons like me to experience the Divine presence, not once but often when the practice of the presence of God becomes my lifestyle.

This book records personal experiences in the discovery of the presence of God by a number of the writers of the "family documents." Included are descriptions of some of the ways these individuals "practiced the presence." Their practice was based upon the hypothesis that the living God will become real and known in the two-way street of God's grace and our openness!

Across the years of my life, filled with the usual mixture of challenge and frustrations, with a few major responsibilities, surrounded by a thousand petty details, I have found the quiet steady sense of God's presence to be very real in the constant unfolding of my life's work. One illustration will suffice. At mid-point in my career as minister-educator and administrator, I was offered a very challenging and rewarding position as Executive Director of a national health care organization. I gave it very serious consideration, since the position offered many opportunities for me to use my experience and training, especially in administration and fund-raising.

Throughout several days of intense reflection, questioning and debate, there never came any clear definitive voice or vision from outside. Quietly and surely there came the confident feeling and understanding that my answer had to be *no* — that I could not turn my back on a quarter of a century of ministry in the church and in higher education.

Nor was there any revelation of next steps to be offered and taken in this my main vocational arena. Again only the deep sense of assurance from God that the future would provide, at the right time and in the right ways, the rounding out of my vocational commitment to ministry and higher education. And so it has been even down to the very writing of this book.

For further understanding of what it means to live within the dimension of hypothesis, turn to the selections under this heading. These writings can help us to sense what it means to live under the hypothesis, God is real and can become a living reality in our lives.

Moving from Knowledge as Information to Experiential Knowledge

Second: consider what happens when we have made the shift from argument to hypothesis; we then move from knowledge as information to experiential knowledge and we find the spotlight focuses on first-hand experience. Under the discipline of this new approach, we aim to discover a quality of knowledge which emerges from personal experience.

All of the selections in this book grew out of the soil of the first-hand experience of the writers of these "family documents." These are *not* arguments about humility, love, joy, detachment, nor debates about the possibility of discovering God. They are insights as to how these spiritual characteristics have been made real in the lives of the authors. They write, *not* to present a rigid and complete "how to" manual, but to offer insights for living out these very special characteristics of the life of the spirit.

While reading these first-hand experiences we may remember similar long-forgotten or perhaps unrecognized experiences of a spiritual nature. This happened to two students in one of the seminars. These two remarkable statements (#6 and #7) of Byron McElroy and Julie Sheetz, upon their reading Anker Larsen's *With the Door Open.* illustrate this principle. A number of students in this same seminar confessed to having had first-hand experience of the presence of God or Christ, and to being afraid to talk freely about these experiences lest they be laughed at, or thought to be queer and abnormal.

Don't be discouraged if out of these readings no immediate or previous experiences emerge. One member in a church seminar told of his experience in dealing with a particular quotation. He commented with some high degree of emotion that when we read, some weeks before, a certain passage about humility, he thought that was the most senseless, unintelligible passage he had ever read. He tried to understand it but failed and ended up wondering why it had been chosen for inclusion in this section on humility. Later he had an experience in which he had needed to practice genuine humility in the very terms of that previously unintelligible insight. He went on to say that this very experience gave him a new basis for "living with" these selections in the market place of his life.

"Who's In Charge Here?"

We come upon a third dimension in seeing life from a different angle when we ask "who's in charge here?" This is the question of external and internal authority and it asks us to look at all our actions and reactions in our daily living. Is our response primarily and only to external authority or are we becoming rooted and grounded through our spiritual living within God's will? If the latter, then increasingly our lives should operate from the base of an inner authority in which God's will becomes the operative and determining control.

Of course, there are external authorities and compulsions under which we live--many of which must be honored if we are to live constructively in our society. Yet for those who discover the presence of God there comes the broadening and strengthening of the foundation of internal authority which must of necessity challenge all external authorities. Inner personal direction and integrity are the central core around which our judgments and commitments increasingly are made and undertaken.

For an illustration of complete inner integrity, see quotation #8.

It is a long hard road to travel in arriving at such complete living under inner authority; and it is in travelling this road that we most frequently compromise and rationalize our acceptance of external authorities, for the pressures and arguments for capitulation are both subtle and overpowering. However, the demand upon us is that we live under this discipline and make advances into action and decision--based upon our developing inner integrity and authority. Persons in these seminars have discovered in themselves an inner depth where dwelling within God's presence makes it possible to live quiet lives of peace and power based on the inner authority of the spiritual life. This idea of internal authority for a fair number of students gave them an awareness "of their own depth and integrity of being so that no one could put them down."

The Unity of the Natural and the Spiritual

There is a fourth way of seeing life from a different angle. We have inherited ways of thinking theologically and philosophically which have split asunder the unity of the natural and spiritual worlds. Nature has been maligned as an evil and degrading influence to be rejected, suppressed, and in the extreme cases of asceticism, annihilated, in order that the life of the spirit may hold full sway. Spiritual freedom and perfection have often been interpreted as flourishing only after the total subjection of nature has been completed.

Thinking persons, reacting against such extremes, have sometimes been led to submerge both humanity and divinity into the realm of nature resulting in some form of pantheism. Neither asceticism nor pantheism are prerequisites to living in the life of the spirit.

Here again we are invited to see life from a different angle, one which relates the natural and spiritual more as two sides of a coin, rather than two separate and opposite entities. When we have made this shift we are then able to regard the reality of the natural world as being the laboratory in which we may engage in experiments for spiritual growth and maturity. Fortunately, in our time there has been a radical shift on the part of scientists, philosophers and students of human nature to a holistic interpretation of the relationship of human nature and the natural world.

The Christian Understanding of Personhood

The final shift in seeing life from a different angle comes in thinking seriously and honestly about our true nature and our true selves from the perspective of our Christian understanding of personhood.

The Christian doctrine concerning our essential humanity rests upon a number of insights which, when accepted as our way of understanding ourselves, give us the basis for living under the disciplined spiritual life. No matter how self-sufficient, how successful our lives are, our deeper insight is that we are finite and dependent. The final victory is the discovery that our lives rest back ultimately upon the living God. In this primary relationship, we discover that we, on many occasions and in various ways, are both guilty and responsible. In making such discoveries we move into the hard realism of understanding both our sinful nature and our essential goodness and redeemability.

The quotations from Baron von Hügel (# 12 and 13) are directly to the point. Here is a man of profound intellect, remarkable spiritual insight, one of the truly great spiritual directors of modern times, who is decidedly clear and forthright about his own finitude. The Reverend Eric M. Coleman, a long time friend, upon hearing of the death of the Baron wrote: "He was a very holy old man and a perfect type of Christian humility."[1]

[1]*Some letters of Baron Friedrich von Hügel*--Privately printed, December 1925--Taken from the *London Times,* Wednesday, January 28, 1925.

Selections from the "Family Documents"

Shifting from Argument to Hypothesis

Here comes a man [Anker Larsen] who has realized that Eternity can flourish in the midst of our daily interests and activities, and that it can be in **us** an ever-flowing fountain that keeps life fresh and sweet. The life of these . . . who carry this Eternity in themselves, is irradiated by a calm beauty, akin to that which gives to the stem and branch of the tree their sure growth and sure repose.

[1]*V. Grönbech*

. . . a certain limited knowledge of God and the things of God enters the mind; and asks of us that honest and humble thought about the mysteries of faith which is the raw material of meditation . . . Christian prayer to God must harmonize with Christian belief about God . . . We pray first because we believe something . . . and with the deepening of prayer, its patient cultivation, there comes--perhaps slowly, perhaps suddenly--the enrichment and enlargement of belief, as we enter into a first-hand communion with the Reality who is the object of our faith.

[2]*Evelyn Underhill*

God does not die on the day when we cease to believe in a personal deity, but we die on the day when our lives cease to be illumined by the steady radiance, renewed daily, of a wonder, the source of which is beyond all reason.

[3]*Dag Hammarskjöld*

Moving from Knowledge as Information to Experiential Knowledge

I looked for it in the theological Faculty. To a thirsting soul, this is like a desert. It reminded me of a time during the war, when one day I entered a café where I hoped to get a cup of coffee, and got something which was called coffee and looked like coffee, but wasn't.

Before my mind's eye I can see them sitting in the crowded

lecture room, in the lectures on exegesis and dogma--all those youthful faces, among them some with good, lively eyes--bowing their heads ingenuously under the theological cobwebs which the professor wafted down upon them. Now they are probably scattered over the country as worthy pastors, and the Life which is weaving behind their half-forgotten theology is communicated to the congregations, and awakens a faint remembrance of the Promised Land. The dyed-in-the-wool theological type was also not wanting among them--may God help their congregations for the pastor doesn't!

[4]*Johannes Anker Larsen*

I had been sitting in the garden working and had just finished. That afternoon I was to go to Copenhagen, but it was still an hour and a half before the departure of the train. The weather was beautiful, the air clear and pure. I lighted a cigar and sat down in one of the easy chairs in front of the house. It was still and peaceful--around me and within me. Too good, in fact, to allow one to think much about anything. I just sat there. Then it began to come, that infinite tenderness, which is purer and deeper than that of lovers, or of **parent toward a** child. It was in me, also came to me, as the air came to my lungs. As usual, the breathing became sober and reverent, became, as it were, incorporeal; I inhaled the tenderness. Needless to say the cigar went out. I did not cast it away like a sin, I simply had no use for it.

This deep tenderness which I felt, first within myself and then even stronger around and above me, extended further and further--it became all-present. I saw it, and it developed into knowing, into knowing all, at the same time it became power, omnipotence, and drew me into the eternal Now.

That was my first actual meeting with Reality; because such is the real life: a Now which *is* and a Now which *happens*. There is no beginning and no end. I cannot say any more about this Now. I sat in my garden, but there was no place in the world where I was not.

During the whole time my consciousness was clear and sober. I sat in the garden and acknowledged it with a smile. There was something to smile over, for time and space, characteristics of the Now which happens were so to speak "outside." But what is the Now which happens? It is the continuously active creation with all its birth throes. I saw time and space as instruments or functions of this creation. They come into existence with it and in the course of it, and with it they come to an end. The Newly Created stands in the Now and discards these tools. The freedom, the real *Being* begins.

But afterwards I had to take the train to Copenhagen. Yes--afterwards--that is a road I have not yet traversed to the end, but it leads through Reality, I may say ever deeper *into* Reality. Because the blessed Now of being and the agonizing Now of happening are one and the same. To make this truth actual--that is the task which arises from the meeting with Eternity. That is to say: to experience within oneself the eternal and the temporal nature of being and to achieve their fusion. In such a practical life, all theories and "views on life," disappear like a fog; reality lies in the clear light of day. Existence is no Maya, no delusion, but we are deluded until we open our eyes in the Now, where the temporal and eternal are merged into a unity, where a workday becomes a holyday, and life a sacrament. In the being Now it is apprehended, in the happening Now it is realized. The eternal sanctifies the temporal, the temporal realizes the eternal.

[5]*Johannes Anker Larsen*

Like Larsen's experience in his garden, there came that beautiful fall day in 1974. I was alone doing some work that did not require much thought or physical exertion, outdoors under trees covered in beautiful fall colors. The sky was clear but for a few distant white billowing clouds and a pleasant breeze rustled the leaves over my head.

Without any provocation on my part, there suddenly came upon me an overwhelming feeling of inner peace, of contentment, of joy, of some sort of wholeness that I probably hadn't experienced since childhood, if I even had such an experience then. It lasted the rest of the afternoon even though I continued the work I was doing. And it came back sporadically several times during the next several days.

I share this in response to Anker Larsen's book because of

the close parallels of our experiences. And in 1974, I didn't understand what was happening to me although I sensed that my seriously fragmented life was suddenly coming together and life became richer and more meaningful. But it wasn't until reading this little book over the past few days that I understand the mystical quality of my experience and the fact that my special experience has seldom recurred because of my entanglement in the cobwebs of the classroom and other demands that prevent me from seeking out within myself those places where the Spirit of God waits patiently.

[6]*Byron McElroy*

The book "spoke to my condition," . . . so significantly because I could resonate with the kind of experiences Anker Larsen describes. I have had those moments of seeing clearly, "honestly and straightforwardly," of celebrating and finding great joy in something simply because it *is*.

As I read *With the Door Open,* I was reminded also of a moment from this past summer, during a solitary hike in the woods. It was the close of a busy, somewhat lonely day; my mood was one of rather bittersweet sadness, but thoughts were not circling around any particular points of focus. I simply *was*, following the trail, looking, listening, absorbing. It was early evening, and everything was cast in the strangely radiant glow of the sun at that hour. The forest was thick, however, and as I ventured deeper into it I was mostly in shadow. At one point, as I came around a turn in the trail, I found myself in a brilliant patch of sunlight which had filtered down through a break in the trees. I could see the light, could feel its warmth in the cool of the evening, and could experience it as especially beautiful. But in a way, that was all at a level once removed (even as writing about it is one step further removed). For, in the first moment, I was there, bathed in light, strangely comforted and exhilarated. I experienced myself as unique and yet part of all that surrounded me. And I experienced God as one who cared for me and who cared for all. It seems that I could not have articulated all that in the moment, but I was drawn in by the light, and through that light to the source of all light.

[7]*Julie Sheetz*

Who's in Charge Here?

Basil of Cappadocia's reply to the prefect of the Emperor, who threatened him with confiscation of his goods, with exile, and finally with a violent death if he would not come over and champion the Emperor's Arian cause, is a fair illustration of . . . fearlessness [and inner authority]. He sent word to the Emperor that he would never yield, that confiscation of his goods would not affect him for he possessed little or nothing, that he would be entirely at home with his God in any place in exile, and that as for the Emperor's taking his life it was all but spent already and would only hasten his communion with God. The prefect replied that no person had ever spoken to him in this way before. Basil answered, "Then you have never until now met up with a Christian Bishop."

[8]*Douglas Steere*

The Unity of the Natural and the Spiritual

The creature has nothing else in its power but the free use of its will, and its free will hath no other power but that of concurring with, or resisting, the working of God in nature.

[9]*William Law*

Know that, by nature, every creature seeks to become like God. Nature's intent is neither food nor drink nor clothing, nor comfort, nor anything else in which God is left out. Whether you like it or not, whether you know it or not, secretly nature seeks, hunts, tries to ferret out the track on which God may be found.

[10]*Meister Eckhart*

Of all the hard facts of science . . . I know of none more solid and fundamental than the fact that if you inhibit thought (and persevere) you come at length to a region of consciousness below or behind thought and different from ordinary thought in its nature and character--a consciousness of quasi-universal quality, and a realization of an altogether vaster self than that to which we are accustomed. And since the ordinary consciousness, with which we are concerned in ordinary life, is before all things founded on the little, local self, and is in fact *self*-consciousness in the little, local sense, it follows that to pass out of that is to die to the ordinary self and the ordinary world. It is to die in the ordinary sense, but in another sense it is to wake up and find that the I, one's real, most intimate self, pervades the universe and all other beings--that the mountains and the sea and the stars are a part of one's body and that one's soul is in touch with the souls of all creatures. Yes, far closer than before. It is to be assured of an indestructible immortal life and of a joy immense and inexpressible--"to . . . sit with all the Gods in Paradise."

[11]*Sheldon Cheney*

The Christian Understanding of Personhood

The fact is that the poor thing that scribbles these lines is the *work of religion*. I weigh my words, Child: I should not be physically alive at this moment, I should be, were I alive at all, a corrupt or at least an incredibly unhappy, violent, bitter, self-occupied destructive soul were it not for religion--for its having come and *saved me from myself* . . . . I also know beyond argument or a moment's hesitation, that my experience is absolutely not an eccentric one; and that, in the long run and upon the whole, humanity itself *realizes* that it cannot do without religion, and that even when and where it does not realise this, it is the less deep, the less tender, the less completely true without it . . . . I feel as though you are now getting thoroughly awake, Child, as though you sincerely long to fight, to drop, to overcome self. Without that dividing up of the true self against the false, without a fear and dread of self that will drive you to God and Christ, without a taking in hand daily, and ever humbly beginning anew, but *not in your own strength*, but *in a despair of self*, which, if true, means *an utter trust in God and Christ*, so utterly near you day and night,--religion is fine talk, at least it has not become fully alive; and without such a life as *that*, Child,--note what I say--you will *never* be happy, you will become feverish, bitter; hard, odious, or will shrink into a poor surface-thing--although I doubt whether you could, whether God would let you achieve the latter.

[12]*Baron von Hügel*

"People often ask me what religion is for," he confided to his niece. "I simply cannot get on without it. I must have it to moderate me, to water me down, to make me possible. I am so claimful, so self-occupied, so intense. I want everything my own way."

[13]*Baron von Hügel*

Reflection and Action

What steps could you take to begin living on the hypothesis that God is real and it is possible for you to center down into God's presence?

Think back across your life to identify those first-hand experiences which have given you experiential knowledge. Write these in your personal journal for future reflection.

Make lists in parallel columns of all those areas of your life dominated by external authority; then do the same for those areas in which internal authority is operative. As you mature in these disciplines, how can your internal authority be enlarged?

LIVING LIFE FROM A DIFFERENT ANGLE

In addition to seeing life from a different angle, life must be lived from a different angle if there is to be growth in the life of the spirit. Here are a number of important shifts in living life from a different angle which require consideration and action.

A Lifetime Adventure

Too long we have reduced religious awakening to a one-time conversion experience with the implication that this once-and-for-all glorious event was the sum total of what it means to become religious or spiritual. The result is that many persons, having experienced a deep personal commitment to God and Christ, are left without any continuing guidance or nourishment, to drift into dutiful, routine religious observance.

To live life from a different angle is to recognize that our very finest religious experience is but a beginning. Actually it is our commitment to a life-long pilgrimage and our "pilgrim's progress" will be rugged, discouraging, frustrating, possibly even despairing. Yet it may well be exhilarating, challenging, encouraging and even joyful.

Our forebears talked and wrote about living with the scriptures until they became the "engrafted word." Such words as love, humility, joy, detachment, when taken into our lives become disciplines for reflection and action. Then with practice, they become characteristics, deep and abiding qualities of our lives.

All that follows in this volume is potentially the source for guidance and nourishment, provided we are prepared to envision this as a lifetime adventure undertaken with openness of heart, mind and soul.

Don't expect, by the time you have completed the first reading and exploration of this material, that you will have it all together in one overwhelming experience. Come, instead, with the expectation that you will find more than enough to validate the reality of the practiced spiritual life, but not enough to short-circuit the glorious, though rugged, pilgrimage of a lifetime into spiritual maturity.

Quotations #14 and 15 illuminate what is meant by the lifetime adventure.

Second: living life from a different angle calls for becoming singly intentioned: our learning to "will one thing."[1]

Becoming Singly Intentioned

In this different way of living we discover a shift that is basic to the growth of all the spiritual disciplines we shall be studying and practicing.

Thomas Kelly, Haverford Professor of Philosophy, called upon twentieth century Quakers to "center down" into the presence of God. He meant by this, learning to will one thing, namely to love God and live only under the Divine Will. When we, with single intention, center down into God's presence, we discover a freedom to reengage in our daily living but in new

[1]Søren Kierkegaard, *Purity of Heart Is To Will One Thing* Translated from the Danish with an Introductory Essay by Douglas V. Steere (New York and London: Harper and Brothers Publishers, 1938). This volume should be read in its entirety to appreciate fully what it means to will one thing!

and often creative ways. Activities and responsibilities which seemed so important will be judged to have lesser value, and may even become insignificant. Then in the light of our recurring attempts to "will one thing" God may challenge us with new responsibilities.

While in no way have I personally achieved the ability always and in every situation to be singly intentioned, the wide variety of career responsibilities which have come to me, as I look in retrospect, have indeed been rooted and grounded in the determination to allow God to provide the leading at every turn in the vocational road. At this point it is important to be clear that persons and institutions always had a very real part in all my vocational decisions, but the constant aim of my life has been the single intention to respond to God's will.

Learning to become singly intentioned requires that we live differently by practicing the art of quiet waiting in silence. To the art of quiet waiting we bring an openness so different from the usual closed circuits in which we are called to operate most of our lives. Openness means stilling our demanding, requesting natures in order to listen.

Since we have so long been conditioned to heavy, forceful, activist ways, quiet waiting may be regarded as evasion through inaction. Far from inaction, it requires a different kind of action to calm both mind and body, reorder our emotions and our thoughts, in order to heighten our potential receptivity and be open to the leading of the Spirit of God. We do not tell God; we bring no hidden agenda to trot out at the right moment. Frantic requests are out of order, no matter how serious or urgent the needs may be.

Quiet waiting may bring clear insight or there may be a new sense of rightness and well-being, or it may be a distinct call to action. Yet there may be no such reaction, only seemingly unending silence. For this reason the friends of God are very clear at precisely this point--quietness and openness may never demand that insight or the word of truth must come each time we meditate. And for these times of unending silence Brother Lawrence calls us to the discipline of "fidelity in times of dryness"--those times when nothing comes in response to our receptivity, when we are surrounded with a seemingly arid desert, not once but several times running.

A third requirement in living life from a different angle leads us to look at a very personal problem.

The Problem of Readiness

There are cycles of the spirit--the tidal ebbing and flowing of awareness and openness. As you read these selections from the "family documents" be sensitive to your present condition.

Don't fret or fight the times of dust and cold, gray ashes. Listen, read, meditate, and at least respect the content and believe in the process. Your spiritual tide may be out, but it will return! I myself made four dismal attempts to read Brother Lawrence's *The Practice of the Presence of God* and only the fifth time brought insight and joy. Just so it may be for you whenever you move to immerse yourself in any of the "family documents." If, after an initial start, it is clear you are not ready, set aside that particular selection or volume without anger or resentment--then try again at a later time or times. The "family documents" are never exhausted, nor fully comprehended at any one sitting or reading. Patience, returning and unhurried sensitivity are called for if we are ever to find ourselves ready to receive the Spirit.

The Practice of Living by Imaginative Forethought

This is an idea which has proven to be of primary assistance to many of the seminar participants in practicing the disciplines of the life of the spirit. Too much of our living is reactive, immediate response to a succession of demands without adequate reflection and calm consideration. Confronted unexpectedly with requests for decisions in conflict situations we give fast answers or we engage in emotional responses as the answer to conflict resolution. The practice of imaginative forethought provides a very different approach to such reactive living.

I first discovered this approach and labelled it imaginative forethought after reading John Woolman's own analysis of an experience he had when, as a young man, he was apprenticed to a tailor in Mount Holly, New Jersey.

> My employer, having a negro woman, sold her, and desired me to write a bill of sale, the man being waiting who bought her. The thing was sudden; and though I felt uneasy at the thoughts of writing an instrument of slavery for one of my fellow-creatures, yet I remembered that I was hired by the year, that it was my master who directed me to do it, and that it was an elderly man, a member of our society, who bought her; so through weakness I gave way, and wrote it; but at the executing of it I was so afflicted in my mind, that I said before my master and the Friend that I believed slave-keeping to be a practice inconsistent with the Christian religion. This, in some degree, abated my uneasiness; yet as often as I reflected seriously upon it I thought I should have been clearer if I had desired to be excused from it, as a thing against my conscience; for such it was.[2]

John Woolman goes on to say that the incident continued to trouble him and that after continued quiet and honest reflection he came to a clear decision that he should have "desired to be excused from such action." And in the light of this decision, the next time a similar request came he did decline the invitation to write another bill of sale for the selling of a human being.

As I reflected on John Woolman's experience, his on-the-spur-of-the-moment argument with himself as well as his later discussion of further reflection leading to conclusion, it came to me that here was an approach to decision making as well as a method of preparing for personal involvement and action that should be developed and practiced well in advance of actual experience. This then can be described as the practice of imaginative forethought. Here is how it works.

When you begin to live by imaginative forethought, you look at your responses to the very practical experiences of your everyday routine, with the honesty of Woolman. In the light of this forthright review, imagine what it would have meant to have stood up for what you know to be right and true. Or you might

[2]John Woolman, *The Journal of John Woolman,* Introduction by Frederick B. Tolles (New York: Corinth Books, 1961), pp. 14-15.

imagine what it would mean to enter into the next day's activities in a difficult work situation, having prayed to God for the help to do everything for and through God's love. Just to pray for such love is to start the whole process of reflecting upon what a loving attitude would be and could do, to change the atmosphere and shift the ground of the issue to a new and more creative level.

Imaginative forethought appealed to me as a practice well worth trying. As minister of a church, I carried my share of pastoral calling, and I decided to put imaginative forethought into my round of calls on members of the church. Under this discipline, before I rang any door bell, I had taken time to reflect, what do I know about the real needs of this family, where are they hurting, what are their joys, what genuine ministry am I called upon to offer in the name of the living God, what word needs speaking, what help is required?

And where I was calling for the first time with a new family or individual, I tried to imagine what might be the needs, the opportunities for ministry to these strangers to whom I was hoping to offer friendship and fellowship.

I have nothing spectacular to relate--only the deeply satisfying knowledge that calling no longer was superficial, stilted, or dutiful. It was an adventure in which unexpected dimensions unfolded. As this happened then, it was possible to build upon the unfolding insights by virtue of the continued practice of imaginative forethought.

This disciplined lifestyle has proven itself as a basic way of living through the tough demands of institutional administration, as well as in interplay of strong and critical staff relationships.

If this idea appeals to you, then begin by taking time to reflect upon Baron von Hügel's beautiful comment, "Caring matters most." Ask yourself questions like these. Where is caring needed most among my family, friends, associates? Where could I begin caring more realistically today? What does it take to care deeply for someone without being maudlin or sentimental? From answers arising out of such serious questioning you then start imagining the various ways in which to practice caring. And when you have decided on next steps you act. Then following your action of caring you return to ask reflectively, what happened, what went wrong, what succeeded, what more do I need to know about the genuine art of caring? And so you begin the next round in the practice of imaginative forethought.

Here is the ultimate imaginative forethought: Hanns Lilje, Bishop of the Free Evangelical Lutheran Church of Germany, spent many months in a Nazi prison under heavy suspicion for an alleged part in the attempted assassination of Adolf Hitler in 1944. In an autobiographical book entitled *The Valley of the Shadow,* Lilje's profound review of the absolute relevance of the practice of Christian faith in living, he tells us at one point of a new dimension he added to his daily meditation.

Every night the guard would come to take prisoners away to be executed. Many of them, when the fatal moment came, were dragged from their cells screaming and fighting. Lilje knew with utmost clarity that if it could be brought off, he too might be summoned any night. Here is his description of how imaginative forethought became his discipline for such a time:

> So, in addition to my rule of Life which I carried on as usual, I added a quarter of an hour of daily meditation on death, in order to prepare myself, gradually, for the possibility of execution. Every day I used to end this quarter of an hour with the prayer that God would not let my knees tremble if I had to step on that stool of which my neighbour had recently told me. Henceforward, I looked up daily to the Son of God, who, in the Garden of Gethsemane, had surrendered to the difficult and holy Will of God, who through His agony and conflict has robbed death of its fears. From Him I learned to endure trembling and anguish, and to say "Yes" to this difficult holy Will of God. This is an agony upon which God's blessing rests; . . . This is a holy conflict with death, against whose dark clouds the rainbow of the Divine Mercy shines out as never before.[3]

[3]Hanns Lilje, *The Valley of the Shadow,* Translated with an Introduction by Olive Wyon (Philadelphia: Fortress Press, 1977), pp. 90-91.

If and when you have put imaginative forethought into practice, you have embraced the central method for all spiritual discipline, the alternation between withdrawal or retreat for reflection, meditation, and prayer; and advance into the market place of your life where you apply to all the tasks and demands the insights and disciplines which your meditation and prayer have revealed to you as sound, true, and worthy of action.

Selections from the "Family Documents"

A Lifetime Adventure

My own conversion came through, or on the occasion of, my first sacramental confession when a precocious, wholesome, much-complicated soul of (turned) fifteen. It was deepened appreciably when at eighteen by the, to me, utterly unforgettable example, silent influence, and definite teaching of a mystically minded but scholastically trained Dutch Dominican [Father Raymond Hocking] in Vienna when I was sickening with typhus fever, when my father had just died, and when "the world" which till then had looked so brilliant to me, turned out so distant, cold, shallow. And the final depth attained so far was mediated for me at forty. I felt at the time and feel still that it came straight from God, yet on the occasion of and by the help of man--by a physically suffering, spiritually aboundingly helpful, mystical saint, a French secular priest [Abbé Huvelin].

[14]*Baron von Hügel*

Von Hügel at 18 made a commitment to "go into moral and religious training." Father Raymond Hocking warned him as follows:

. . . "You want to grow in virtue, to serve God, to love Christ? Well, you will grow in and attain these things if you will make them a slow and sure, an utterly real, mountain-step plod and ascent, willing to have to camp for weeks in spiritual desolation, darkness and emptiness at different stages in your march and growth. All demand for constant light, all attempt at eliminating or minimizing the cross and trial, is so much soft folly and puerile trifling." And what Father Hocking taught me as to spirituality is of course, also true, in its way, of all study worthy of the name.

[15]*Baron Von Hügel*

Becoming Singly Intentioned

A pure heart is one that is unencumbered, unworried, uncommitted, and which does not want its own way about anything but which, rather, is submerged in the loving will of God, having denied self. Let a job be ever so inconsiderable, it will be raised in effectiveness and dimension by a pure heart.

[16]*Meister Eckhart*

We ought to keep hold of God in everything and accustom our minds to retain God always among our feelings, thoughts, and loves. Take care how you think of God. As you think of God in church or closet, think of God everywhere. Take God with you among the crowds and turmoil of the alien world. As I have said so often, speaking of uniformity, we do not mean that one should regard all deeds, places, and people as interchangeable. That would be a great mistake; for it is better to pray than to spin and the church ranks above the street. You should, however, maintain the same mind, the same trust, and the same earnestness toward God in all your doings. Believe me, if you keep this kind of evenness, nothing can separate you from God-consciousness.

[17]*Meister Eckhart*

Even though your works are lowly, and unimportant in themselves, perform them solely for God and with as much care as if you were binding up the wounds of Christ . . . . Have diversity in your works, but simplicity in your intention.

[18]*Henry Suso*

Dietrich Bonhoeffer, a brilliant young theological scholar, had come to America and had become one of the outstanding Protestant theologians. His writing and teaching was of such high calibre, there was no question but what he was headed for a highly distinguished career in this his chosen field.

Yet at the outset of the Second World War, he felt compelled to return to Germany to cast his lot with the Christian forces against National Socialism. He was well aware of the high risk involved in this commitment. Yet for him this was "the willing of one thing" in obedience to God.

Who stands fast? Only the man whose final standard is not his reason, his principles, his conscience, his freedom, or his virtue, but who is ready to sacrifice all this when he is called to obedient and responsible action in faith and in exclusive allegiance to God--the responsible man, who tries to make his whole life an answer to the question and call of God. Where are these responsible people?

[19]*Dietrich Bonhoeffer*

The success of this work much depends upon the frame of thy heart . . . Get thy heart as clear from the world as thou canst. Wholly lay by the thoughts of thy business, troubles, enjoyments, and everything that may take up any room in thy heart. Get it as empty as thou possibly canst, that it may be the more capable of being filled with God . . .

[20]*Olive Wyon quoting Richard Baxter*

The Problem of Readiness

. . . we all pass through periods when all reality seems to have faded out of prayer, when we are not so much unhappy as bored; religion and all its practices have become deadly dull. St. Bernard gives a vivid description of this state of soul; he says that when he is in this condition: "My heart is dried up, and my soul like a land without water . . . . I find no savour in the Psalms; I have no pleasure in reading good books. Prayer does not recreate me. The door is not open to meditation. I am lazy in my work, sleepy in my watchings, prone to anger, obstinate in my dislikes, free in my tongue, and unrestrained in my appetite." Various names are given to this state of mind by spiritual writers: one is "dryness;" when this develops into suffering it is called "desolation." When we are suffering from "dryness" or "aridity" the danger is that we may be tempted to neglect prayer for something more "useful." But quiet persistence in prayer, in spite of our feelings or lack of emotional response, will have a very purifying effect; for we are now learning to care for God for Himself; we are being moved into a higher class in the school of prayer, and we are learning lessons which will stand us in good stead for the rest of our life. We are beginning to approach maturity.

[21]*Olive Wyon*

"These are times of great fruitfulness," writes Baron von Hügel, "provided we will be patient, force nothing, change no regulation, decide nothing capable of being put off, but gently busy ourselves with other things . . . ." In another letter he speaks more fully about the way in which we should react to the "stress of dryness and darkness." He admits that such passages are very trying, but insists that they are "*irreplaceably profitable.*" "If you but gently persevere through them, you will come out at the other end of the gloom sooner or later into ever deeper, tenderer day."

[22]*Olive Wyon*

Reflection and Action

Are you willing to be open to living with these spiritual disciplines for your lifetime?

How would you describe your readiness or lack of it right now with regard to becoming singly intentioned?

How could you begin to practice being singly intentioned and willing one thing?

Imaginative forethought has been one of the most exciting and helpful proposals in this entire book. What problem or personal situation are you facing this week that could use an application of imaginative forethought? Try it and see what happens.

Selection Footnotes

1. *With the Door Open*, p. 12. V. Grönbech, editor, and author of the Introduction.
2. Evelyn Underhill, *The School of Charity* (London and New York: Longmans, Green and Co., 1934), p. 7.

3. Dag Hammarskjöld, *Markings*, Translated by Leif Sjöberg and W. H. Auden with a Foreword by Auden (New York: Alfred A. Knopf, 1964), p. 56.

4. *With the Door Open*, pp. 23-24.

5. *With the Door Open*, pp. 72-75.

6. Byron McElroy, unpublished paper, Winter, 1980.

7. Julie Sheetz, unpublished paper, Winter, 1980.

8. Douglas V. Steere, *On Beginning From Within* (New York and London: Harper and Brothers Publishers, 1943), p. 145.

9. William Law, *A Serious Call to a Devout and Holy Life--New Bedford's Andrew Gerrish, Jr., 1821.* Quoted by Dorothy B. Phillips, *The Choice is Always Ours* (New York: Richard R. Smith, 1949), p. 41.

10. *The Choice is Always Ours,* edited by Dorothy Phillips (New York: Richard Smith, 1948), p. 5, abridged quotation from *Meister Eckhart* A Modern Translation, edited by Raymond Bernard Blakney (New York and London: Harper and Brothers Publishers, 1941).

11. Sheldon Cheyney, *Men Who Have Walked with God* (New York: Alfred A. Knopf, 1946), pp. 378-379, quotation from Edward Carpenter, *The Art of Creation* (London, 1907).

12. *Spiritual Counsel and Letters of Baron Friedrich von Hügel*, edited with an Introductory Essay by Douglas V. Steere (New York and Evanston: Harper and Row Publishers, 1964), pp. 60-61.

13. *Spiritual Counsel and Letters of Baron Friedrich von Hügel*, p. 11.

14. *Spiritual Counsel and Letters of Baron Friedrich von Hügel*, pp. 3-4. Original letter given to Douglas Steere by Emelia Fogelklow Norlind. Used by permission of Douglas V. Steere.

15. *Spiritual Counsel and Letters of Baron Friedrich von Hügel*, p. 4.

16. *Meister Eckhart,* A Modern Translation, edited by Raymond B. Blakney. (New York and London: Harper and Brothers, Publishers, 1941), p. 4.

17. *Meister Eckhart*, p. 8.

18. Henry Suso, *The Exemplar,* Vol. II. Translated by Sister M. Ann Edward, (Dubuque, Iowa: The Priory Press, 1962), p. 288.

19. Dietrich Bonhoeffer, *Letters and Papers from Prison,* Revised and Enlarged Edition. Copyright c. 1953, 1967, 1971, by SCM Press, Ltd., p. 5.

20. *The School of Prayer*, p. 100.

21. *The School of Prayer*, p. 89-90.

22. *The School of Prayer*, p. 90.

CHAPTER

III

SPIRITUAL DISCIPLINES FOR EVERYDAY LIVING

Douglas V. Steere

1901--

Courtesy: Douglas V. Steere and Haverford College.

After serving on the faculty of Haverford College from 1928-1964, Douglas Steere is now the Emeritus T. Wistar Brown Professor of Philosophy.

Combining deep personal faith with profound scholarship, he has provided us with many "family documents" from his own writings and lectures: On Beginning from Within, Prayer and Worship, and Work and Contemplation. His interpretations of other devotional writers include Doors Into Life and his translation of Kierkegaard's Purity of Heart. His editing and introduction of von Hügel's Spiritual Counsel and Letters of Baron Friedrich von Hügel enrich our legacy of great writings concerning the life of the spirit.

"Hastening unto God and hastening into the world" has been characteristic of Dr. Steere. An organizer of Quaker relief work in Finland in 1948; for ten years the chairman of the Work Camp Committee of the American Friends Service Committee; official observer at the Second Vatican Council and initiator in the formation of the Ecumenical Institute of Spirituality, he has related the contemplative life to the life of social action, renewal and reconciliation.

We were privileged to have Doulgas Steere direct a number of our early seminars over a two-year period at Crozer, and I am personally indebted to him for the gracious and scholarly criticism he has given in the final preparation of this book.

Chapter III

INTERRELATEDNESS

We are required at the outset, as well as for the duration of our spiritual pilgrimage to become serious students of human nature. Any pilgrimage with God is a one-with-one encounter between God and a person. In order for this encounter to be shared and vital, we need to understand our own humanity; our strengths and weaknesses; our interrelationships with all others and our essential individuality. This is the work set before us in this chapter and in Chapter IV. Both are preparation for Chapter V, The Practice of the Presence of God.

First we delve into what it really means to be inescapably interrelated.

OUR ESSENTIAL UNITY

John Donne's famous and often quoted line, "No man is an island," takes us directly to the fact of our underlying essential unity. Just as an island beneath the surface of the water is integrally connected to the mainland, so, despite our individuality, our visible independence, and the appearance of being alone, we are all integral parts of one humanity. We are by nature interrelated. In this section we shall attempt to be open to every insight which will help us understand what it means to be interrelated and how we may end up on the positive, creative side of living in these interrelationships. In the next chapter we shall concentrate on the importance of maturing selfhood.

Where and how are we informed about this essential unity we all share as human beings? I am indebted to one of the seminar students, Karen Davis, whose helpful observations point to several dimensions of knowledge through which we may be informed about our interrelatedness. She writes,

> The whole concept of the interrelatedness of all Reality might be more easily understood by being

> introduced at the level of the physical and material, rather than the spiritual level. For example, a book on biology, such as *Lives of a Cell* by Lewis Thomas, or on atomic physics, *The Tao of Physics* by Fritzof Capra, enables the reader to "see" interrelatedness in "this world" and could thus facilitate the "jump" to the spiritual realm. I would [also] recommend some volume on the economic interrelatedness of the entire world, perhaps something by Schumacker, or Buckminster Fuller on ecology . . . it might be helpful to stress that interrelatedness is an ontological fact, i.e., it is the actual architecture of Reality.[1]

The Judeo-Christian scriptures give us clear readings concerning our interrelatedness.

The Psalmist sharpens our understanding of our unique individuality, shared by all humanity when he asks of God, "What is man that thou art mindful of him and the son of man that thou dost care for him? Yet thou hast made him little less than God and dost crown him with glory and honor."[2] Now consider Saint Augustine's beautiful prayer, "Thou hast made us for thyself and our hearts are restless until they find rest in Thee." These two poetic utterances introduce us to the biblical understanding that we share the common inheritance of a potentially realistic relationship with God.

The scriptural passage known popularly as the golden rule is rooted in this same understanding of our interrelatedness. "So whatever you wish that men would do to you, do so to them."[3] The force of the concept of our essential unity is apparent in Matthew 7:1-12.

The greatest commandment of all sums up the whole matter. "You shall love the Lord your God with all your heart, and with all your soul, and with all your strength, and with all your mind, and your neighbor as yourself."[4] Every one of these spiritual

[1]Karen Davis, Student Evaluation paper; unpublished, Winter 1980.

[2]Psalm 8:4-5. *The Holy Bible*, Revised Standard Version.

[3]Matthew 7:12. *The Holy Bible*, Revised Standard Version.

[4]Luke 10:27. *The Holy Bible*, Revised Standard Version.

disciplines will provide insight and give us direction for the keeping of this commandment. The longer I live with these spiritual truths, the more I discover each leads me back to the great commandment. Clearly, it becomes the recurring theme of this entire book.

Humanity's fall from grace as described in Genesis makes it perfectly clear that we are all one in our inheritance of easy capabilities to sin against God and all persons everywhere. Take time to reflect upon the many ways in which our shared sinfulness mars, hurts and impedes our interrelatedness. These selections (#1 through 6) call for careful and thorough reflection, for they may well furnish us with further insight about the nature of our essential unity.

Selections from the "Family Documents"

Here are a number of profound insights by Lawrence LeShan, a man who engaged in a nine-year scholarly investigation concerning the reality of the life of the spirit. The results of his arduous work are to be found in *The Medium, the Mystic and the Physicist*. To describe the world of spirit and its consequent life-giving potential he speaks of the Clairvoyant Reality as being just as real as the Sensory Reality, the world of nature.

I might start by asking what is most important about ***Mary Smith or*** John K. Jones. Clearly, the most important thing about ***them*** is that ***they are*** individuals, unique ***persons***, John K. Jones ***and Mary Smith*** . . . the seventh that ***they are*** fields of energy interacting with other energy fields of all kinds . . . until we come to what is ordinarily considered the *least* important thing about ***them***; that ***they are*** part of the total cosmos, that, ***each*** is one with all and everything, with the total universe . . . . We usually tend to consider that the most important aspects are the ones clustering around the unique and individual end of the spectrum.

In the special moments of paranormal perception, I discovered from the writings of the clairvoyants, this consideration is reversed . . . It is the *unity* of all things that is seen as most important, their *relationships* rather than their individual and unique characteristics that are seen as crucial.

[1]*Lawrence Le Shan*

Further, there is an ethical aspect implicit in the Clairvoyant [Spiritual] Reality. If I *know* that in a real and profound sense you and I are one and are both integral parts of the total One, I treat you in the same way I treat myself. In addition, I treat myself with love and respect because I am part of the total harmony of the universe . . . If I regard you and me as separate, and do not accept that we are part of one another, I tend to treat you differently than I treat myself.

[2]*Lawrence Le Shan*

If, however, instead of the necessary, practical goals of the biological and physical world which we can work toward so well in the Sensory Reality, we wish to work toward another type of goal, we need the Clairvoyant Reality. If we wish to choose as our goals a sense of serenity, peace, joy in living, being fully at home in the cosmos, a deeper understanding of truth, our fullest ability to love, we need the world of the One. Beyond this, however, is the crucial fact that to attain our full humanness we need both.

[3]*Lawrence Le Shan*

The deepest goal is to integrate the two in our lives, so that each viewpoint is heightened and sharpened by the knowledge of the other. This is the lesson of the magnificent Rodin statues which shade off into the raw unfinished rock of our planet. The tremendous individuality and uniqueness given by the finished parts of the statue, the vibrancy and thrust of being they provide, is accented by the part that shades into the raw stone and thus into oneness with the stuff of the world. The background of the One heightens our perception of the specialness and uniqueness of the individual, as the special quality of the individual note of music may be accentuated by its being a part of the symphony.

[4]*Lawrence Le Shan*

No man is is an Island, intire of it selfe; every man is a piece of the *Continent*, a part of the maine; if Clod bee washed away by the *Sea, Europe* is the lesse, as well as if a *Promontorie* were, as well as if a Mannor of thy *friends* or of *thine owne* were; any man's *death* diminishes *me*, because I am involved in *Mankind*; And therefore never send to know for whom the *bell* tolls; It tolls for *thee*.

[5]*John Donne*

For this turning to the light and Spirit of God within Thee is thy *only true* turning unto God; there is no other Way of finding ***God*** but in that Place where ***God*** dwelleth in Thee. For though God be everywhere present, yet ***God*** is only present to Thee in the deepest and most central Part of thy Soul. Thy natural *Senses* cannot possess God or unite Thee to ***God***; nay, thy inward Faculties of *Understanding, Will*, and *Memory*, can only reach after God, but cannot be the *Place* of ***God's*** Habitation in Thee. But there is a *Root* or *Depth* in Thee from whence all these Faculties come forth, as Lines from a *Centre*, or as Branches from the Body of the Tree. This depth is called the *Centre*, the *Fund* or *Bottom* of the soul. This depth is the *Unity*, the *Eternity*, I had almost said, the *Infinity* of thy Soul; for it is so infinite, that nothing can satisfy it, or give it any Rest, but the infinity of God.

[6]*William Law*

Reflection and Action

- Why should we love our neighbors as ourselves?
- Has there ever been a time when you have been aware of your essential oneness with others?
- After reflection about these selections try writing about your understanding of your own essential unity.

PRACTICE REQUIRES CREATIVE, WHOLESOME, RESILIENT INDIVIDUALS

To understand fully what it means to be interrelated we must begin with our essential unity, which is the primary relationship. Then we can turn to grasp the meaning and importance of becoming creative, wholesome, resilient individuals who are capable of nourishing and fulfilling human relationships. Without an essential "me," whose authenticity is genuine and maturing, our essential unity is less than adequately expressed or discovered.

"It takes two to tango" is more than a clever comment; it takes us to the heart of the matter. Relatedness is possible only when there are at least two persons between whom (inter) there is potential action, recognition and response (relatedness). The second group of quotations (#7 through 9) are worthy of serious reflection and discussion as you come to appreciate the importance of being a strong, creative, yet genuinely humble and open person in your own right. In several seminars, the group found Rollo May's concept of an individual's "meaning-matrix" a very stimulating and challenging way to talk about our individuality (see #8).

In practice, when I have discovered more about the reality of the "me," the core of my life, how I came to be this collection of values, insights, feelings--my "meaning-matrix," then I am free to take a different view of the person opposite me who may appear as friend, co-worker, advocate or adversary. Would you believe this ends in several very practical consequences? First I no longer make snap judgments in situations where it is all too easy to look at surface facts without considering the person or persons involved. Second, this different view gives me a better chance to ask the right questions in any given situation where human beings are involved. Asking the right question helps get at the truth of the issue at hand.

The writer of one of the *Letters of the Scattered Brotherhood* describes this center core of oneself as the smallest ring at the center of an ever-widening series of concentric rings, the outermost of which is the surface level of our lives filled with detail, demands, decisions, interruptions as well as all the necessary pursuits of life.

Sociologists and psychologists have long pointed to the "role playing" nature of our lives. They describe our roles as parents, husbands, wives, friends, breadwinners, club members, church members, and a host of other accepted parts we play in the drama of life. Yet in this very natural response in fulfilling many roles, as we mature, we discover the significance of having a solid core at the very center, the "Real Me," the person that is the reality functioning with integrity, reliability and joy.

This core must be vital, resilient, vigorous and fully aware of its own identity. Without such a center which I consciously recognize as the *Real Me* my life is simply a series of reactions, and involvements strung together like beads, but hollow at the center. How thoroughly do we see this and realize its implications for our maturity?

The full, free and joyous acceptance of the reality of the Real Me at the center of the inward life is the important factor in the disciplined spiritual life. The Real Me is the role player, whose existence is in creative solitude.

Here is a very specific application of these insights. In an organization in which I served as executive director I was getting criticism about the lack of performance of one of my staff members who was not answering the hundreds of detailed budget requests for which he was responsible. Because this man was also a close personal friend I stepped back from my first reaction to call him in and tell him to "shape up today." Fortunately I had at my disposal an excellent review of my friend's strengths and weaknesses (his "meaning-matrix"). I took time to review this before taking any action.

The review made it clear that here was an individual who became more frustrated and inoperative as the amount of detail to be handled increased in geometric proportions. With this fact, it was then possible to begin to ask a few right questions such as these. How important is the handling of budgetary details to the total job performance? The answer was, it was not really of great importance. It was a routine matter that should be handled easily and without heavy consumption of time and energy. Then came the question: if this is true, then are there other ways of getting this detailed phase of the job done? Yes, there was a way; sitting right in our office was a person who had reached a peak in the level of responsibility, a person who enjoyed detail and all the routine work involved. This person was given a new title with the added responsibility of all this detailed work. Overnight the field flak disappeared--one person stretched up to new responsibility and the departmental head was freed up to function even more effectively in areas where his leadership was most needed and appreciated.

Selections from the "Family Documents"

What does the interrelatedness of the individual and the "all" have to do with the day-to-day business of raising children? That is what we will be looking at in this book. Western psychology throughout years of competitive individualism has been more interested in the development of "autonomy"--our struggle to become independent, learn skills, leave home--and presents the autonomous "ego" as the ultimate in human development. Yet, although from the time egg and sperm meet we are constantly becoming more unique, more "ourselves," at the same time we are always embedded in a larger nurturing field, beginning with the womb, but not limited to it. The growth of a human being always and simultaneously involves both differentiation and unity.

The more we can experience our "ego" as part of this field, this unity, the less frightened, lonely, and insecure we will be, as children or adults. And the more we can experience our interconnectedness, the less willing we will be to destroy each other and our world.

[7]*Annette Hollander*

Every person, sane or insane, lives in a meaning-matrix which ***she or*** he, to some extent, makes . . . but . . . makes it within the shared situation of human history and language. This is why language is so important: it is the milieu within which we find and form our meaning-matrix, a milieu which we share with our fellow human beings . . . . I must be able to participate in my patient's meanings but preserve my own meaning-matrix at the same time, and thus unavoidably, and rightfully, interpret for him ***or her*** what he ***or she*** is doing--and often doing to me. The same thing holds true in all other human relationships as well: friendship and love require that we participate in the meaning-matrix of the other but without surrendering our own. This is the way human consciousness understands, grows, changes, becomes clarified and meaningful.

[8]*Rollo May*

Harry Stack Sullivan . . . gave abundant evidence that we love others to the extent that we are able to love ourselves, and if we cannot esteem ourselves, we cannot esteem or love others.

[9]*Rollo May*

Reflection and Action

- How would you describe your "meaning-matrix" or the "real me"?

- What are the most creative, wholesome and resilient features of the real you?

- In what ways can you be free to really see, understand and appreciate other persons?

- What does it mean then to be free to ask the right questions in those various situations involving you with other persons?

THE CONSEQUENCES OF INTERRELATEDNESS

When we become creative, wholesome and resilient individuals by participating completely in our own essential unity and in our basic interrelatedness, we will find ourselves caring about other persons and seeking to enrich and strengthen all our human relationships.

Consider first that *caring matters most*. Once we have come to appreciate our essential unity and have discovered what it means to participate more completely in this, our basic interrelationship, by being creative, wholesome and resilient individuals, we find that we are moved to care about persons and about the enrichment and the strengthening of these human relationships.

Out of the counseling, teaching, preaching assignments which have been mine in recent years, the constantly recurring concern is this: who around us is in need of caring? What are our particular talents which can be expended in caring for others? How do we find out about the real unmet needs of others? Let these writings concerning caring provide us with the means to step out with imaginative forethought to start caring for others.

Out of caring issues what may be the ultimate in being interrelated, namely learning and practicing the highly sensitive art of *intercessory prayer*. Once we have come to care supremely about a person or persons we have laid down the basis of loving concern which makes it possible to release a wide variety of creative and helpful influences in support of those for whom we pray. The validity of intercessory prayer rests upon the certainty that within the oneness of the spiritual world in which all of us may be inheritors, there are spiritual currents and energies available to give strength, encouragement, and insight to those for whom we care.

Read, re-read and meditate on the following selections (#16 through 19) concerning intercessory prayer and seek to understand the importance of caring and praying for others in enriching our experience of interrelatedness.

Selections from the "Family Documents"

Our great hope is in Christianity--our only hope. Christ recreates. Christianity has taught us to care. Caring is the greatest thing--caring matters most. My faith is not enough--it comes and goes. I have it about some things and not about others. So we make up and supplement each other. We give and others give to us . . . remember, no joy without suffering--no patience without trial--no humility without humiliation--no life without death.

[10]*Baron von Hügel*

Care is a state in which something does *matter*; care is the opposite of apathy. Care is the necessary source of eros, the source of human tenderness.

[11]*Rollo May*

But care is always caring *about* something. We are caught up in our experience of the objective thing or event we care about. In care one must, by involvement with the objective fact, do something about the situation; one must make some decisions. This is where care brings love and will together.

[12]*Rollo May*

This is the mythos of care. It is a statement which says that whatever happens in the external world, human love and grief, pity and compassion are what matter. These emotions transcend even death.

[13]*Rollo May*

Care is . . . a feeling denoting a relationship of concern, when the other's existence matters to you; a relationship of dedication, taking the ultimate form of being willing to get delight in or, in ultimate terms, to suffer for, the other.

[14]*Rollo May*

Hanns Lilje says this of his friend and fellow prisoner, Freiherr von Guttenberg:

He had retained a complete capacity for thinking of others; and the reason for this was the simple fact that he was a Christian. His example showed us that kindness and courage are mysteriously related. Genuine kindness is the privilege of great and fearless souls. Most human beings cannot be kind in this way, because they are afraid. Who but a fearless man could have exercised this quiet kindness which he gave us during these nights of danger? . . . But he lived in that spirit of kindness that springs from a holy fearlessness. He is one of those who kept alight in this building the pure, clear flame of human dignity and greatness.

[15]*Hanns Lilje*

LeShan describes this interrelatedness at the level of prayer in the Transpsychic Reality in this fashion:

Prayer is one way of conceptualizing the mode of action and communication in this reality, and true prayer must be done purely. One can only really pray for the best for another part of the whole, for its increased harmony. Prayer that is specific beyond this disrupts the Transpsychic Reality. It implies greater knowledge of what is "best" for one part of the All by another part, and thus leads to a division and separation of the parts from the whole that disrupts this way of being-in-the-world and returns one to the Sensory Reality. Certainly the compassion one feels for another's pain or illness can lead one to pray for ***that person***, to go into the Transpsychic Reality, and sometimes this seems to lead to quite startling results. "Religion," wrote R. H. Blyth, is "the infinite way we do finite things." In addition, the prayer must be "pure," that is, without reference to one's own best interests.

[16]*Lawrence LeShan*

Those who deal much with souls soon come to know something about the strange spiritual currents which are at work under the surface of life, and the extent in which charity can work on the supernatural levels for supernatural ends. But if you are to do that, the one thing that matters is that you should care supremely about it; care, in fact, so much that you do not mind how much you suffer for it. We cannot help anyone until we do care, for it is only by love that spirit penetrates spirit.

Consider for a moment what is implied in this amazing mystery of intercession; at least in the little that we understand of it. It implies first our implicit realization of God, the infinitely loving, living and all-penetrating Spirit of Spirits, as an Ocean in which we all are bathed. And next, speaking still that spatial language to which our human thinking is tied down, that somehow through this uniting and vivifying medium we too, being one with ***God*** in love and will, can mutually penetrate, move and influence each other's souls in ways as yet unguessed; yet throughout the whole process moulded and determined by the prevenient, personal, free and ever-present God. The world ***God*** has been and is creating is a world infused through and through with Spirit; and it is partly through the prayerful and

God-inspired action of ***persons*** that the spiritual work of this world is done. When a man or woman of prayer, through their devoted concentration, reaches a soul in temptation and rescues it, we must surely acknowledge that this is the action of God . . ., using that person as an instrument.

[17]*Evelyn Underhill*

Can we make *all* our relations to our fellows relations which pass ***through God***? Our relations to the conductor on a trolley? Our relations to the clerk who serves us in a store? How far is the world from such an ideal! How far is Christian practice from such an expectation! Yet we, from our end of the relationship, can send out the Eternal Love in silent, searching hope, and meet each person with a background of eternal expectation and a silent, wordless prayer of love. For until the life for ***each of us*** in time is, in every relation, shot through with Eternity, the Blessed Community is not complete.

[18]*Thomas Kelly*

Because Charles Whiston's book, *Teach Us to Pray*, is out of print, I have with his permission used extensive quotations here as well as in other chapters.

What follows is a series of excerpts from his most excellent Chapter 9, entitled *Intercession*. If you can find a library copy or find one for sale in a second hand or rare book store, you will want to read that chapter.

. . . God cares, and cares redemptively for each and every . . . creature . . . But it is only slowly over the years that we learn through adoration and self-giving that caring is not Christian caring until it is caring for all. (pp. 115, 116)

The basic motif of intercession is simple to grasp. We turn to God to offer our strength, love, energies, time--our whole life in its entirety--in order that God may use them . . . for the blessing of some other person . . . In Christian intercession we seek nothing for ourselves, but only the glory of God and the salvation of another person. (pp. 120, 121)

We, with our limited freedom, may not be able to enter into another person's inner life, but God in . . . perfect freedom and prevenience can work in and upon the person's life with the energy and love which we have offered. (p. 122)

Our first act of intercession will be that of turning to God and our second act of intercession will be to offer our life to God for ***the ones for whom we pray***. We say: "O God, I give thee myself--all that I am, and all that I have." And then: "Take me and all that I have; purge and cleanse it, and use it as may be most for thy glory and thy blessing . . . ." (p. 122)

All that we need to do is to turn our hearts toward God; name the person; then offer to God our loving and unselfish concern for ***that person***. (p. 124)

God also links our lives with strangers, whom we know not by name and whom we may never meet again; we are walking on the street and notice the strained and anxious face of a person who passes by; we notice the fatigue written in the face and posture of the ***individual*** seated across from us in the train; . . . we overhear another's vile language: for all of these strangers we offer unselfishly to God our loving intercession, that they may be saved by God. (p. 127)

We do not need to see or fully understand how God uses our offered energies. Our belief in the power of intercession is rooted primarily in our faith, responding to the prevenience of God. God . . . cares redemptively for every ***person***. We cannot believe that when we turn to ***God*** and unselfishly offer our love and energy for one . . . needy ***creature, God*** will pay no attention to our offering. Does God care less than we do? We have faith that God takes whatever we offer . . . for others, purges it, directs it, and uses it . . . for the blessing and saving of that person. This is not however to claim that ***God*** uses it just ***as*** we expect or desire, but only . . . in . . . wisdom and love. As we practice this intercessory work over the years, we are given by God . . . to know and see something of the mighty power of Christian intercession upon the lives of those for whom we pray. (p. 128)

This work of intercession has very real consequences. The first and foremost result is that it actually conforms us to God's redemptive concern for all. We find our lives sharing more and more in ***God's*** love for all. We find ourselves living less and less for ourselves, and like God, living more and more for others. We find that we are given by God deeper and truer insight into the real needs of those for whom we intercede. We enter into richer and fuller companionships with people, just because they are rooted in praying.

Moreover intercession is a great source of health and purity of life. There is a marked difference in power and cleanliness between a mountain stream and a stagnant pool. The mountain brook never stays still. All that it receives from on high, it at once passes on. The stagnant pool receives, holds fast, and will not give out freely. It thus becomes dirty and foul. So too it is with our lives. The selfish life holds fast and will not give out in intercession. The intercessory life at once gives out and passes on to others all that it has received from God, in order that others may thereby be blessed and saved.

But there is also a real and objective power upon those for whom we intercede . . . . The energy and love which we offer, ***God*** uses it to bless and save others. Behind every ***person's*** salvation lies hidden much Christian intercession. Often God uses us indirectly for the salvation of another person. Sometimes ***God*** uses us directly for when we pray unselfishly for another, God often gives us concrete opportunities of implementing our praying with action. We are also given through intercession a much deeper insight into the essential meaning of the Church--that great fellowship of all those whose lives are knit together by God in Jesus Christ. (pp. 133, 134)

[19]*Charles Whiston*

Reflection and Action

- Why should caring matter most?
- Who needed caring this past week and you passed by on the other side of the road?
- Using imaginative forethought, who among those you know, love and work with are in need of caring this week? What can you do about it?
- Why and how are caring and intercessory prayer related?

Selection Footnotes

1. Lawrence LeShan, *The Medium, the Mystic, and the Physicist.* (New York: Ballantine Books, 1975); pp. 34, 35.
2. *The Medium, the Mystic, and the Physicist,* p. 52.
3. *The Medium, the Mystic, and the Physicist,* pp. 58-59.
4. *The Medium, the Mystic, and the Physicist,* p. 60.
5. John Donne, *Devotions Upon Emergent Occasions,* XVII, 1623.
6. The Works of The Reverend William Law in Nine Volulmes: Volume VII, *The Spirit of Prayer,* in Two Parts (London: Printed for M. Richardson in *Pater-noster Row,* 1749), p. 28.
7. Annette Hollander, M.D. *How to Help Your Child Have a Spiritual Life.* (New York: A & W Publishers, Inc., 1980), pp. 17-18.
8. Rollo May, *Love and Will.* (New York: W. W. Norton and Co., Inc., Delta Books, 1973), pp. 261-262.
9. *Love and Will,* p. 84.
10. *Spiritual Counsel and Letters of Baron Friedrich von Hügel,* p. 34.
11. *Love and Will,* p. 289.
12. *Love and Will,* p. 291.
13. *Love and Will,* p. 302.
14. *Love and Will,* p. 303.
15. *The Valley of the Shadow,* pp. 78-79.
16. *The Medium, the Mystic, and the Physicist,* p. 159.
17. Evelyn Underhill, *Concerning the Inner Life with The House of the Soul.* (New York: E. P. Dutton and Co., Inc., 1953), pp. 49-50.
18. Thomas R. Kelly, *A Testament of Devotion.* (New York and London: Harper and Brothers, Publishers, 1941, 10th edition), p. 88.
19. Charles Francis Whiston, *Teach Us to Pray,* with an Introduction by Nels F. S. Ferré (Boston, Pilgrim Press, 1948), pp. 115-134, selected portions.

CHAPTER

IV

SPIRITUAL DISCIPLINES FOR EVERYDAY LIVING

Howard Thurman
1900 - 1981

Courtesy, Mrs. Howard Thurman and Colgate Rochester-Bexley Hall-Crozer Seminaries. This portrait given to Dr. Thurman's alma mater, now hangs in the Howard Thurman Black Church Studies Resources Room--a room established in his honor by the seminaries.

A graduate of Morehouse College and Rochester Theological Seminary, he was an outstanding leader in the world of twentieth century religion. His spiritual leadership found expression as a preacher, teacher, poet, theologian, counsellor and author. Influential in his own spiritual maturation were Rufus Jones, Rabindranath Tagore and Mahatma Gandhi.

In 1944 he became the co-founder and co-pastor of the Church for the Fellowship of All Peoples, a congregation of interracial, intercredal and international membership.

He was dean of Marsh Chapel at Boston University and professor of Spiritual Disciplines and Resources in the School of Theology, 1953-65. His twenty-one books reflect his Christian faith lived out in keeping with the disciplines of the spiritual life, and enrich the enduring collection of the "family documents."

Chapter IV

ON BEING ALONE:

FROM LONELINESS TO SOLITUDE

We have discovered that we are equally interconnected, forever destined to search for those lasting and joyous relationships with others of the human family, and yet, we are uniquely individual, forever destined to be ourselves.

This paraphrase from Dietrich Bonhoeffer says it very precisely. Let all who cannot be alone beware of community, and let all who are not in community beware of being alone.

OUR OWN ENDURING CENTER

We turn now to give serious consideration to the discovery of our own enduring center in creative solitude. There is a major segment of your life which is yours and only yours. This became very real to me at the time of my father's death when I was nineteen and an only child. My mother and I together experienced his dying, and while we shared that traumatic event, I realized that there was a segment of that experience which was highly individualistic and unsharable--for my mother had been wife and lover, and I had been son and friend. In no way could either of us enter completely into the complex of emotions, or understanding of the other at the level of these essential relationships. We both had to deal in our own way with our own distinctive sorrow, grief and dismay arising from our totally different relationship to him.

Just so with the sum total of each of us--no other living soul does possess or can possess all of us, for only we ourselves are the sum total of our experiences. Similar though many experiences may be, they can never be totally absorbed by any other human being. Each person is both filter and receptacle and this is our own unique individuality which can and must be mature and wholesome.

In our unique individuality we are alone. This aloneness is in the very nature of our true being, and it is essential we grow into full acceptance of that fact until our enduring center is the base from which all our creative living comes.

Look about you and talk with others concerning their feelings about aloneness. Take time to review your own reactions to being alone especially extreme moments of isolation which do come to all of us.

In so doing we discover that we ourselves and many others have called aloneness--loneliness. When we regard these experiences as loneliness we then rush out to seek many ways to fill the void. If we are unsuccessful in filling the emptiness we may end in boredom, or despair, hopelessness or alienation.[1]

It is essential that we expose loneliness for what it is, a short circuit which takes us away from the rugged but creatively powerful understanding of the very nature of our beings; an entire segment of our lives is ever and always uniquely independent and alone.

Only when we have freely and fully accepted this truth about ourselves are we able to begin to explore and move to living in creative solitude. Such acceptance leads to a dawning awareness of what it means to be in possession of this enduring center--ourselves in our aloneness. There is no fear here. There can be the beginning discovery of power and strength which sustains us in such solitude. Then it becomes abundantly clear: here is the place where God meets us.

Selections from the "Family Documents"

Howard Thurman takes us directly to the heart of the matter in this meditation about having "a sense of Presence."

. . . It is the solitariness of life that makes it move with such ruggedness. All life is one, and yet life moves in such intimate circles of awful individuality. The power of life perhaps is its aloneness. Bernard Shaw makes Joan of Arc say that . . . aloneness . . . ***is God's*** strength. There are thresholds before which all ***of us*** stop, over which only God may tread--and even ***God***, in disguise. Each soul must learn to stand up in its own right and live. How blissful to lean upon another, to seek a sense of everlasting arms expressed in the vitality of a friend! We walk a part of the way together, but on the upper reaches of life, each path takes its way to the heights--alone. Ultimately, I am alone, so vastly alone that in my aloneness is all the life of the universe. Stripped to the literal substance of myself, there is nothing left but naked soul, the irreducible ground of individual being, which becomes at once the quickening throb of God. At such moments of profound awareness I seem to be all that there is in the world, and all that there is in the world seems to be myself.

[1]*Howard Thurman*

"It is ***your*** enduring center, ***your*** seed that will endure. Search yourself for this constant within . . . you will not find it in your brain, look for it rather in the region of the heart; or more accurately, in the intangible sensations which have no organic position . . . . There is nothing more important than creating this abode of emotional security, spiritual order and demonstrable strength."

[2]*Betty Stewart*

Everyone has a divine spark and it is realized for the most part, forgotten often. All we bring to you is the prayer, the sympathetic suggestion that you keep it alight. Blow on it until it becomes a reality, for it will consume and burn away dross . . . . Your first task is to blow upon your divine spark and each one is alone . . . in this regard. It isn't enough that we come together and receive renewed strength, surcease and inspiration; the battle is alone with yourself in a material world. You have the instructions, you have the chart, the course is laid. It is for you now at this great time to dedicate your inward life to the manifestation of that which is invisible, this secret personal industry. You will come away with refreshment, encouragement and help from your common communion, but the actual work is yours alone.

[3]*Letters of the Scattered Brotherhood*

[1]For a fuller understanding of what loneliness can do to us, read *Loneliness* by Clark Moustakas, *Reaching Out* by Henri Nouwen, and *The Loneliness of Man* by Raymond Chapman. It would be appropriate either in a seminar group or in individual pursuit, to take time for a thorough mastering of these three important works. (See Bibliography.)

To get at the core of ***God's greatness***, one must first get into the ***individual*** core of ***oneself*** at . . . least, for no one can know God who has not first known ***oneself***. Go to the depths of the soul, the secret place of the Most High, to the roots, to the heights; for all that God can do is focused there.

[4]*Meister Eckhart*

There is an outer ring of yourself surrounded by turbulence, chaos and anxiety; great moments swirling about, cosmic in potentiality. Within this ring is another circle outside of which are your responses to all these alarms and insistent shocks, excitements and dismays. Inside this ring is another ring. This is a place where you sense your ignorances, your unawarenesses, your inadequacies. Here is where you are sorely tried, for this is your human self. And so these rings get smaller as you near the center where you find a place in you that longs for peace, calmness and spiritual understanding. Finally there is the center which seems to the imagination within a very small circumference. Here is where you are, here is a place where you decide; here is where you are yourself. Most people seldom find it except in great moments; and yet when found and realized it encircles the universe. This is the quietness, this is the peace promised to those who seek. For this center lifts you high and clear of all the rings into eternal omniscient vision; here, when your mind is fastened to it and all your thoughts and all desires are pointed toward it, is the Spirit that will lead you through the valleys of the shadows of death, violence and hates and all the confusion that beset you and your country and your world at this time.

Hold to this center. You can only reach it in silence, you can only keep it in quietness, you can only feel it in serenity; this is the place of the pearl of great price.

[5]*Letters of the Scattered Brotherhood*

Life is meant to be lived from a Center, a divine Center. Each one of us can live such a life of amazing power and peace and serenity, of integration and confidence and simplified multiplicity, on one condition--that is, *if we really want to.*

[6]*Thomas Kelly*

Without the solitude of heart, the intimacy of friendship, marriage and community life cannot be creative. Without the solitude of heart, our relationships with others easily become needy and greedy, sticky and clinging, dependent and sentimental, exploitative and parasitic, because without the solitude of heart we cannot experience the others as different from ourselves but only as people who can be used for the fulfillment of our own, often hidden, needs.

The mystery of love is that it protects and respects the aloneness of the other and creates the free space where he ***or she*** can convert . . . loneliness into a solitude that can be shared. In this solitude we can strengthen each other by mutual respect, by careful consideration of each other's individuality, by an obedient distance from each other's privacy and by a reverent understanding of the sacredness of the human heart. In this solitude we encourage each other to enter into the silence of our innermost being and discover there the voice that calls us beyond the limits of human togetherness to a new communion. In this solitude we can slowly become aware of a presence of him who embraces friends and lovers and offers us the freedom to love each other, because he loved us first. (see I John 4:19)

[7]*Henri Nouwen*

Reflection and Action

- Can you identify that segment of yourself which is uniquely you alone?
- Are you willing to accept your aloneness and begin to live creatively in solitude?
- At what points are you living in anxiety with fear of loneliness?

THE PRACTICE OF CREATIVE SOLITUDE

Penelope Colman who has been my most careful, rigorous, and encouraging editor, has provided us with these insights as she was seriously trying to understand what it meant to live in creative solitude.

She discovered, for example, that such living is impossible if we are weary and fatigued. So rest is a discipline for the spiritual life! She also found we cannot do much with creative solitude when we are preoccupied. Silence and quieting of the mind, sense, and emotions are important disciplines! She came to an awareness of the importance of having a safe environment which frees us to take the next steps in living creatively with solitude. The requirement for safe environment includes both internal and external guarantees from psychic stress and physical danger. Here again, "the practice of the presence of God" is the heart of the matter, for here is the essential security, integrity and safety which produces utter fearlessness.

In the midst of learning to accept and live in creative solitude, we discover God at the center of our lives. God is to be found in creative solitude. In our aloneness, the presence of God may become real and totally sufficient. Read and reflect on all the quotations (#8 through 16), then resolve to live with this insight, for the creative side of solitude is the way in which we open ourselves to God's presence.

The testimony of Hanns Lilje (#11) and Alfred Delp (#3) in Chapter V came from the extremity of imprisonment and solitary confinement. We do not have to be in prison to discover that "God alone suffices." The "family documents" invite us to explore and experience the presence of God as being central to our growth into the life of the spirit.

In the next series of selections we also discover more about what it can be like at the center of our lives. These are descriptions by individuals out of their own experience. For us to expect exactly the same experience would be wrong. Our own experiences in creative solitude may lead us to selflessness. We may be illumined and clear in our thinking and discovery of new truth, or we may move into an all-pervading sense of infinite quiet and peace based on an inner integrity and power. We may take any or all of these and live with them as potentially possible for the nurture and growth of our own inner selves. At the same time we should take the initiative in exploring other possibilities of living creatively within ourselves.

Selections from the "Family Documents"

I want to prepare you, to organise you for life, for illness, crisis and death. Live all you can--as complete and full a life as you can find--do as much as you can for others. Read, work, enjoy--love and help as many souls--do all this. Yes--but remember: Be alone, be remote, be away from the world, be desolate. Then you will be near God!

[8]*Baron von Hügel*

Finally, be not afflicted nor discouraged to see thyself faint hearted; ***God*** returns to quiet thee, ***and to*** stir thee; because this divine Lord will be alone with thee . . . that thou mayest look for silence in tumult, solitude in company, light in darkness, forgetfulness in pressures, vigour in despondency, courage in fear, resistance in temptation, peace in war and quiet in tribulation.

[9]*Letters from the Scattered Brotherhood*
Entire quotation from Miguel de Molinos, 1640-1697.

Use this indwelling spirit! How many pray to it and then go about their affairs under tension, taking upon themselves the burden from which they have asked to be freed, not trusting the God to whom they have prayed! In the *realizing oneness* with the Spirit do you find your working godhood; the beauty descending and ascending is your freedom. God moves in you now, through limitless space. Cast off your mooring from the land of fear and doubt, leave the prisons of despair and melancholy and set sail on a guided journey . . . .

[10]*Letters from the Scattered Brotherhood*

We cannot truly be alone, if ***we*** cannot be alone with God. In point of fact the tragedy of ***our*** earthly existence comes out in the fact that ***we*** can no longer endure solitude . . . .

But for myself, and for many others in this building, it was a fundamental truth that we were only able to overcome this final terrible solitude by our meeting with God. At some time in ***our lives***, and probably more than once, ***we*** must stand completely alone, over against God, as ***we*** will have to face ***God*** at ***our*** last hour, before ***we*** know that ***we*** must be responsible to God for ***our*** existence on earth, and before ***we*** can understand what it means for our life on earth that the Son of God has hallowed all our solitude by allowing Himself to suffer the final desolation on the Cross.

[11]*Hanns Lilje*

I dare not believe, I do not see how I shall ever be able to believe: that I am not alone . . . . Didst Thou give me this inescapable loneliness so that it would be easier for me to give Thee all?

[12]*Dag Hammarskjöld*

. . . *You will either be disciplined by events or you will make your own discipline.* Therefore make your own discipline and so contribute to great events. Be emotionally strong and firm, spiritually strong as steel, but controlled so that you can bend to shocks and not be uprooted by panics.

All that matters is your response to challenging events. If you are left alone to the inflowing and outflowing of human emotional relationships and the onslaughts of their passing moods you will find that your responses are immediate, you are undefended and emotionally exposed, quick to take fire. The value of these communions and of your silences is that in them you are strengthened and given poise; you are lifted high above the flood and you are given something strong, serene and healing. This is what is meant by the great words, "of myself I do nothing;" you discipline yourselves so that you may receive, and you turn to complete acceptance of the outpouring gift of the Spirit.

[13]*Letters of the Scattered Brotherhood*

. . . Few seem to grasp the true meaning of religion; to many it is a hope through formalized prayers and dogmas to achieve a state of comfort and protection. But this is seldom realized because they leave religion to the teachers. In your adventure toward freedom you have taken an active part in your own development; you have sought sincerely and honestly a working method by which you could live as a channel for the Holy Spirit to flow through for your healing and cleansing and as a way to bring it into the world. You have become aware of receiving comfort and the protection that faith gives, and you know that the core of you is an inward calm, that it is steady and not subject to change. In a sense you have built an ark so that in this flood of emotion, of terror and uncertainty, you are safe. And by that I mean when tempted to dismay and bewilderment by the steady onslaught of news, you can open the invisible door and melt into the steadfast, quiet and confident center of your being.

The old disciplines of the monastic orders were devised to remind the stubborn flesh that it must not come first; the angelus, matins and vespers and the wayside crosses help many to remember the Spirit within. Today, instead of the hair shirt, the cruelty upon the body of the race drives us to the need of awareness of ***God*** to ease our hearts and sustain us, and hard as it is to believe, when you, each in turn, come to your God alone, within, by so much is this holocaust diminished; there is no greater way to practice the love of God, the ***love of persons***, and the fellowship of the Holy Spirit. Within this center of infinite quiet and peace lies resolution to action that is born of love and wisdom. Whenever challenged by the horrors or irritations of human living, you know that through the mind you can touch all that is august, deathless beauty and immortality.

[14]*Letters of the Scattered Brotherhood*

. . . You can only reach God in stillness, in calmness. What is a week, a month in this august destiny? Play the part nobly and refuse this frantic littleness; stand and wait . . . Be comforted, be comforted and learn that destinies are controlled by the delicacy of your calmness within, by your turning to the divine companion who never leaves nor forsakes thee . . . Come where the eternal Spirit, Love itself, untangles, loosens and pulls away from you all that binds, for it unshackles these imprisoning chains, these iron bands of thought and silences the gongs of fear and dismay.

In your outer active life translate humble things into divine things; use this actual outside living as a way to God. Take the serene and timeless peace of a great mountain, feel its vast serenity when you write a letter or stamp an envelope or perform what seems to you very unimportant labors. Bring the divine power into actual life and beautify it.

So peace be unto your hearts and great stillness and calm. Seek this creative peace within; here there is no struggle. Here are beauty and truth and protection and joy in abundance. Here is order; and here, locked away, is the divine plan. When you dissolve and become still, holy in that oneness with the infinite holiness, the divine plan cometh to pass and you are free . . . The secret is to lean on no one but your inner self, through which you touch the tenderness and the power of the almighty Spirit.

[15]*Letters of the Scattered Brotherhood*

Try dissolving your universe, as you have been told before, into spiritual and mental concepts; consider yourself a feeling that has been led about by the events of your time. Character is, in its last analysis, a collection of feelings. A good ***individual*** is a trust feeling. If you dissolve all people to thought and examine your own thought as you carry it about you will see with greater clarity how destructive it is to be a Fear. If you are a Fear, you at once become a vortex which attracts to you currents of obstacles and blockings. But if you are a Confidence going through the unseen, as your true world really is, if you are a spirit of courage, calm and loving, you act like a sun on all about you and grateful faces will turn to you as you touch the creative impulse everywhere. It is as simple as this. Guard yourself from states and when you find yourself sinking into one and you stand before the walls of your Jericho, blow your silver bugle and your clear note of prayer will be heard. Great and good forces are your companions; you do not walk alone, Christ is in your heart.

[16]*Letters of the Scattered Brotherhood*

Reflection and Action

- How have you run away from loneliness (aloneness) this past week or month?

- How can you stop running?

- How can you embrace your aloneness with expectancy? How does #11 answer this?

- Have you ever sensed the presence of God at the center of your aloneness? If never, which of these selections have helped you see that such discovery is possible?

THE CONSEQUENCES OF BEING ALONE

The final series of quotations(#17 through 20) make it clear that this discipline of discovering our true identity through creative solitude is no "cop-out," no withdrawal from "real" life. On the contrary, it is the true source of ultimate power and love which comes from God enabling us to move out into our everyday world with different understanding and far more effective ways of dealing with persons, issues and the problems of our own making as well as the social issues of our time.

Here again it will take serious and continuing reflection to broaden our understanding of this important truth. If we persist in meditation and if we pursue our reading in depth of the "family documents," there will be growing evidence as to these consequences resulting in action.

Karen Davis, in reflecting upon the movement from aloneness as loneliness to aloneness as creative solitude, found that for her it meant the uncovering of her own spiritual qualities, and with such discovery came the touching of the "edge of God's presence." "Here," she says, "it should be emphasized that being created in the image of God means being imbued with spiritual qualities (the combination of, and expression of that which is unique in each individual). Discovery of these qualities in ourselves leads us back to their source--or to God."

Sue Comstock, in reading Thomas Kelly's selection, was reminded of a deep personal experience she had in discovering the "last rock," an experience she recorded in this very moving poem. Kelly's writing was for Sue a refreshing challenge to follow the "path of faith."

"I believe, help my unbelief"

The pain rises over my head.

My feet search for a rock on which to rise
above the tide.

I find one and for a moment I surface and
see the sun.

But, I wonder, is there a rock tall enough to
help me stay near the surface?

And I know somewhere deep in my soul that
there is and it is called God.

And the path of faith is the way to the rock.

What will be the consequences of all this for each of us? We cannot say until we have lived our way into creative solitude. When this is done, we may well have any number of excellent illustrations to offer in support of this. In the meantime, the "family documents" offer a number of ways of experiencing aloneness which turns into creative solitude, and leads us in our pilgrimage into discovering the presence of God.

Selections from the "Family Documents"

. . . But if we *center down*, as the old phrase goes, and live in that holy Silence which is dearer than life, and take our life program into the silent places of the heart, with complete openness ready to do, ready to renounce according to ***God's*** leading, then many of the things we are doing lose their vitality for us. I should like to testify to this, as a personal experience, graciously given. There is a reevaluation of much that we do or try to do, which is *done for us*, and we know what to do and what to let alone.

[17]*Thomas Kelly*

. . . In the late autumn of 1937 after the publication of this book, a new life direction took place in Thomas Kelly. No one knows exactly what happened, but a strained period in his life was over. He moved toward adequacy. A fissure in him seemed to close, cliffs caved in and filled up a chasm, and what was divided grew together within him. Science, scholarship, method, remained good, but in a new setting.

[18]*Douglas V. Steere*

The consequences of this transformed life were evident in a series of lectures Thomas Kelly gave at the Germantown Friends' Meeting in January of 1928. Douglas Steere tells us that:

At Germantown, people were deeply moved and said, "This is *authentic.*" His writings and spoken messages began to be marked by a note of experimental authority. "To you in this room who are seekers, to you, young and old who have toiled all night and caught nothing, but who want to launch out into the deeps and let down your nets for a draught, I want to speak as simply, as tenderly, as clearly as I can. For God *can* be found. There *is* a last rock for your souls, a resting place of absolute peace and joy and power and radiance and security. There is a Divine Center into which your life can slip, a new and absolute orientation in God, a Center where you live with ***God*** and out of which you see all of life, through new and radiant vision, tinged with new sorrows and pangs, new joys unspeakable and full of glory." It was the same voice, the same pen, the same rich imagery that always crowded his writing, and on the whole a remarkably similar set of religious ideas. But now he seemed to be expounding less as one possessed of "*knowledge about*" and more as one who had had unmistakable "*acquaintance with.*" In April 1938, he wrote to Rufus Jones, "The reality of Presence has been very great at times recently. One knows at first hand what the old inquiry meant, "Has Truth been advancing among you?"

[19]*Thomas Kelly*

All this might sound like a new sort of romanticism, but our own very concrete experiences and observations will help us to recognize this as realism. Often we must confess that the experience of our loneliness is stronger than that of our solitude and that our words about solitude are spoken out of the painful silence of loneliness. But there are happy moments of direct knowing, affirming our hopes and encouraging us in our search for that deep solitude where we can sense an inner unity and live in union with our fellow human beings and our God.

I vividly remember the day on which a man who had been a student in one of my courses came back to the school and entered my room with the disarming remark: "I have no problems this time, no questions to ask you. I do not need counsel or advice, but I simply want to celebrate some time with you." We sat on the ground facing each other and talked a little about what life has been for us in the last year, about our work, our common friends, and about the restlessness of our hearts. Then slowly as the minutes passed by we became silent. Not an embarrassing silence but a silence that could bring us closer together than the many small and big events of the last year. We would hear a few cars pass and the noise of someone who was emptying a trash can somewhere. But that did not hurt. The silence which grew between us was warm, gentle and vibrant. Once in a while we looked at each other with the beginning of a smile pushing away the last remnants of fear and suspicion. It seemed that while the silence grew deeper around us we became more and more aware of a presence embracing both of us. Then he said, "It is good to be here" and I said, "Yes, it is good to be together again," and after that we were silent again for a long period. And as a deep peace filled the empty space between us he said hesitantly, "When I look at you it is as if I am in the presence of Christ." I did not feel startled, surprised or in need of protesting, but I could only say, "It is the Christ in you, who recognizes the Christ in me." "Yes," he said, "He indeed is in our midst," and then he spoke the words which entered into my soul as the most healing words I had heard in many years, "From now on, wherever you go, or wherever I go, all the ground between us will be holy ground." And when he left I knew that he had revealed to me what community really means.

[20]*Henri Nouwen*

Reflection and Action

- Reflect upon the one or two insights which now give you the basis upon which to live in creative solitude instead of suffocating loneliness.

- What are the next steps you can take toward living your way into joyous solitude?

- How would the discipline of silence help you?

Selection Footnotes

1. Howard Thurman, *Deep Is the Hunger* (New York: Harper and Row, 1951), pp. 169-170.
2. Cornelia Brunner, "Betty, A Way of Individuation," *Inward Light*, 37, Fall 1950, p. 20.
3. Mary Strong, editor, *Letters of the Scattered Brotherhood* (New York: Harper and Brothers, Publishers, 1948), p. 147.
4. Meister Eckhart, *Fragment #37*, p. 246.
5. *Letters of the Scattered Brotherhood*, pp. 180-181.
6. *A Testament of Devotion*, p. 116.
7. Henri J. M. Nouwen, *Reaching Out, The Three Movements of the Spiritual Life* (Garden City, New York: Doubleday & Co., Inc., 1975), p. 30.
8. *Spiritual Counsel and Letters of Baron Friedrich von Hügel*, p. 176.
9. *Letters of the Scattered Brotherhood*, p. 139.
10. *Letters of the Scattered Brotherhood*, p. 137.
11. *The Valley of the Shadow*, p. 58.
12. Sven Stolpe, *Dag Hammarskjöld: A Spiritual Portrait* (New York: Charles Scribner's Sons, 1966), p. 74.
13. *Letters of the Scattered Brotherhood*, p. 132.
14. *Letters of the Scattered Brotherhood*, pp. 133-134.
15. *Letters of the Scattered Brotherhood*, pp. 127-128.
16. *Letters of the Scattered Brotherhood*, pp. 122-123.
17. *A Testament of Devotion*, p. 118.
18. *A Testament of Devotion*, p. 18.
19. *A Testament of Devotion*, pp. 18-19.
20. *Reaching Out*, pp. 30-31.

Reflection and Action

[illegible]

CHAPTER

V

SPIRITUAL DISCIPLINES FOR EVERYDAY LIVING

Bishop Hanns Lilje

Courtesy: Fortress Press.

Prior to the second World War, Dr. Hanns Lilje was, for ten years, general secretary of the German Christian Students World Union. He served as a secretary of the Lutheran World Federation; and later was elected Bishop of the Evangelical Church of Germany. In August 1944 he was arrested in the purge which followed the July 20th assassination attempt on Hitler. Although he had not been actively involved in the plot, his ties with national and international Christian organizations, and his personal and pastoral relationship with many of those involved in resistance to Hitler and the Fascist state were enough to cause his imprisonment.

In his book, The Valley of the Shadow, Lilje describes his time of imprisonment under the Nazis. This book provides rare and penetrating insights concerning the strength and vitality of Christian faith lived under spiritual discipline in a time of intense crisis and in confrontation with radical evil. It too is one of the 20th century classic "family documents."

Chapter V

THE PRACTICE

OF THE PRESENCE OF GOD

This chapter is pivotal: In understanding our essential unity as well as the center of our aloneness we have caught glimpses of God's presence. We have been introduced to the firsthand experiences of Hanns Lilje, Johannes Anker Larsen and John Woolman. Now in this chapter we will be introduced to the personal experience of God as described by three additional writers. We will explore what it means to practice the presence of God and reflect about the consequences of such practice. In subsequent chapters we will discover in additional disciplines of the life of the spirit further ways in which God's presence is the very heart of the entire pilgrimage.

THE EXPERIENCE OF GOD'S PRESENCE

In addition to the testimony of firsthand experience of God from these writers of the "family documents," it is essential to attend to this witness within the Holy Bible. The Psalms are full of the poetic expression of this. The entire prophetic tradition is firmly rooted in the realities of individuals' deep and radical experience with God.

Our Lord, standing in this prophetic tradition, is the supreme example of a God-centered person. And in the conversion of Saul of Tarsus to Paul the Apostle we are confronted with the continuing evidence of the reality of such personal experience. Out of this heritage has come a succession of pilgrims with God and Christ whose lives and writings show us the way to begin our pilgrimage with God.

Selections from the "Family Documents"

In the year that King Uzziah died I saw the Lord sitting upon a throne, high and uplifted; . . . And I said: "Woe is me: For I am lost; for I am a man of unclean lips, and I dwell in the midst of a people of unclean lips. For my eyes have seen the King, the Lord of hosts!" Then flew one of the seraphim to me, having in his hand a burning coal which he had taken with tongs from the altar. And he touched my mouth, and said: "Behold, this has touched your lips; your guilt is taken away, and your sin forgiven." And I heard the voice of the Lord saying, "Whom shall I send, and who will go for us?" Then I said, "Here I am! Send me."

[1]*The Holy Bible: Isaiah*

M. Beaufort recorded this conversation with Brother Lawrence.

The first time I saw *Brother Lawrence* was upon the third of August 1666. He told me that GOD had done him a singular favour, in his conversion at the age of eighteen.

That in the winter, seeing a tree stripped of its leaves, and considering that within a little time the leaves would be renewed, and after that the flowers and fruit appear, he received a high view of the Providence and Power of GOD, which has never since been effaced from his soul. That this view had set him perfectly loose from the world, and kindled in him such a love for GOD, that he could not tell whether it had increased in above forty years that he had lived since.

[2]*Brother Lawrence*

And that brings me to my own affairs. Have I grown in stature in the past year? Have I increased my value to the community? How do things stand with me?

Outwardly they have never been worse. This is the first New Year I have ever approached without so much as a crust of bread to my name. I have absolutely nothing I can call my own. The only gesture of goodwill I have encountered is that the jailor has fastened my handcuffs so loosely that I can slip my left hand out entirely. The handcuffs hang from my right wrist so at least I am able to write. But I have to keep alert with one ear as it were glued to the door--heaven help me if they should catch me at work!

And undeniably I find myself in the very shadow of the scaffold. Unless I can disprove the accusations on every point I shall most certainly hang. The chances of this happening have never really seriously occupied my thoughts for long although naturally there have been moments of deep depression--handcuffs after all are a symbol of candidature for execution. I am in the power of the law which, in times like the present, is not a thing to be taken lightly.

An honest examination of conscience reveals much vanity, arrogance and self-esteem; and in the past also a certain amount of dishonesty. That was brought home to me when they called me a liar while I was being beaten up. They accused me of lying when they found I mentioned no names except those I knew they knew already. I prayed hard, asking why . . . God permitted me to be so brutally handled and then I saw that there was in my nature a tendency to pretend and deceive.

On this altar much has been consumed by fire and much has been melted and become pliable. It has been one of God's blessings, and one of the signs of ***God's*** indwelling grace, that I have been so wonderfully helped in keeping my vows. ***God*** will, I am confident, extend . . . blessings to my outward existence as soon as I am ready for the next task . . . . From this outward activity and intensified inner light new passion will be born to give witness for the living God, for I have truly learned to know ***God*** in these days of trial and to feel ***the*** healing presence. *God alone suffices* is literally and absolutely true. And I must have a passionate belief in my mission to mankind, showing the way to a fuller life and encouraging the willing capacity for it. These things I will do wholeheartedly *in nomine Domine.*

[3]*Alfred Delp*

Finally, there must be a matured and maturing sense of Presence. This sense of Presence must be a reality at the personal level as well as on the social, naturalistic and cosmic levels. To state it in the simplest language of religion, ***we*** must know that ***we are children*** of God and that the God of life in all its parts and the God of the human heart are one and the same.

Such an assurance will vitalize the sense of self, and highlight the sense of history, with the warmth of a great confidence. Thus, we shall look out upon life with quiet eyes and work on our tasks with the conviction and detachment of Eternity.

Whenever ***my*** mind . . . has been uplifted; whenever I have frustrated the temptation to deny the truth within me, or to betray a value which to me is significant; whenever I have found the despair of my own heart and life groundless; whenever my resolutions to be a better man have stiffened in a real resistance against some form of disintegration; whenever I have been able to bring my life under some high and holy purpose that gives to it a greater wholeness and a greater unity; whenever I have stood in the presence of innocence, purity, love and beauty and found my own mind chastened and my whole self somehow challenged and cleansed; whenever for one swirling moment I have glimpsed the distinction between good and evil courses of conduct, caught sight of something better as I turned to embrace something worse; whenever these experiences or others like them have been mine, I have seen God, and felt ***God's*** presence winging near.

[4]*Howard Thurman*

Reflection and Action

- Take time to think quietly back across your experiences--small, medium or large, until you come upon one in which you can say you have sensed God's presence. Write about that experience in your personal journal.

- Think intently about Brother Lawrence's experience of God, then about the different descriptions of Anker Larsen; Byron McElroy and Julie Sheetz, Chapter II, or Hanns Lilje, Chapter IV, and the Alfred Delp selection above. Where have you encountered descriptions of the presence by others?

- If such has never been your experience, do you think God might possibly be available? Could you be open to this possibility without insisting upon it or demanding it in a bargaining way?

THE PRACTICE ITSELF

How do we, each one of us, love God with all heart, soul, strength and mind? In this chapter we shall find some answers; and as we move through the entire work it will become clear that this is the basic question for the whole pilgrimage and that other insights and answers may well be forthcoming as we progress along the way.

The practice begins when we concentrate on loving God with our whole beings without ulterior motive--that is without conditioning that love with our personal expectation, our secret motives or goals. Only in the free space in which there are no demands, no secret hopes, no urgent needs to be satisfied, may we truly love God. This in no way means we will not have demands, needs, expectations, hopes, and motives. What it does mean is this: all such baggage must be set aside, checked if you will, until our love for God and God only is pure and direct. Out of such unconditional loving it is possible to return to pick up all these conditional aspects of our lives, in new and far more genuine ways.

After reading quotation #5 in one of the graduate seminars I asked if students thought it possible to write term papers or take examinations without any view to pleasing the professors. One previously reticent graduate student, responded spontaneously saying that during the previous semester she had driven herself to distraction and mononucleosis trying to please everyone with her papers. When in bed and completely down in mind and spirit, she had time to think through why she was in Seminary and consider the true purpose of all that writing. Only after she found that the true purpose was not that of pleasing professors was she freed up to read and write effectively.

Once we are free from ulterior motives and really false motivation, we are able to begin to enter into the joy of doing everything "purely for the love of God."

The following illustration was for me a major concrete experience in what it means to live and work under God's loving care without ulterior motive. This came during the years I was President of the Crozer Theological Seminary, 1962-1970.

The Crozer family had founded both the Seminary and the Crozer Hospital and established two boards of directors with an interlocking relationship. As a member of the Hospital Board and its Executive Committee, I was party to the merger of the Crozer Hospital and the Chester Hospital into a new Crozer-Chester Medical Center. The creation of the new five-hundred bed medical center gave us the solid base for establishing a bachelor of science nursing program.

It fell to my lot to give the primary leadership in founding and developing the College of Nursing of the Crozer Foundation, offering a Bachelor of Science degree in Nursing. As I moved into this heavy responsibility I tried to keep my activity free from personal ulterior motives. I found in following Brother Lawrence's suggestion, that everything be done purely for the love of God was applicable to this endeavor, and that I could be freed from personal motivation. I was then able to act in the interest of providing high quality nursing education for all students in eastern Pennsylvania, New Jersey, and Delaware.

After two years of planning and preparation we began with thirteen students. Today, fifteen years later, there are over 500 students and the College of Nursing is one of the professional schools of Widener College. When the time came for us to give the College of Nursing to Widener College (by then we had fifty students enrolled), I found that I could participate in that transfer with enthusiasm and full endorsement in the confidence that we were giving to Widener an excellent and solid institution.

Several of my close friends and associates who participated in the whole process have asked in several different ways, "How could you put so much into the founding and development of the College of Nursing and then give it away without suffering personally?" The answer I honestly believe lies at the place of beginning without ulterior motive of a personal nature, and of scrupulously holding to this discipline. Now again I must be clear about the fact that, of course, I rejoice in the success of the endeavor, I'm pleased to have had a major part in the creation of such an institution, and I delighted in working through all of the various essential features of the entire enterprise--raising the funds, securing the faculty, creating the corporation with appropriate charter, planning an effective recruitment program. The point is, the satisfaction and rejoicing comes at the end and is never posited at the beginning as a necessary conclusion. And as I look back to the beginning and review all the events and activities which contributed to the success of our College of Nursing I am persuaded the power and love of God was quietly at work in all that we did.

The quotations which follow offer specific directions as to how we may wish to begin the practice of the presence of God. Individuals on their own or in the seminars have made a choice for their beginning disciplines. Some have undertaken to follow Brother Lawrence's practice of continuing conversation with God, or his practice of carrying "high notions" of God at all times, or doing all his business purely for the love of God. In the seminars, people were able to report about their successes and failures in attempting these practices.

Selections from the "Family Documents"

How do we prepare ourselves for the possible visitation of God's presence? Here are suggested disciplines used by those who are the writers of the "family documents."

That the most excellent method which he had found of going to God, was that of *doing our common business* without any view of pleasing men, and (as far as we are capable) *purely for the love of GOD.*

[5]*Brother Lawrence*

That we ought not to be weary of doing little things for the love of GOD, for ***God*** regards not the greatness of the work, but the love with which it is performed.

[6]*Brother Lawrence*

The presence of God calms the mind, gives peaceful sleep and rest, even during the day in the midst of all our work; but we must be God's without any reservation . . . we must lift ourselves to the point of loving ***God*** purely for love of ***God*** without any idea of self-interest.

[7]*François Fénelon*

Lift up your heart to God with humble love: and mean God . . . and not what you get out of ***God***. Indeed, hate to think of anything but God . . ., so that nothing occupies your mind or will but only God.

[8]*The Cloud of Unkowing*

"How am I to think of God?" . . . yet of God . . . can no ***one*** think. Therefore I will leave on one side everything I can think, and choose for my love that thing which I cannot think! Why? Because ***God*** may well be loved, but not thought. By love ***God*** can be caught and held, but by thinking never. Therefore, though it may be good sometimes to think particularly about God's kindness and worth, and though it may be enlightening too, and a part of contemplation, yet in the work now before us it must be put down and covered with a cloud of forgetting. And you are to step over it resolutely and eagerly, with a devout and kindling love, and try to penetrate that darkness above you. Strike that thick cloud of unknowing with the sharp dart of longing love, and on no account whatever think of giving up.

[9]*The Cloud of Unknowing*

We said of humility that it was mysteriously and perfectly summed up in this little, blind loving of God, beating away at this dark cloud of unknowing, all else buried and forgotten. We may say this, however, of all the virtues, and in particular of charity. For charity is nothing else than loving God . . ., above all created things, and loving ***people*** in God just as we love ourselves. It is quite right that in contemplation God should be loved . . . alone above all created things, for as we have said already, this work is fundamentally a naked intent, none other than the single minded intention of our spirit directed to God . . . alone.

I call it "single-minded" because in this matter the perfect apprentice asks neither to be spared pain, nor to be generously rewarded, nor indeed for anything but God . . . .

[10]*The Cloud of Unknowing*

The following quotations from the conversations of Brother Lawrence can be for us exercises in the practice of the presence of God.

That we should establish ourselves in a sense of GOD'S Presence, by continually conversing with ***God***. That it was a shameful thing to quit . . . conversation ***with God*** to think of trifles and fooleries.

That we should feed and nourish our souls with high notions of GOD.

That we ought to give ourselves up entirely to GOD, with regard both to things temporal and spiritual, and seek our satisfaction only in the fulfilling of ***God's*** will . . . .

That there was need of fidelity in those times of dryness or insensibility and irksomeness in prayer, ...

That he had always been governed by love without selfish views; and that having resolved to make the love of GOD the *end* of all his actions, he had found good reason to be well satisfied with his method. That he was pleased, when he could take up straw from the ground for the love of GOD seeking ***God*** only and nothing else, not even ***God's*** gifts.

That when an occasion of practising some virtue offered, he addressed himself to GOD, saying, LORD, *I cannot do this unless Thou enablest me*; and that then he received strength more than sufficient.

That when he had failed in his duty, he simply confessed his fault, saying to GOD, *I shall never do otherwise, if Thou leavest me to myself; 'tis Thou must hinder my falling, and mend what is amiss*. That after this, he gave himself no farther uneasiness about it.

That we ought to act with GOD in the greatest simplicity, speaking to ***God*** frankly and plainly, and imploring ***God's*** assistance in our affairs, just as they happen. That GOD never failed to grant it as he had often experienced.

[11]*Brother Lawrence*

Let this actual thought often return that God is omnipresent . . . . "Whither shall I go from thy Spirit?"

Make an act of adoration.

Let everything you see represent to your spirit the presence, the excellency, and the power of God.

In your retirement, make frequent colloquies, or short discoursings between God and your own soul.

Represent and offer to God *acts of love and fear* [Webster's dictionary defines fear: "*to have reverence or awe*--mixed feeling of reverence, fear, and wonder caused by something majestic or sublime; profound respect inspired by greatness, superiority, grandeur."]

God is in every place.

God is in every created being or thing; be cruel towards none, neither abuse any by intemperance.

[12]*Jeremy Taylor's*
Rules for the Practice of the Presence of God.

We must not wait for free hours in which we can close the door. The moment in which we regret recollection can serve to make us practise it as well. We must turn our hearts to God in a simple, familiar way, full of confidence. All the most preoccupied moments are good at all times, even while eating, while hearing others talk. Idle and boring stories, instead of tiring us, refresh us by giving intervals of liberty to recollect ourselves. Thus all things turn to good for those who love God.

[13]*François Fénelon*

You may reasonably say: This is all very well, and on general religious grounds we shall all agree about the beauty and desirability of such prayer. But how shall we train ourselves, so persistently called off and distracted by a multitude of external duties, to that steadfastly theocentric attitude? This brings us to the consideration of the further elements necessary to the full maintenance of the devotional life--its food and its education. If we want to develop this power of communion, to correspond with the grace that invites us to it, we must nourish our souls carefully and regularly with such noble thoughts of God as we are able to assimilate; and must train our fluctuating attention and feeling to be obedient to the demands of the dedicated will. We must become, and keep, spiritually fit.

We shall of course tend to do this feeding and this training in many different ways. No one soul can hope to assimilate all that is offered to us by the richness of Reality. Thus some temperaments are most deeply drawn to adoration by a quiet dwelling upon the spaceless and changeless Presence of God;

some, by looking at Christ, or by meditating in a simple way on His acts and words, as recorded in the Gospels, lose themselves in loving communion with Him. Some learn adoration best through the sacramental life. We cannot all feel all these things in their fullness; our spiritual span is not wide enough for that. Therefore we ought to practise humbly and with simplicity those forms of reflective meditation and mental prayer that help us most; and to which, in times of tranquility, we find ourselves most steadily drawn.

[14]*Evelyn Underhill*

Reflection and Action

- What does it mean to love God without ulterior motive? How can you carry on a continuous conversation with God? With what high notions of God could you nourish your spirit? When have you been faithful in times of dryness? What straw have you taken up from the ground purely for the love of God? What does this mean?

- How can you begin to practice Jeremy Taylor's rules? With which could you start this week? How can we see God in everything?

THE CONSEQUENCES OF PRACTICING THE PRESENCE OF GOD

The quotations help us begin to turn our thoughts to understanding the consequences of the practice of the presence of God. Be very clear in accepting this discipline, this is no blue print that guarantees God's presence to you. All we are doing is placing ourselves in such attitudinal positions as to make it possible for God's spirit to be operative in our lives. When, for example, we are made more charitable through our meditations on the love of God, we then dare try loving all persons for God's sake and for their own. When this happens and becomes a green and growing discipline, it is entirely possible God's presence may be known to us.

There are many evidences of God's special activity in our disciplined lives, but never any contractual guarantees, nor a manual of practices which will produce the desired results. This is an adventure in faith in which we open our very special selves to the possibilities of God's love and presence.

Selections from the "Family Documents"

. . . that the first concern of a fully Christian life is with the realm of Being; with God . . ., to whom each one in our ceaseless series of outward acts and experiences must be related. And its second concern is with the bringing of the values of that world of Being into the world of Becoming, the physical world of succession and change. That, of course, is putting the situation in a roughly philosophic way. We put it in a more religious way if we say that such a scheme of life commits us to carrying on in our own small measure the dual redemptive and illuminating work of Christ; and this by such a willing and unlimited surrender, such love, humility and diligence, as shall make us agents of the Eternal within the world of time. All this means once more, that when in our own practice we really develop a creative inner life, we are sure to find that it involves us in a twofold activity; an activity directed both to God and to other souls.

Thus the complete life of the Christian worker is and must be, in more than a metaphorical sense, a continuous life of prayer. It requires a constant inward abiding in God's atmosphere; and unhesitating response to ***God's*** successive impulsions; a steady approximation to more and more perfect union with ***God's*** creative will. We can test the increase of our souls in depth, strength, and reality, by the improvement in our ability to maintain this state.

[15]*Evelyn Underhill*

This God does not say, "I am that I am," but as Buber translates it, "I shall be there *as* I shall be there."

[16]*Maurice Friedman*

Faith is a state of the mind and the soul. In this sense we can understand the words of the Spanish mystic St. John of the

Cross: "Faith is the union of God with the soul." The language of religion is a set of formulas which register a basic spiritual experience. It must not be regarded as describing, in terms to be defined by philosophy, the reality which is accessible to our senses and which we can analyse with the tools of logic. I was late in understanding what this meant. When I finally reached that point, the beliefs in which I was once brought up and which, in fact, had given my life direction even while my intellect still challenged their validity, were recognized by me as mine in their own right, and by my free choice. I feel that I can endorse those convictions without any compromise with the demands of that intellectual honesty which is the very key to maturity of mind.

[17]*Dag Hammarsköld*

Reflection and Action

- List four persons, one from your family, one from your place of business, a neighbor, one from your church; then put down under each name the ways in which you could dare to love them for their own sakes.

- What would it take and what would it mean for you to become an agent of the Eternal Charity?

Selection Footnotes

1. *The Holy Bible*, Isaiah 6:1-8, Revised Standard Version.
2. *The Practice of the Presence of God*, p. 9.
3. Alfred Delp, *The Prison Meditations of Father Alfred Delp*, with an Introduction by Thomas Merton (New York: Herder and Herder, 1963), pp. 11-12.
4. *Deep Is the Hunger*, pp. 144-145.
5. *The Practice of the Presence of God*, p. 21.
6. *The Practice of the Presence of God*, p. 22.
7. François Fénelon, *Christian Perfection*, (New York and London: Harper and Brothers, Publishers, 1947), pp. 27, 33.
8. Anonymous, *The Cloud of Unknowing*, Translation and Introduction by Clifton Wolters (Baltimore: Penguin Books, 1974), p. 53.
9. *The Cloud of Unknowing*, pp. 59-60.
10. *The Cloud of Unknowing*, pp. 83-84.
11. *The Practice of the Presence of God*, pp. 10-13.
12. Jeremy Taylor, *The Rule and Exercise of Holy Living*, edited with an Introduction by Thomas S. Kepler, (Cleveland & New York: The World Publishing Co., 1936), pp. 39-42.
13. *Christian Perfection*, p. 29.
14. *Concerning the Inner Life*, p. 29.
15. *Concerning the Inner Life*, pp. 46-47.
16. Maurice Friedman, *Touchstones of Reality*, (New York: E. P. Dutton, 1972), p. 142.
17. *Dag Hammarskjöld: A Spiritual Portrait*, pp. 23-24.

CHAPTER VI

SPIRITUAL DISCIPLINES FOR EVERYDAY LIVING

Dag Hammarskjöld
1905 - 1961

Courtesy: The United Nations, U.N. Photo 40308.

Born the son of a Swedish prime minister, Dag Hammarskjöld spent his life in government service both nationally and internationally. At the age of 36, he was chairman of the board of the Bank of Sweden. He then served on the Swedish cabinet, after which he was delegate to the United Nations and served as chairman of his country's delegation to the seventh session. In 1953, he was elected Secretary General of that body, a position he held until his death in 1961.

Throughout his public career, he worked with quiet tact and persistence for causes of peace and justice. Since his death he has been honored not only as a statesman, but also as a person of great spiritual depth. The insights and struggles of his own personal journey of faith are poignantly revealed in his posthumously published diary, entitled *Markings*, which takes its place as one of the contemporary "family documents."

Chapter VI

GENUINE HUMILITY

Recall for a moment the Copernican Revolution. In the time of Copernicus the earth was regarded as the center of the universe. Through study, experimentation and reflection Copernicus demonstrated the fact that the sun was the center of the universe. This radical revolution in approaching our universe provided scholars of science with new freedom for theorizing, experimentation, and invention.

GOD THE CENTER AND SOURCE OF GENUINE HUMILITY

To understand the full meaning of the discipline of humility requires a spiritual Copernican Revolution. Instead of the "I, Me, and Mine" being the center of our lives, God is found to be the center for vital creative living. When the revolution takes place, we accept the fact that we can be pleased and satisfied with ourselves in our successful dealing with each other and in our performance of our work, providing we keep in proportion, in all honesty, the contribution we actually made, as well as the fact that we now live constantly within the Divine perspective.

It is when we shift the base of our satisfactions and genuine self-confidence to the conclusion that success is completely our own doing, false pride takes over. We then slip into the attitude that it is our right to be successful; and that our successes should be rewarded because of who we are. By these successive steps, we have arrived in a totally self-centered world. We then bend all our energy and effort to proving and sustaining the "great I am."

Reflect on the ramifications and consequences of this lifestyle--how far has this happened to you? Where do you see this rampant in other persons with whom you work and live? Just as people think and feel their way into self-centeredness, so those of the practicing humble spirit will gradually but assuredly become God-centered.

Genuine humility emerges from the recognition of our essential finitude, our limitations, and shortcomings. Even in times of our greatest success, our finest achievements, under this discipline of humility, we discover we have been aided, strengthened, from beyond ourselves. We are the instruments of God's peace and power. All our strengths as well as weaknesses are available when we "center down" in true humility in the presence of the living God.

As the "centering down" into God's presence has taken place in my life (and the process is by no means complete), I have found that creative solutions for difficult problems which have come to me are not of my own making; and when they come, there is an inherent "rightness" about them which makes them dependable when adopted. Even at the level of deciding which is the best approach to a difficult issue in human relations, living within the divine frame of reference makes a difference. Out of quiet reflection which begins with the honest recognition that left to my own skills and know-how I would more than likely choose the wrong method, there come clear and often simple insights which enable me to sort out the real issues or problem. This makes it possible to ask the right questions and to move the antagonists to a different ground upon which the search for truth can then be undertaken to the mutual advantage of all concerned.

Thus it is possible to become a reconciler through the practice of genuine humility since in such "working through" one is surrounded with the abiding presence ready and willing to respond to an open, non-demanding, honest spirit.

Selections from the "Family Documents"

The year that Dag Hammarskjöld was appointed Secretary General of the United Nations he began his 1953 diary with this quotation.

> "--Night is drawing nigh"--For all that has been--Thanks!
> To all that shall be--Yes!
>
> [1]*Dag Hammarskjöld*

This next quotation comes from this same period of time when according to his biographer, Sven Stolpe, Hammarskjöld spoke unhesitatingly about the reality of God.

It *did* come--the day when the grief became small [Hammarskjöld's suffering from a deep sense of isolation, according to Stolpe]. For what had befallen me and seemed so hard to bear became insignificant in the light of the demands which God was now making. But how difficult it is to feel that this was also, and for that very reason the day when the joy became great. Not I, but God in me.

[2]*Dag Hammarskjöld*

When a lowly and loving man considers that God has served him so humbly, so lovingly, and so faithfully; and sees God so high so mighty, and so noble, and man so poor, and so little, and so low; then there springs up within the humble heart a great awe and a great veneration for God. For to pay homage to God by every outward and inward act, this is the first and dearest work of humility . . . .

[3]*John of Ruysbroeck*

In Augustine the enmity to God is no longer charged to matter or body versus mind, or to the biological versus the psychological. The reluctance to yield to God is laid to pride and is thus placed within the mind itself. By placing the whole struggle within the mind or the will . . . Augustine has placed it in that very part of ***us*** for which . . . ***we are*** uniquely responsible, and hence ***we are*** made to bear the full brunt of the responsibility for ***our*** defiance of God. Now it is proud, self-centered mind . . . against a thankful, responsive God-centered mind. And the whole tussle is depicted as a psychological struggle between the hard, proud bent to self- sufficiency and autonomy on the part of the restless, active mind, and the willingness of one who becomes a loving, tender, humble agent of God to yield to the Christ-mind. It is the split mind versus the whole mind.

[4]*Douglas Steere*

It is the will of God that thou shouldst be holy, says St. Paul. Now holiness is to know God and the self aright, then to love all things only in God, and finally to offer the self to God, as a good and fitting tool. . . .

[5]*Rudolf Otto*

That we are not able to see God is due to the faintness of desire and the throng of things. To desire high things is to be high. To see God, one must desire high: know that earnest desire and deep humility work wonders. I say that God can do anything, but ***God*** cannot deny anything to the person who is humble and yet has high desires . . . .

[6]*Meister Eckhart*

"The best and most wonderful thing that can happen to you in this life, is that you should be silent and let God work and speak."

[7]*Dag Hammarskjöld*

Humility does not rest, in final count, upon bafflement and discouragement and self-disgust at our shabby lives, a brow-beaten, dog-slinking attitude. It rests upon the disclosure of the consummate wonder of God, upon finding that only God counts, that all our own self-originated intentions are works of straw. And so in lowly humility we must stick close to the Root and count our own powers as nothing except as they are enslaved in ***God's*** power.

[8]*Thomas Kelly*

The God-blinded soul sees naught of self, naught of personal degradation or of personal eminence, but only the Holy Will working impersonally through ***self***, through others, as one objective Life and Power . . . . But the humility of the God-blinded soul endures only so long as we look steadily at the Sun. Growth in humility is a measure of our growth in the habit of the Godward-directed mind. And ***we*** only ***are*** near to God ***when we are*** exceedingly humble.

[9]*Thomas Kelly*

A saint is one in whom God or Christ is felt to live again.

[10]*Douglas Steere*

Only in the perspective of the life-awakening Thou of God ***do we*** recognize ***ourselves*** without anxiety and without disgust. Indeed, then ***we do*** not need frantically to demonstrate ***our*** autonomy, for ***we*** know that ***we are*** held in existence. ***We*** come to ***ourselves*** when ***we are consciously*** obligated to that love which illuminates all with its brightness.

[11]*Bernard Häring*

Reflection and Action

- What are the dominant features that are driving you to self-centeredness? Begin by asking: Of what am I prideful?
- How has your own pride alienated you from others?
- Where have you seen pride in others operating destructively in human relations?
- Can you accurately describe your own finitude in times of failure? in times of success and achievement?
- When, if ever, have you felt the reenforcing sense of the essential rightness of your decisions?
- Which of these quotations gave you added insight as to God being the center and source of your humility?

THE PRACTICE OF GENUINE HUMILITY

The next time you find yourself "in the middle" of a rugged confrontation between people (one of your children and the other parent, your best neighborhood friends, your co-workers at the office or in the plant or the school or the hospital where you work), begin to move toward a creative working through the tension and conflict by turning to the Presence of God there to admit your inadequacy and ignorance to deal with these antagonists by yourself.

Then reflect quietly and patiently on the question: what is the real issue, what is really at stake in this argument or fight? When the real issues become clear, then it is time to seek for ways of asking the *right* questions of both antagonists which will get them to focus on the real issues and concerns.

Even if what you thought were the right questions prove to be less than perfect, the chances are that in the response from both persons there will be a further clarification of the underlying cause of their antagonism to each other. Careful, open listening--done with a sense of God's presence--in the very midst of the confrontation will enable you to take the next step either in further "right questioning" or, if it seems right, a tentative outlining of one or more alternative solutions.

Here again your reactors may strongly object to your questions or your possible alternatives. Out of their reactions will come further insights which may even help you to begin to see how one of the alternatives may be the genuine solution. In all such probing and searching, by your very attitude rooted and grounded in humility, you are conveying the quiet assurance that there can be discovered a mutually acceptable and satisfying solution for all of you. At the same time, such a process moves all of you to new ground upon which to proceed in the discovery of the truth. Whereas the old ground upon which these antagonists fought was emotion, fear, prejudice, arrogance, this new ground will make it possible to redirect emotion into seeking a newly definable solution, to transmit fear into an open willingness to consider the issue to eradicate prejudice, and to outdistance arrogance and pride by inviting each one to bring his or her best to the solution of the real issues at hand.

Furthermore, as you bring genuine humility into the "act," you are under no compulsion to pull off a great victory. You do not have a solution previously prepared on academic grounds. You are one who together with the others involved will discover the truth and share in the achievement of reconciliation. Then there will be genuine satisfaction and joy for all those participating persons who will have discovered the way in which, within the framework of God-directed thinking, human relations are redeemed, reconstructed, and improved.

As I mature in humility, I no longer find it necessary to drive myself by comparison with others. Søren Kierkegaard in his book entitled *Purity of Heart* has a long section in which he exposes the shortcomings of living under the drive of comparison with others. He says in several ways that in the final analysis, God does not care about what you did in comparison to someone else. God simply cares and asks what did you do with what you had. The only legitimate comparison is between your poorest and your best--out of which may come the energy and joy to live up to your best.

Humility, then, is the discipline of rejecting my own heavy tendency to measure my life in comparison to others. It is the exposing of the folly and waste of energy, time and talents when we live in the tension of radical competition. Meditate on this as you expose your own competitive drives. Reflect upon the evidence of such folly as it is lived out in the lives of so many persons all about you. Then return over and over again to ask for more insight as to what you may do--indeed what God may even expect you to do with what you have.

Once we have understood how in humility we accept our strengths and weaknesses, we are then able to live and move calmly beyond our hang-ups and our limitations, and we are able to accept joyfully all praise and success as responding to the glory of God rather than to self-glorification.

The most overlooked feature of genuine humility is the quiet acceptance of our strengths--those qualities God-given which are just as surely ours as our limitations and weaknesses. Perhaps we are beautiful, handsome, intelligent, naturally loving, outgoing, capable in management--whatever our strengths--these are to be brought under discipline for use by the living God for *the* world and for *people*, our brothers and sisters. With this essential concept, we are then free to realize that, as finite creatures, we carry in our unique individuality strengths as well as weaknesses.

Yet when it comes to talking about humility, the traditional emphasis has been to demean and belittle human nature, and to view humility as the way of concentrating on our shortcomings.

John of Ruysbroeck's earlier quotation used the traditional language such as "so poor," "so little," and "so low." Gospel hymns use terms such as "mean," "wretched," and "miserable." All of this has turned us off from an honest review of our weaknesses: our pride, our short temper, our drive to perfection, our modest intellect, our lack of follow-through, our jealousy.

In the practice of genuine humility, we acknowledge these weaknesses for what they are. We begin to eradicate them from our lifestyle, and when like weeds, they keep growing back, we keep weeding and cultivating. Likewise we continue to nourish and cultivate our strengths.

When Brother Lawrence says that God does not regard the greatness (or smallness) of the work, but only the love with which it was performed, he points in the right direction for dealing in humility with our strengths and weaknesses. To understand that our total selves are rooted and grounded in God, and if our performance has been for the love of God, then we are free to rejoice in our successes and quietly without despairing, to acknowledge our failures and let them fall away into oblivion.

It is important to understand that when we have learned to rejoice with God about our strengths, we are much more capable of dealing with our shortcomings, our inadequacies, and our weaknesses. Equally important, we are free to be much more appreciative and understanding of every other person's strengths and weaknesses.

A final insight about living in genuine humility is this: such humility enables us to be utterly fearless. The quotation #15 from Thomas Merton will serve as a springboard for your meditation about the truth that humility leads to fearlessness.

Having centered down into God's presence, we need not be afraid of failure nor defeat even though we may fail or we may be defeated in our next immediate endeavor. This does not mean we sit back with folded hands and leave it up to God. No, it means we tackle the issues--the problems before us--having given our best reflective thought and prayer to the necessary action we believe needs to be taken. We may not even be conscious of God's presence in the thick of the encounter, but we live with the sense of his support and his inspiring spirit.

When the attack from the opposition is heaviest, this is the very time the truly humble person, operating within the sense of God's presence, remains calm and unafraid; and in so doing, is free to defuse the antagonism and redirect the arguments into the search for what is true and right.

Selections from the "Family Documents"

[Think before you pray for humility] . . . many who pray for humility would be extremely sorry if God were to grant it to them. [Because in praying for humility] . . . they forget that to love, desire, and ask for humility is loving, desiring, and asking for humiliations, for these are the companions, or rather the food of humility, and without them it is no more than a beautiful but meaningless idea . . . if the bare thought of humiliation fills us with horror . . . if pride and self-love get the better of us on every occasion . . . we are flattering ourselves if we think we love humility.

[12]*Jean Nicholas Grou*

A humble ***person*** is not disturbed by praise, . . . is no longer concerned with ***self***, and . . . knows where the ***personal*** good . . . comes from. ***Such an individual*** does not refuse praise, because it belongs to . . . God . . ., and in receiving it . . . keeps nothing for ***self*** but gives it all, with great joy, to . . . God . . . .

[13]*Thomas Merton*

The humble ***person*** receives praise the way a clean window takes the light of the sun. The truer and more intense the light is, the less you see of the glass.

[14]*Thomas Merton*

A humble ***individual*** can do great things with an uncommon perfection because he ***or she*** is no longer concerned about incidentals, like ***personal*** interests and . . . reputation, and therefore . . . no longer needs to waste ***any*** effort in defending them. For a humble ***individual*** is not afraid of failure, . . . is not afraid of anything, even of ***self***, since perfect humility implies perfect confidence in the power of God, ... Humility is the surest sign of strength.

[15]*Thomas Merton*

A first step to inner gentleness is thus to gratefully love myself as a unique divine gift and to admit and accept my weakness which makes me the fragile earthen vessel of this treasure. As long as I pretend that I am strong, that I by myself can live up to the unique eminence God calls me to in Christ, I cannot be gentle with myself. Gentleness with self is possible only when I recognize and "own" also the vulnerability of the treasure I am. I must be able to look at myself with a forgiving eye. This may seem almost impossible because there is something in me that tells me that I cannot forgive myself.

[16]*Adrian von Kaam*

Reflection and Action

- How does the practice of humility assist us in asking the right questions in a wide variety of situations from rugged confrontations, to vocational decisions, to administrative decisions, or choices for our families?

- What advanced stage of comparison and competitiveness can you cut from your lifestyle, beginning now?

- Write down your two or three greatest strengths--are there others? Then look honestly at your reaction to this suggested action. What false concepts of humility almost kept you from doing this exercise? If however you did it, did you begin to sense a new level at which humility operates to let you freely accept your strengths as God-given abilities?

- Now do the same for your two or three most serious weaknesses--are there others? What are the dynamics of the practice of humility that will enable you to overcome these limitations and shortcomings?

- Do you receive praise "as a clear window receives sunlight?"

- How does humility move us beyond fear of failure?

CONSEQUENCES AND ACTION

There are two very particular human experiences in which humility is an essential ingredient in genuinely mature and creative living: humility and suffering, and the relationship of humility and love.

Consider first the role of humility in our personal grappling with suffering. The problem of suffering escapes rational and logical solution and is the thorniest of all issues with which theologians must deal. In no way do these quotations nor those in Chapter IX, *Joy and the Lifted Heart*, provide carefully thought-out philosophical or theological answers. They are, instead, creative ways of living with the suffering that comes into our lives. These are ways of experiencing suffering from a different angle, for here we discover that suffering once we accept it, and acceptance requires genuine humility, then we are free to discover how we may use our suffering in the service of others.

In suffering we are driven back to the honest recognition of our own limitations and finitude. We are not perfect, nor indestructible. We are full of imperfection, subject to breakdown--physical, mental, and emotional. Once we accept these insights, we are free to discover the ways in which we may use it for the redemption and reconciliation of other persons.

How does the discipline of humility relate to love? The final series of quotations #22 through 27 concern the relationship of humility to love. The invitation here is to begin to discover the interaction between these two disciplines, humility and love. Humility helps make love possible and is the basis for courageous selfless service. Humility helps prepare the human heart for the practice and experience of love.

Yet in the midst of all this God is operative in motivating and challenging us to move toward the all-pervading source of divine energy--love. God's love revealed to us in Christ calls us to discipleship, the first step of which is humble acceptance.

Selections from the "Family Documents"

It is only suffering *meekly accepted, willed, transfigured by love of God, of Christ*--It is only such, that will purify or cure anything.

[17]*Baron von Hügel*

Holy suffering is the very crown of holy action. And God is no pedant: He can and does look to the substance of our suffering, and knows how to penetrate beyond our surface restlessness or murmurs. Indeed, part of the great work suffering effects in the soul doubtless springs from the way in which, when acute, it almost invariably humbles us: we can much less easily cut a fine figure in our own eyes over our sufferings, than we can over our actions when in peace and plenty.

[18]*Baron von Hügel*

. . . [Prayer is] the final humility of the spirit. The greatest things in existence will only be given to those who pray. In suffering one learns to pray best of all.

[19]*Peter Wust*

This "final humility of the spirit," prayer, may be expressed so simply that it would seem almost a violation of its nature to elaborate the aspects of it . . . . Francis of Assisi prayed through the night, "My God and my All, what art Thou and what am I?"

[20]*Douglas Steere*

I wonder whether you realise a deep, great fact? That souls--all human souls--are deeply interconnected? That (I mean) we can, not only pray for each other, but *suffer* for each other? That these long, trying wakings, that I was able to offer them to God and to Christ for my child--that He might ever strengthen, sweeten, steady her in her true, simple, humble love and dependence upon Him? Nothing is more real than this interconnection--this gracious power put by God Himself into the very heart of our infirmities. And, *it is the Church* (which, *imperfectly* understood, "dumbs" my bewildered Child)--it is the Church which, at its best and deepest, is just *that*--that inter-dependence of all the broken and the meek, all the self-oblivion, all the reaching out to God and souls, which certainly "pins down" neither my child nor this her old groping Father--which, if it "pins down" at all, does so, really only--even taken simply intellectually--as the skeleton "pins down" the flesh. What a hideous thing the skeleton, taken separately, is, isn't it? Yet even Cleopatra, when in the splendour of her youth, she had such a very useful, very necessary, quite unavoidable skeleton inside her, had she not?

[21]*Baron von Hügel*

Humility is the emphasis of superabundant love which finds its way to the lowliest in order to raise ***an individial*** out of the dust; it is the bright glance of a love which looks more at the worth and dignity of others than at its own excellences. The humble ***person*** discovers the hidden values even in little things; true greatness is revealed ***at a*** glance. Unaffected humility is the expression of the fact that one is standing in the right place and in ***one's*** heart accepts and loves ***one's*** circumstances.

[22]*Bernard Häring*

Humility is the courage for selfless serving, and this very courage truly to seek the Thou of the other in serving is the glowing ratification of the richness of love.

[23]*Bernard Häring*

The entire history of God with ***humanity*** is the history of ***God's*** love at once sublimely holy and humble. It is the inner-most impulse of all the religions of the world. This mystery comes to its perfect manifestation in Jesus Christ.

[24]*Bernard Häring*

The original and first expression of *creaturely* humility is petition and gratitude to God, the worshiping response to that love from which everything good comes. And the more richly ***we are*** endowed by God, the easier it becomes for ***us*** to perceive that the nobility of bestowed dignity fulfills itself in the *courage to serve.*

[25]*Bernard Häring*

Humility gets all its power and beauty from love. From love it receives its clear vision for the merits of the neighbor which make ***an individual*** lovable, even if these merits perhaps disconcert the lover. Pride, on the other hand, constantly lives in the dark fear of being set in the shadows by the accomplishment and dignity of the other. Love, the queen of all the virtues, grants even humility a royal dignity. Humility is for its part entirely a service to love. It is the most wonderful task of humility to open the human heart to love and to prepare it to receive gracious, joy-bringing love.

[26]*Bernard Häring*

Humility, therefore, is more than modesty which recognizes the limits of its own ability and its own worth and is content with a low place. The humble person is prepared to accept God's call to great things. It would be a concealed form of pride to limit oneself arbitrarily to the insignificant instead of trusting in God's ability to do great things . . . through ***persons***. The humility of the magnanimous love often proves itself in little things, but it is also always ready to accept gratefully the commission to great things. Indeed, only in its confidence in God's grace is it not frightened of ***God's*** sublimity, for the lover sees that the received gift is always greater than the task commissioned with it.

[27]*Bernard Häring*

Reflection and Action

- What first steps can you take in understanding the relationship between humility and suffering?
- What do you understand to be the ways you can relate love and humility in your life?
- Put in your own words a paragraph which describes your understanding of the close connections between our relationship to God in humility and utter fearlessness.

Selection Footnotes

1. *Markings*, p. 89.
2. *Markings*, p. 90.
3. John Baillie, *A Diary of Readings*, (New York: Charles Scribner's Sons, 1955), Day 221. Quotation from John of Ruysbroeck.
4. *On Beginning From Within*, p. 105.
5. Rudolph Otto, *Mysticism East and West*, (New York: Collier Books by arrangement with the MacMillan Co., 1962), p. 196.
6. *Meister Eckhart*, p. 233.
7. *Markings*, p. 156, written in his Diary, 9/26/57.
8. *A Testament of Devotion*, p. 62.
9. *A Testament of Devotion*, p. 63.
10. *On Beginning From Within*, p. 11.
11. Bernard Häring, *Christian Maturity*, translated by Arlene Swidler (New York: Herder and Herder, 1967), p. 90.
12. *A Diary of Readings*, Day 29, Quotation from J. Nicholas Grou.
13. Thomas Merton, *New Seeds of Contemplation*, (New York: New Directions Publishing Corp., 1972), p. 188.
14. *New Seeds of Contemplation*, p. 189.
15. *New Seeds of Contemplation*, p. 190.
16. Adrian vanKaam, *Spirituality and the Gentle Life*, (Denville, NJ: Dimension Books, Inc., 1974), p. 21.
17. *Spiritual Counsel and Letters of Baron Friedrich von Hügel*, p. 90.
18. *Spiritual Counsel and Letters of Baron Friedrich von Hügel*, p. 91.
19. *On Beginning From Within*, p. 79.
20. *On Beginning From Within*, p. 79.
21. *Spiritual Counsel and Letters of Baron Friedrich von Hügel*, pp. 78-79.
22. *Christian Maturity*, p. 89.
23. *Christian Maturity*, p. 90.
24. *Christian Maturity*, p. 91.
25. *Christian Maturity*, p. 92.
26. *Christian Maturity*, p. 93.
27. *Christian Maturity*, p. 94-95.

Selection Footnotes

CHAPTER VII

SPIRITUAL DISCIPLINES FOR EVERYDAY LIVING

Martin Buber
1878 - 1965

Courtesy: Charles Scribner's Sons.

Jewish philosopher and theologian, Martin Buber was born in Vienna, the grandson of the rabbinic scholar, Solomon Buber. His life combined active leadership in public affairs, particularly in the Zionist movement, with profound and sustained scholarship in the fields of Jewish religion, ethics, and social philosophy. A professor at the University of Berlin, he was finally forbidden by the Nazis to lecture in Germany. In 1938 he moved to Israel, and was a professor at the Hebrew University until his retirement in 1951.

Central to his philosophy is an understanding of reality as fundamentally dialogical at the level of the human-divine encounter. It was said of him at the time of his death that "he had harmonized thought and action, word and deed into an integrated experience of living." His sensitivity for the life of the spirit as found in the Hasidism (a mystical movement of the 18th and 19th centuries in East European Jewry) may well have given him the motivation to begin bridge-building between Judaism and Christianity. His masterpiece I and Thou and his two volume edition, Tales of the Hasidim are representative of the "family documents" from within Judaism.

Chapter VII

"THE GREATEST OF THESE IS LOVE"

Understanding and undertaking the practice of love is the most difficult of all disciplines. Every day we are up against human behavior which often evokes in us anger, hostility, mistrust, and, if nothing else, simply wears us down. Because we are surrounded by popular, romantic notions of love it is all too easy to think that by finding someone to love us, we can find peace, harmony and security.

OUR LOVE OF GOD AND GOD'S LOVE FOR US

In this chapter we are introduced to insights into the nature of love of a different quality and kind--love which is adequate for a life of peace and power. We are being invited to live with these insights, working them into our thinking and practice over the years.

The quotation section begins with the New Testament passages for they make clear the cosmic nature of God as the ultimate source of love and describe fully what it means for us as persons to be related in love to God and to each other.

Next comes a series of insights which are variations of this scriptural theme of God's love for us and the nature of our love for God. These quotations introduce us to the broader notion of love as the central field of force, the all-pervading universal "holy energy . . . the essential activity of God." Here we are invited to stretch our imaginations until we begin to live within this vital force by returning to make love operative especially in our common business, for after all most of us live most of our lives with common business. Rarely is there "uncommon" business needing our attention!

Selections from the "Family Documents"

Here it is important to begin with the New Testament witness to the meaning of love as revealed in Jesus' life, death, and resurrection. Jesus' own teaching is central to all our living.

I have loved you just as the Father has loved me. You must go on living in my love. If you keep my commandments you will live in my love just as I have kept my Father's commandments and live in his love. I have told you this so that you can share my joy and that your happiness may be complete. This is my commandment: that you love one another as I have loved you. There is no greater love than this--that a man should lay down his life for his friends.

[1]*The New Testament in Modern English*

If I speak with the eloquence of men and of angels, but have no love, I become no more than blaring brass or crashing cymbal. If I have the gift of foretelling the future and hold in my mind not only all human knowledge but the very secrets of God, and if I also have that absolute faith which can move mountains, but have no love, I amount to nothing at all. If I dispose of all that I possess, yes, even if I give my own body to be burned, but have no love, I achieve precisely nothing.

This love of which I speak is slow to lose patience--it looks for a way of being constructive. It is not possessive: it is neither anxious to impress nor does it cherish inflated ideas of its own importance.

Love has good manners and does not pursue selfish advantage. It is not touchy. It does not keep account of evil or gloat over the wickedness of other people. On the contrary, it is glad with all good men when truth prevails.

Love knows no limit to its endurance, no end to its trust, no fading of its hope; it can outlast anything. It is, in fact, the one thing that still stands when all else has fallen . . . .

In this life we have three great lasting qualities--faith, hope and love. But the greatest of them is love.

[2]*The New Testament in Modern English*

My children, let us love not merely in theory or in words--let us love in sincerity and in practice.

[3]*The New Testament in Modern English*

[Love, for Ruysbroeck] is hardly an emotional word at all, and never a sentimental one; rather the title of a mighty force, a holy energy that fills the universe--the essential activity of God. . . . This Love, in fact, is the dynamic power which St. Augustine compared with gravitation, "drawing all things to their own place," and which Dante saw binding the multiplicity of the universe into one. All Ruysbroeck's images for it turn on the idea of force. It is a raging fire, a storm, a flood. He speaks of it in one great passage as "playing like lightning" between God and the soul.

[4]*Evelyn Underhill*

Reflection and Action

- Morton Kelsey, in contrasting the essential difference between Christianity and the Eastern religions, writes "The basic difference between the two is whether one sees ultimate reality as a Lover to whom one responds, or as a pool of cosmic consciousness in which one seeks to lose identity."

- Can you describe your present feelings and understanding of God as the center and source of love?

- Have you ever sensed God's love as a mighty force, a holy energy that fills the Universe? If not, what steps could you take to connect with such "holy energy?"

- What popular notions of romantic love need to be discarded in your thinking to clear the way for deeper insight into the nature of God's love and our relationship to that love?

THE PRACTICE OF LOVING GOD

In order to participate in the all-pervading divine energy of God's love consider that our discipline of love really begins when we start doing all things without ulterior motive. How frequently we are motivated by ego-centric love or with an eye to pleasing others? How rarely we do anything purely for the love of God.

Yet the difficult concept for our comprehension is this idea of God's universal love for all persons in general and in particular: a love which any or all persons are free to reject or accept; and a love which leads us into an honest acceptance and love of our best selves--something quite different from self-centered love.

The discipline of love begins with learning as Brother Lawrence did to do "little things for the love of GOD;" "doing our common business without any view to pleasing persons . . . purely for the love of GOD," Baron von Hügel's letter to his niece about her packing, #6 makes the same point.

Such loving transforms us as individuals and redeems all our human encounter. Here we are asked to set aside all intellectualizing about God. We are invited to seek the divine presence by loving God only and always.

Within the quotations under this heading are suggestions as to how we may begin the practice of loving God. Choose a practical place for beginning and live with your choice.

Selections from the "Family Documents"

So likewise in his business in the kitchen (to which he had naturally a great aversion), having accustomed himself to do everything there for the love of GOD, and with prayer, upon all occasions, for ***God's*** grace to do his work well, he had found everything easy during the fifteen years that he had been employed there.

[5]*Brother Lawrence*

(To G.G.September 1, 1919)

I want this little scribble to reach you on your starting your packing-fortnight. I want to put, very shortly, what has helped myself, so greatly, for now a generation.

Well,--you are going pack, pack and unpack, unpack for a fortnight. What is it that I would have you quietly set your mind and heart on, during that in itself lonesome and dreary bit of your road, Child? Why, *this*! You see, all we do has a *double-relatedness*. It is a link or links of a chain that stretches back to our birth and on to our death. It is part of a long train of cause and effect, of effect and cause, in your own chain of a life--this chain variously intertwisted with, variously affecting, and affected by, numerous other chains and other lives. It is certainly your duty to do quietly your best that these links may help on your own chain and those other chains, by packing well, by being a skillful packer.

Yes, but there is also, all the time, another, a far deeper, a most darling and inspiring relation. Here, you have no slow succession, but you have each single act, each single moment joined directly to God--Himself not a chain, but one Great Simultaneity. True, certain other acts, at other moments, will be wanted, of a kind more intrinsically near to God--Prayer, Quiet, Holy Communion. Yet not even these other acts could unite you as closely to God as can do this packing, if and when the packing is the duty of certain moments, and if, and as, the little old daughter does this her packing with her heart and intention turned to God her Home, if she offers her packing as her service, that service which is perfect liberty.

Not even a soul already in Heaven, not even an angel or archangel, can take your place there; for what God wants, what God will love to accept, in those rooms, in those packing days, and from your packing hands, will be just this little packing performed by you in those little rooms. Certainly it has been mainly through my realising this doctrine a little, and through my poor little self-exercising in it, that I have got on a bit, and you will get on faster than I have done with it. You understand? At one moment, packing; at another, silent adoration in Church; at another, dreariness and unwilling drift; at another, the joys of human affections given and received; at another, keen suffering of soul, of mind, in apparent utter loneliness; at another, external acts of religion; at another, death itself. All these occupations every one can, ought, and will be, each when and where, duty, reason, conscience, necessity--God--calls for it; it will all become the means and instruments of loving, of transfiguration, of growth for your soul, and of its beatitude. But it is for God to choose these things, their degrees, combinations, successions; and it is for you just simply, very humbly, very gently and peacefully, to follow that leading.

[6]*Baron von Hügel*

There is an old, old story that the gateway to deep religion is self-surrender. Dr. Coomaraswamy, writing upon the art of India, says that all developed religions have as their center the experience of becoming unselfed. But falling in love is an old, old story in the history of the world, yet new to each individual when first it comes. Descriptions of the unselfing which comes with the Invading Love are no substitute for the immediacy of the experience of being unselfed by the Eternal Captain of our souls. Nor is there a freedom so joyous as the enslaving bonds of such amazing, persuading Love.

But according to our Christian conception of the unselfing in religion, to become unselfed is to become truly integrated as a richer self. The little, time-worn self about which we fretted--how narrow its boundaries, how unstable its base, how strained its structure. But the experience of discovering that life is rooted and grounded in the *actual*, active, loving Eternal one is also to experience our own personal life firm-textured and stable. For we are no longer imprisoned between birth and death, between yesterday and tomorrow, but Eternity is our home, while our daily affairs are coordinated in that supernal light. Profound immersion in the Divine Love is a shaking experience. But it is not an unsettling experience; one becomes at last truly *settled*, a coordinated, integrated personality.

This is the life beyond earnestness, beyond anxiety, beyond strain. Its strength sets in when we let go. This is a way fraught with danger, for it is easy to *deduce* human passivity from divine initiative. But the root *experience* of divine Presence contains within it not only a sense of being energized *from* a heavenly Beyond; it contains also a sense of being energized *toward* an earthly world. For the Eternal Life and Love are not pocketed in us; they are flooded *through* us into the world. There is an element of transmissiveness in the experience of being energized by the Divine Life . . . . We are significant terminals of Love and Power, ends of Love; we are also transmitting channels, means and ends of creative Love. Through us the hungry world must be fed. We dare not oppose the divine urgency. Great things may be done for ***people***, for we do not do them; they are done through us. We do not carry the load, in anxious balance. The living waters sweep through us to make green the fields of ***humanity***. We are at peace. If we succeed, it is God who had succeeded, if we encounter defeat, then it is part of that strange resistance within History which God permits in a going world. Gladly we become anonymous, like the writer of the *Theologia Germanica*, for to God belongs all the praise . . . .

[7]*Thomas Kelly*

. . . every day until they die ***people*** weep for lack of love. Even in the presence of your dead your grief is doubled by the thought that during life you gave them less love than they had needed. Prepare a good sleep, loving well by day. Prepare a good death, loving well in life.

[8]*Constancio Vigil*

. . . every Christian is obliged to make frequent acts of the love of God. From the fact that one cannot exactly determine how many such acts should be made in a month, or in a week, we may conclude that it is not possible to make them too often, and that we ought not to be satisfied with our dispositions on this point until we have reason to think that God is satisfied: and this takes us further than we might think: God not being satisfied with us until we love him with all our heart, all our mind and all our strength.

But how can we make as many acts as God wishes? What are the means we should take in order to do so? Here we reply, the way is simple, easy, and, at the same time, it is the *only* way: there is absolutely none other. Let God . . . rule these acts, and not you yourself: and, indeed, you could only produce them through ***God***. Begin, then, by making ***God*** the entire Master over your heart and all its movements. Then pray . . . every morning and beg ***God*** to make your produce, during all that day, just so many acts of love as shall please ***God***, for ***God's*** glory and for your sanctification. After that, keep yourself all the day recollected in ***God***, sufficiently recollected, that is, and sufficiently attentive to ***God's*** inspirations, not to miss any one of those . . . offered you. Make, at least, this strong resolution: renew it every time when you find yourself getting distracted, and reproach yourself sharply and sincerely. You will find great advantage from this method, before you have used it long. If you can say that it is, doubtless, a sure way, but that it does not seem to you easy, that is because you do not love and do not wish to love. Embrace it courageously and God will make it easy to you. Would it not be strange if you should profess to practise the love of God without it costing you anything, any effort, any violence? Remember that your nature, which is corrupted by sin, recoils with all its strength from the love of God. Remember that you have increased its repugnance by your personal faults. Remember, in short, that the aim of the love of God is to destroy in you the work of sin, to raise you above nature, and to transform the animal ***being*** into a ***person*** all spiritual and even divine. And you wish to suffer no difficulty in the exercise of this love!

[9]*Nicholas Grou*

Reflection and Action

- Can you do all things this week purely for the love of God, without any view to pleasing anyone?

- After reflecting on #5 and 6, ask yourself what are the small, tiresome duties I can offer in loving service to God? How, in the offering of such seemingly insignificant service is there perfect liberty? Have I ever known such liberty? If not, how could I find it?

- What does it mean to become "unselfed" in our religion? Try rewriting #7 in your own words and include analysis and description of how it is with you. For example, when you begin to rewrite the sentence, "The little time-worn self about which we fretted, how narrow its boundaries, how unstable its base, how strained its structure," go on and spell out how fretful and worn you are, define its narrow boundaries, describe the insecurities you feel, be straighforward in writing about the tensions and strains in your life.

- Can you sleep well tonight because you have loved well today? If you were to die today would yours be a good death because you loved well all your life long?

THE CONSEQUENCES OF LOVING

Over these past years I have attempted to do my everyday business for the love of God. What has happened? First I found it is exceedingly difficult to be consistent. The immediacy of tensions surrounding many of the human situations in which I find myself often overwhelm any good intention I may have had to put the love of God at the center. Or it may be the heavy pressure to *decide*, or the tangled lines of half truth, misrepresentation, even deliberate falsehood, either of which trigger immediate reaction which is self-centered, not God-centered.

Yet as I have kept bringing myself back again and again to attempt to do everything purely for the love of God, there have been those times, in increasing numbers when keeping this divine perspective at the center of my thinking and acting has made a radical difference in the actual situation as well as in its outcome. For example, when we are confronted on occasion by persons so emotionally upset that they are carried to extremes in making accusations against us, if we are trying to respond to such an adversary purely for the love of God, we do respond differently. We do not react from wounded pride or from feeling personally affronted or demeaned. If nothing else, we are able to let all the irrational, irrelevant and unrealistic charges and issues fall by the way without defense. We can quietly point to whatever real issues exist and leave with an open-ended commitment to work at solving the real issues.

Haven't we all experienced those times in our lives when our love of family was more tender, our friendships with others more open and sensitive? Even our working with others at the shop, plant, office was freer and more inspired because the tidal flow of love in its own mysterious way had expanded our horizons, our sensitivity and helped us see all persons in a new light.

Then we fall back into the old ways and we wonder for how long we must endure. The ebbing of the tide can be shortened and the flow of love lengthened by our living under the discipline of love. These "family document" selections can be the means of living our way into a fuller and more abiding lifestyle of love.

Here then in these next selections are glimpses of what it means for us to become "agents of the Eternal Charity" acting in accord with and response to this "holy energy" at the heart of all things.

Selections from the "Family Documents"

Human beings are saved by a Love which enters and shares their actual struggle, darkness and bewilderment, their subjection to earthly conditions. By a supreme exercise of humility the deep purposes of God are worked out through ***our*** natural life with all its powers, humiliations, conflicts and sufferings, its immense capacity for heroic self-giving, disinterested love; not by means of ideas, insights, and spiritual experiences even of the loftiest kind. Charity, generosity, accepting the vocation of sacrifice, girding itself with lowliness as one that serveth and then going straight through with it, suffering long, never flinching, never seeking its own, discloses its sacred powers to us within the arena of our homely everyday existence; and it is by the varied experiences and opportunities of that daily existence, that our dull and stubborn nature shall be trained for the glorious liberty of eternal life.

[10]*Evelyn Underhill*

Less clear is the element of action in the relation to a human You. The essential act that here establishes directness is usually understood as a feeling, and thus misunderstood. Feelings accompany the metaphysical and metapsychical fact of love, but they do not constitute it; and the feelings that accompany it can be very different. Jesus' feeling for the possessed man is different from his feeling for the beloved disciple; but the love is one. Feelings one "has;" love occurs. Feelings dwell in man, but man dwells in his love. This is no metaphor but actuality: love does not cling to an I, as if the You were merely its "content" or object; it is between I and You. Whoever does not know this, know this with his being, does not know love, even if he should ascribe to it the feelings that he lives through, experiences, enjoys, and expresses. Love is a cosmic force. For those who stand in it and behold in it, men emerge from their entanglement in busy-ness, and the good and the evil, the clever and the foolish, the beautiful and the ugly, one after another become actual and a You for them; that is, liberated emerging into a unique confrontation. Exclusiveness comes into being miraculously again and again--and now one can act, help, heal, educate, raise, redeem. Love is responsibility of an I for a You: in this consists what cannot consist in any feeling--the equality of all lovers, from the smallest to the greatest . . . .

[11]*Martin Buber*

"When the evening of this life comes," says St. John of the Cross, "you will be judged on love." The only question asked about the soul's use of its two-storied house and the gifts that were made to it, will be: "Have you loved well?" All else will be resumed in this; all thoughts, beliefs, desires, struggles and achievements, all complex activities . . . . For Faith is nothing unless it be the obscure vision of a loved Reality; and Hope is nothing unless it be the confidence of perfect love. So too with all the persons, events, opportunities, conflicts and choices proposed for the soul's purification and growth. Was everything that was done, done for love's sake? Were all the doors opened that the warmth of Charity might fill the whole house; the windows cleaned that they might more and more radiate from within its mysterious divine light? Is the separate life of the house more and more merged in the mighty current of the city's life? Is it more and more adapted to the city's sacred purpose--the saving radiation of the Perfect within an imperfect world? For this is Charity; the immense expansion of personality effected by the love of God, weaving together the natural and the supernatural powers of the soul and filling them with its abundant life. Overflowing the barriers of preference, passing through all contrary apearance, it mediates the Divine pity and generosity to every mesh and corner of creation and rests at last in God, Who is the life and love of every soul.

[12]*Evelyn Underhill*

When we are drowned in the overwhelming seas of the love of God, we find ourselves in a new and particular relation to a few of our fellows . . . . It is wonderful. I have been literally melted down by the love of God.

[13]*Thomas Kelly*

But Holy Fellowship . . . lives in the Center and rejoices in the unity of ***God's*** love.

And this Fellowship is deeper than democracy, conceived as an ideal of group living. It is a theocracy wherein God rules and guides and directs **us, the** listening children. The center of authority is not in ***a person***, not in the group, but in the creative God . . . .

[14]*Thomas Kelly*

Another aspect of the same awakening of the soul-tenderness is the new love of the world. Before, we had loved the world because it enriched our lives--we were the receiving centers. But now all is new, even the nature of love itself. Our families, our dear ones, they are reloved. For family love is now understood in the light of an Eternal Love that endures to the end for its beloved ones. And just as the infinite Love of God enfolds us, so we know that infinite Love enfolds all things in our love. Yet it is not our love, but the love of God, loving its way, through us to this world. Would that we could encounter all needs, bear all burdens, dry all tears, fulfill all . . . dreams. But the three score years and ten close in upon us and the geographical and historical necessities put bounds upon us. Yet in *intention*, we love all, suffer with all, and rejoice with all, and laugh with all. In the tendering sense of the Eternal Presence we come to the burden-bearing, Calvary-re-enacting life which is the heart of Christian living . . . .

[15]*Thomas Kelly*

Reflection and Action

- How have you dealt with, or how could you deal lovingly with an irrational, highly emotional confrontation between yourself and another person?

- Think back across your life and set down in your personal journal a description of those tender or sensitive times which have come to you. Try to remember what were the elements and conditions that made these possible. Then imagine what steps you could take to prepare yourself for new tendering and sensitivity.

- What are your genuine qualities that make self-love possible? Reflect on #17 and 18 (see also More Selections from the "Family Documents," for Chapter VII) until you come to a fuller understanding of how we can be delivered from this "ego-fissure?"

- In answer to the question, "Have you loved well?" what can you say about your love for family, co-workers, strangers, enemies? What can you do about living into a broader and deeper love with all such persons?

Selection Footnotes

1. *The New Testament in Modern English*, translated by J. B. Phillips. (New York: The MacMillan Company, 1959), John 15:9-13, p. 223.
2. *The New Testament in Modern English*, I Corinthians 13, pp. 370-371.
3. *The New Testament in Modern English*, I John 3:17-18, p. 520.
4. Evelyn Underhill, *An Anthology of the Love of God*. (New York: David McKay Co., Inc., 1953-1955, Oxford: printed by A. R. Mowbray), p. 33.
5. *The Practice of the Presence of God*, p. 14.
6. *Spiritual Counsel and Letters of Baron Friedrich von Hügel*, pp. 81-82.
7. Thomas R. Kelly, *The Eternal Promise*, edited by Richard Kelly. (New York: Harper and Row Publishers, 1966) pp. 24-26.
8. Constancio C. Vigil, *The Fallow Land*. (New York: Harper and Brothers, Publishers, n.d.), pp. 26-27.
9. Jean Nicholas Grou, *Meditations on the Love of God*. (London: Burns, Oates and Washbourne, 1948), pp. 23-24.
10. *The School of Charity*, p. 53.
11. Martin Buber, *I and Thou*, translated by W. Kaufmann. (New York: Charles Scribner's Sons, 1970), p. 66.
12. *Concerning the Inner Life with The House of the Soul*, (New York: E. P. Dutton, 1947, 1953), pp. 148-149.
13. *A Testament of Devotion*, pp. 20-21.
14. *A Testament of Devotion*, p. 84.
15. *The Eternal Promise*, pp. 30-31.

CHAPTER

VIII

SPIRITUAL DISCIPLINES FOR EVERYDAY LIVING

Adrian van Kaam, C.S.S.P.

1920--

Born in the Hague. Holland, Adrian van Kaam joined the order of the Spiritans in 1940. Theology. philosophy, psychology and education formed the basis of his years of scholarly discipline which culminated in his receiving the Ph.D. degree in Psychology from Western Reserve University in 1958. Father van Kaam has developed a unique theory of Christian personality and a research methodology in spiritual formation. His twenty-nine books covering many aspects of the life of the spirit establish him as one of the foremost modern authors of the "family documents."

For Father van Kaam, teaching and writing issued in action. While teaching at his seminary in Holland he became involved in a unique educational experiment for young working adults. These "Life Schools" attracted thousands of young people to week-end courses, where they learned to integrate the spiritual inspiration of their religion with the main dimensions of their daily living.

After coming to Duquesne University to teach in the Department of Psychology, Dr. van Kaam began to concentrate on his major interest--the study of human and Christian formation in the life of the spirit. He was founder and first director of the Institute of Formative Spirituality. Currently he is Director emeritus of the Institute and Professor of foundational formation. He continues to write and lecture throughout the nation and the world.

Chapter VIII

THE ULTIMATE DISCIPLINE: ATTACHMENT WITH GOD

By now we have begun to sense that our primary grounding is in our personal relationship with God. In this chapter we shall seek to discover what it means to live our way into this ultimate discipline, our attachment with God.

THE BASIC CONCEPT

This concept has always been the central affirmation of the Judeo-Christian faith--God is the center of our lives. We find it in the Psalmist's command, "Be still and know that I am God," in the descriptive experiences of the Old Testament prophets, and in Jesus' numerous references to his relationship with God. Great theological formulations have also made this clear. Martin Buber's penetrating writings shed much insight on the "I-Thou" relationship. Likewise the great theological writers of the Roman Catholic, Greek Orthodox and Protestant traditions have in a variety of ways established the intellectual reality of this ultimate discipline.

Here in this chapter we shall concentrate upon those insights which have come from the personal experience of the writers of the "family documents" as they have reflected upon, and discovered something of the meaning of attachment to God. This has come because they worked their way through the practice and consequences of living with involuntary and voluntary detachment, and out of the process of re-examining and reordering their attachments.

Through it all is the clear message that our basic attachment is in a living relationship with God. As we work our way through to new levels of insight concerning our attachments and detachments, we may well be drawn closer to the living God as the constant center and source of our everyday existence.

Selections from the "Family Documents"

This decidedness in a Christian is not to be confused with the decidedness of the bigot, or the ***person*** with a one-string gospel. It is not a decidedness about a particular doctrine. Such "decided" Christians are plentiful, but they are not the answer to the world's need. True decidedness is not of doctrine, but of life orientation. It is a commitment of life, thoroughly, wholly, in every department and without reserve, to the Inner Guide. It is not a tense and reluctant decidedness, an hysterical assertiveness. It is a joyful and quiet displacement of life from its old center in the self, and a glad and irrevocable replacement of the whole of life in a new and divine Center. It is a life lived out from an all-embracing center of motivation, which in glad readiness wills to do the will of ***God***, so far as that will can be discerned. It is a life of integration, of peace, of final coordination of all one's powers, within a singleness of commitment. It is the final elimination of all *tolerated* double-mindedness, and the discovery of the power which comes from being "in the unity."

[1]*Thomas Kelly*

To become strong and peaceful, I must rid myself of interests that distract and agitate me inordinately. Gently I must stem the flow of superficial thoughts, emotions, and memories that crowd my life. The unity I seek presupposes that I can detach myself at certain moments from the rush of fleeting days and establish zones of silence and recollection. I ready myself to find God and self when I distance myself from the flood of images thrown at me by billboards, journals, magazines, and countless television and radio programs.

[2]*Adrian vanKaam*

In this modern prison my cell was smaller than that in Lehrterstrasse. It was only five paces wide; but it was quite clean, and in these silent days of autumn, when the sun shone through the bars, it had something of the austere beauty of a monk's cell. The more clearly I saw my destiny approaching, the more deeply did I enter into quietness, both within and without. The world seemed to fade away, and the voices of daily life were silent. There was no telephone to break the stillness; no interviews, no committees, no discussions, no obligations, to fill my day with activity. Even the bars of my window, and the chains on my wrists seemed no longer to have much meaning. My surroundings were of the simplest--just a few necessary things--a spoon and a plate--a table and a plank bed. No longer was there anything to excite me or to distract me. My mind was rested and free to receive essential impressions. The stream of time flowed on quietly and majestically towards God. In point of fact this is always the case, but here in the stillness I was enabled to see it more clearly. In those days it was granted me to tread the shores of that land which lies on the outermost fringe of time, upon which already something of the radiance of the other world is shining. I did not know that an existence which is still earthly and human could be so open to the world of God. It was a stillness full of blessing, a solitude over which God brooded, an imprisonment blessed by God . . . .

[3]*Hanns Lilje*

To reach at oneness with ***God***, I must free myself from the deceptive ties that bind me to the world. I free myself *from* attachment to things to free myself *for* deeper attachment to God. Detachment is not a negative act. It is a way of distancing myself from the temporal world to bind myself more intimately to the eternal that shines forth in it.

[4]*Susan Muto*

Reflection and Action

- What kind of a decided Christian are you?

- Have you experienced the quiet displacement of life from its old self-centeredness? If so, what is it like moving toward the divine center? If not, how can you imagine and describe the possible transition, by eliminating the "tolerated double mindedness" (Selection #1) of your present life? What double mindedness do you tolerate?

- How do we go beyond fear to the "yes" of attachment to God? What clues do you find in #3 and 4, to give some answer to this question?

PRACTICING THE ULTIMATE DISCIPLINE

To become intentionally related to God, at the very center of our lives, we must fully comprehend, accept and assimilate our experiences of detachment and attachment.

To describe this relationship as "the reciprocating principle of attachment and detachment" is an interesting way of beginning to talk about these twin disciplines which are really two sides of the coin of our essential unity and our unique aloneness.

"To reciprocate," according to Webster's dictionary, is *"to move alternatively back and forth."* We live all our lives within the reciprocating principle of attachment and detachment. Begin by taking a clear look at the way the natural process of attachment operates in our lives. By our very natures we accept, we possess, we acquire; we actively seek to hold or own things, and we enter into human relationships in which our expectations are for lasting ties and permanent love or friendships. The work we do rests upon this very same principle and our having and holding our job, or of letting it go voluntarily or involuntarily. The causes we espouse, the organizations we join are based upon the operation of this reciprocating principle. So too, our relationships to our immediate families and our wider relationships with uncles, aunts and cousins, call for attachment and detachment in a wide variety of ways.

Take time to think about your present assorted attachments. How did you get involved; why are you so attached in some facets of your life, and so loosely related in others? What is the intensity and the quality of these attachments? What are your underlying expectations and how demanding are these expectations? What of their validity and vitality and what are the possible invalid and detrimental features of any of these attachments?

In all of this we are recognizing the inherent rightness of having and holding, and we are saying that attachment is essential for creative living. The discipline of attachment is also a process. Early enthusiastic attachments may be displaced by more considered long-lasting havings and holdings. All is not lost and often much is gained when we let go of present attachments and move into new and challenging relationships.

So here we are embedded in our attachments sometimes even to the point of imprisonment. Then suddenly, often without warning, *involuntary* detachment breaks in upon the smooth operation of our lives. All experiences of involuntary detachment, it should be noted, are within the parentheses of those two ultimate experiences of such detachment common to all of us, birth and death.

How then does involuntary detachment operate in our lives? When, where, and how have we been cut loose from our moorings? What have been the pressures forcing us to let go? What were those external events that ruthlessly cut us loose from our attachments? Looking honestly at our lives we discover that involuntary detachment is a frequently recurring fact of our existence.

More than sixty years ago my father and I built the largest, most beautiful kite we had ever made. That sleek, streamlined pink creation we took to an open field for a holiday morning of glorious kite-flying, for it was an ideal day. On its first trial flight when it was about two-thirds of the way up, a sudden strong current of wind snapped the string and my beautiful kite went its erratic and uncontrolled way out of my life. To this day I still remember the scalding tears of disappointment, frustration and utter loss. This was a small boy's early experience with enforced detachment made all the more vivid because of his personal involvement in the creation and construction of that kite--a prelude to a series of other inevitable detachments which come to all of us.

Phillips Brooks, the great American churchman, experienced such detachment in this way. After completing his studies leading to teaching, he taught for a year. At the end of the year he was called before the headmaster and told that he would not be rehired and that in no way should he consider teaching to be his chosen vocation.

In the death of a beloved person, husband, wife, mother, father, child or friend, we are confronted with the most radical detachment of all, where most if not all of our attachment is broken asunder, and the residue of loving memories seems thin and ephemeral.

How then do we come to terms with these experiences of externally enforced detachment? We begin by recognizing that, even though we had no choice, we were not destroyed, since, if nothing else, the instinct for survival is strong enough to carry us through to more than dull unthinking acceptance.

This very fact of our not being destroyed or permanently hurt beyond repair is the important place of beginning. After the traumatic loss of the pink kite, I soon was back at making more kites. We do know that Phillips Brooks found his way into the Christian ministry and became one of the great preachers of the American pulpit. Again, in experiencing the death of a beloved person, we can recover and move on into new effective and often creative living.

In all such experiences, when we find ourselves intact and even under the necessity of rebuilding our lives, we can experience a new sense of freedom and fearlessness in which reconstruction and new growth takes place. Here's how it can develop.

Such freedom may arise from our recognition that what was taken from us was not as important as we thought. If, at the other extreme our loss was of someone loved and cherished, we discover a new dimension of freedom in the recognition of our extreme good fortune in having had such an attachment; and the cherished memories of that attachment have healing and nourishing qualities for our developing lives. We also realize that we have no inherent guarantee that such blessed attachments are forever; and we are then able to open ourselves to the possibility of forming new and equally fulfilling affiliations without heavy feelings of guilt and disloyalty to the past. It is at just this point that the spiritually disciplined person begins to ask of God, "What are the next attachments for me, within the perspective of your divine will?" All this is the model of training and discipline by which we discover the reality of God's availability in the midst of our natural existence. At the same time we are freed from ever having to be afraid of any future unexpected involuntary detachment which may confront us.

This then is a process in which we frequently become aware of the reenforcing sense of the presence of God. Then as other experiences of involuntary detachment come, we begin to experience further fearlessness and freedom, and we continue to open ourselves to the reality of God's presence.

The next step in moving into the ultimate discipline of

attachment with God comes when we begin to see the possibilities of *voluntary* detachment. If out of our previous experiences with externally enforced detachment we have discovered something of the reality of God's presence, we then are free enough to raise the question of voluntary detachments from our affiliations and commitments.

Now we are free to begin realistically sorting out the lines and motivations of our present attachments. Here we learn to let go of possessions, ego demands, our shabbier human relationships, a dull enervating job, and even some of our previously thought to be "favorite causes." Here much of the baggage of our lives is exposed for just what it is--excess--non-essential for genuinely full creative living under God.

By the exercise of imaginative forethought we can begin to examine all our attachments in the light of our growing desire to "do everything purely for the love of God." In so doing, we find it possible to begin to *voluntarily* cut loose from some of our previously unexamined attachments, in order to prepare the way for entering into new and more vitally significant relationships.

Two further insights are necessary if we are to move close to this ultimate discipline of attachment with God.

First, there is an elemental factor which must be operative in learning the art of detachment and attachment. Consider how subtly, how thoroughly we have become ego-centric in all our thinking and living. We tend to act as though we really are, somehow, responsible for the very nature and essence of all that is. In reality we are totally immersed in a physical, social, and spiritual world which is given to us by God, and is already there.

It is, therefore, a liberating step through detachment when we understand our place in the universe. Our responsibility is in the molding, shaping, constructing of our inheritance at every level. Our will, our intellect, our motivation together with our learning and our discipline are important features of our stewardship.

Thus, at the center of our thinking and living is a gratitude and joy in acknowledgement of the given, and in our relationship to it. Our responsibility rests at the level of our stewardship of this given. Now we are free to have and to hold, and to let go and to examine and fashion new ways of allowing this reciprocating principle of attachment and detachment to function for ourselves and for all persons everywhere, and in all phases of life, physically, socially, politically, economically, and religiously.

Second, the meaning of attachment and detachment involves an awareness of who I am as a person. In order for us to form an attachment with God, there must be an essential *Me*--whose health and maturity is capable of entering into such a relationship. Only those who have wrestled through to an understanding of the essential *Me* and have let go at this deepest level are able to take hold and accept the gifts of the given in new and significant ways.

Douglas Steere's illustrations of "dying little deaths" (#8) help us in grasping the meaning of this concept. Hanns Lilje's profound insight regarding our essential existence in solitude (#3) is equally applicable in our coming to know that there may well be those several times when in the midst of total detachment we stand utterly alone with the living God. Does it require imprisonment and solitary confinement for all of us in order for us to experience God? Not at all, if we come to practice the art of detachment.

What Douglas Steere is suggesting is that all of these experiences leave us in possession of the essential core of our beings--the essential *Me* which finally resides in the presence of the living God. It is for each of us to pursue those steps in letting go which we may take voluntarily, and then accept with joy those involuntary events of detachment which will come to all of us.

In the cheerful clarity of mind, heart and soul we learn to let go some of the practical realistic holdings of our present existence. This is never easy, yet it can be done and with practice it can be done with good grace, even cheerfully!

Now consider some very practical ways of practicing attachment and detachment. Consciously establish zones of silence and recollection in which to center down to the reality of God's living spirit. In these times we quietly and calmly set aside useless expectations, false pressures, unrealistic goals, superficial values as we work to become "decided Christians" who will come finally to will one thing, who will strive to do all things purely for the love of God. Yet we can use imaginative forethought in the service of learning to let go. For example, take time to review reflectively and in depth how you think you would react and feel if suddenly your most cherished friendship was broken asunder by the transfer of that friend to another part of the country. Imagine what it would be like to be called in and told you were fired.

My wife and I discovered how imaginative forethought could help us detach and attach ourselves when we moved from serving our first church to a second church. We were beginning to feel sorry for ourselves as the day of departure approached--sorry that we were leaving such good and choice friends as we now had in this first church. Then one night as we were lamenting our approaching loss, we began to try to imagine what kinds of new friends we would find in this next situation. We were then able to look back in love and appreciation as we considered how these present friendships had been formed. Again we tried to imagine how new friendships would develop, and under what entirely different circumstances the next friendships might emerge. New and lasting friendships have been made and sustained over the years, through at least a half dozen moves. By the use of imaginative forethought, detachment and attachment in personal friendships have given us a treasury of special friends in many locations.

Now some of us will say, "Yes, that's fine for you who have moved about and it is much easier in those circumstances than for those of us who have lived, and will continue to live out our days in one place." Yes, of course, you are right. Try a good healthy application of imaginative forethought not once but often, asking where are the places, people and groupings of people in our present clubs and organizations where new and creative attachment could be possible if we take the initiative. And such reflection may even require that we imagine a wide variety of ways for taking the initiative. We may even have to go all the way down the line to imagine ourselves into taking the first step, in which we detach ourselves from our old entrenchments and move with vigor and keen anticipation into new adventures in attachment.

Only after we have come through to creative handling of *involuntary* and *voluntary* detachment are we then ready to move into a clear acceptance of the ultimate discipline of attachment with God and the consequences of this for all other attachments which follow. For remember this, our attachment with God does not end in glorious isolation from the world; it is the very center and source of motivation, inspiration, yes even demanding involvement in new and challenging attachments.

Right here let us also be clear that in the early stages of faith, along with acceptance of other's testimony--for example, these quotations from the "family documents," the ultimate in experience comes for us in an unfolding process. Our new attachments emerge from our faith and knowledge put into experimental practice. Therefore, for each of us this is a highly individualized growth; and as such it must always be free from the false legislation or unrealistic expectation of others no matter how genuine their experiences may have been for them, or how desperately they may want us to share their exact experience.

Selections from the "Family Documents"

One must first have a place before leaving it. One can abandon only what one has got. One can give up only what one has received . . . leaving a thing is a free act.

In all things there is a time for attachment and a time for detachment. ***When we do*** not attach ***ourselves*** properly at the time for attachment ***we*** cannot detach ***ourselves*** properly either at the time for detachment. (pp . 98-99)

It would be absurd and unjust to urge detachment upon a ***person*** who had never received the thing in question . . . . The rich young man was told by Jesus to sell his goods (Mark 10:21). The young man had first received his goods, had enjoyed them and had become attached to them, and Jesus does not blame him for that. But now the time for detachment has come, so that he may be able to attach himself to the person of Jesus ("and come, follow me," Jesus says). Thus there is a rhythm between attachment and detachment . . . one must first possess, in order to be able to give up. (p. 99)

We must always be letting go what we have acquired, and acquiring what we did not possess, leaving one place in order to find another, abandoning one support in order to reach another, turning our backs on the past in order to thrust wholeheartedly towards the future. I have even seen many people so accustomed to misfortune that they could not believe in good fortune when it came. Suffering was their place, and they could not leave it without experiencing such distress that it spoilt their happiness. (p. 164)

But no one can go on receiving and acquiring indefinitely. And even if ***we receive*** beyond ***our*** expectations, ***we have*** not yet had the fundamental experience of life, which is always of the order of the second movement. When ***we have*** received much, ***we*** must come some day to the turning-point in ***our*** destiny when ***we*** must let go what ***we have*** received, on pain of remaining its prisoner and becoming lost in it. (pp. 144-145)

. . . when a ***person*** hesitates in my consulting-room ***and*** is faced with the need to give something up, I understand what it is that is stopping ***her or*** him: it is not only an instinctive attachment to . . . old habits, and ***the*** fear of losing the familiar place which lent . . . support. It is also a presentiment of that middle-of-the-way anxiety . . . ***each one*** must cross that painful supportless zone [alone]. (p. 164)

In these circumstances what can I make my support as I start off once more? What can I use as a thread to guide me forward through the darkness of this moment? I need a sort of radar that would enable me to take off and land blind. That radar, I think, is my conviction that God has a purpose for me, a purpose for each one of us, and at every moment of our lives. I believe that God can lead me, even when I cannot yet see the road clearly in front of me. I believe that my illness is not fortuitous, but a part of God's purpose, and that all the problems it raises are opportunities to learn something about ***God***, to undergo new experiences under ***God's*** guidance. (p. 167)

[5]*Paul Tournier*

Tournier tells of a Dutchman who had been a prisoner of the Japanese who said with deep emotion,

"You can't imagine the sense of freedom I had after they had taken from me everything I had."

[6]*Paul Tournier*

Hanns Lilje describes his friend and fellow prisoner Moltke as a free and fearless person.

He said--"Don't have any illusions! If you have done what you have just told us, you will be hanged." His calmness was not stoical, because it sprang from an inward detachment which was almost cheerful, and he tried to persuade us to give up all illusions about our fate, and challenged us to prepare for death.
He did this himself in an exemplary manner, without the slightest self-deception about his probable end; he lived in a cheerful clarity of soul, the most shining example of a resolute attitude, due to his faith. As a Christian, he was the most convinced and the most certain of all of us. His faith was completely solid and real . . . . He had already achieved what is only possible on the borderland of death--the conflict lay behind him. No cloud of temptation dimmed his confidence and his faith. I can bear witness that I only saw him cheerful and calm . . . . The letters he wrote during this period are marvelous in their certainty and clearness. Up to the last he was inwardly completely free, friendly, helpful, thoughtful for others, a truly free human being, with inward nobility, in the midst of a world of meanness and cruelty.

[7]*Hanns Lilje*

Douglas Steere has a remarkable chapter entitled, "Death's Illumination of Life," in his choice book, *On Beginning from Within*. In this chapter is a section headed, "Practice in Dying Little Deaths." These quotations from this section provide clear insight into the practice of detachment.

How good to remember, now, that time in life when as a parent we saw a child off to school that first morning, to feel the wrench of his departure, to know that now he must make his own way, be taught by others than ourselves, risk life by accidents and suffer in countless ways from which we can no longer shield him! We trusted him to life that morning, and as he disappeared from sight, we died a little death. But in that death something still stronger inside us seemed to emerge and he was more our own because we had let him go.

How good to remember the first day we gave a daughter in marriage to a young man who was not bone of our bone and who could scarcely be expected to understand and to treat this precious daughter as we knew so well to do at home! How great the risks and uncertainties of love and marriage! How important this girl's future was to our heart! And then the scene cleared, and we gave her away to this young man. And we died another little death, only to feel a new dimension of caring for these two rise up in us and the meaning of an old Sanscrit proverb come clear: "That which is not given away is lost."

How good to remember the time that I knew that I should die if I owned to another my guilt in some affair, and how I owned it and died, only to discover that what had died in me in that miniature death was my egotistical pride and that beneath the death of humiliation there is still the true *Me* that lives and breathes more freely for this loosening of its bond!

How good to remember those sleepless nights when I feared to relax to sleep lest I should meet there what I was afraid of, and lest I should not be able to stand the encounter; and to remember how I slowly discovered that to die the little death of sleep meant trusting the goodness and the forgiving character of the conserver of the *Me*, and how I learned to let go to the source of life as the earth lets go to the spring and how I was carried away and refreshed and strengthened and restored!

How good to remember that illness in which, my body stale, torpid, dull and apathetic to my demands upon it, I practiced dying. I practiced wearing my body like a loose garment! There I discovered that instead of quenching the *Me*, the utter weakness of my body seemed to intensify the *Me's* claims to possess a life of its own.

How good to remember how I have let go what went before and have faced and welcomed each age of my life as it came, and in mature age how I have discovered that the dying back of my body has given me more occasion to be at home, and to keep my own heart warm by living in it! Until that time I had never fully grasped what that seventeenth-century writer had meant when he suggested that it was a wonderful thing to recognize the advanced age of a person less by the infirmity of . . . body, than by the maturity of . . . soul.

The remembrance of these exercises in dying the little deaths helps to make us able to inhabit a *Me* whose nature it seems to be to die into life, to discover an invisible means of support as it is loosened from its tightly clutched settings which masquerade as life.

[8]*Douglas Steere*

Reflection and Action

- List all of your present attachments. How intensively are you bound by these?

- Recall an experience of involuntary detachment, in which you were not destroyed. Reflect on the influence this experience has had on your life. What were the elements that preserved your essential self?

- What persons, places and things have shaped the "essential Me" that you know at the present time in your life. Consider how these influences represent the creative flow of attachment and detachment for you. Consider what meaning this creative flow has had on your relationship with God.

- Choose an attachment from which you would like to become more detached. Think about the benefits of becoming detached from that attachment; think of the challenges.

- Do you begin to see how you could practice voluntary detachment? What steps would you take? What is the most crucial single attachment which must be voluntarily jettisoned, if you are to be free to respond to God?

- Reflect upon the remarkable quotations of Douglas Steere, above. When in your life have you "died into life," and in so doing discovered that divine source which supports your essential self?

THE CONSEQUENCES OF LIVING UNDER THIS ULTIMATE DISCIPLINE

For ten years 1952-62, I had the privilege of providing executive leadership to a national church board. In these ten years we were given resources and therefore had sufficient staff to do some creative experimentation along with expansion and growth in program. My predecessor had had ten years of curtailed budgets, limited staff, restricted programming, in which he had no chance to reverse these trends.

In the midst of success, I came to the full realization that a very large part of my achievement was due to the positive reenforcement of the era, times and persons in which and with whom I functioned. Then it dawned on me that if the neutral and negative factors in my predecessor's situation had been my inheritance, my success quotient would have been minimal.

I also recognized that in all likelihood there would come a time in my life when the combination of given factors would operate to frustrate and minimize any chance of success and achievement. This did happen in a four-year period, 1970-1974, when as president of a small private church-related college the combination of events and the realities of declining enrollment meant that we had only modest achievements in some areas to offset the drastic curtailment and reductionism which was dictated by the exigencies of our given situation. Yet we were able to do what we had to do, and survive with good grace because we were able to let go and not be devastated. And even the difficult measures that had to be adopted were not of the desperation variety but were sufficiently realistic to provide the foundation upon which recovery is well underway.

At the outset of my service to the college we all thought it would be a period of stabilized enrollments in which we could set about the task of further delineating the nature and function of the Christian college. All too soon, the radical shift took place in which survival was the foremost demand. Such traumatic shift in the givenness of our situation called for a new definition of expectations and an understanding that there would be no glamour, very limited creative experimentation--only tough, difficult decisions and planning which at best would issue in nothing more than survival. Only the long discipline of detachment gave me the inner strength to live with and through such a radical change in vocational demand and responsibility. Only a consciousness of my ultimate relationship with God made it possible for me to take the initiative to release the college from its final year's contract with me in order to free them up to find a new person who would be free to give leadership without the burden of responsibility which had fallen on me in those years of drastic curtailment. At 61 years of age and with no immediate offer of another position, this was voluntary detachment in its most drastic form. Yet the validity of this discipline was vindicated.

The spiritual discipline of attachment and detachment requires us to constantly evaluate our vocational life and our whole lives by asking the right questions about our reasons for doing what we are doing, and to reconsider the expectation and demands we place upon our work. Here is another illustration of imaginative forethought in the practice of voluntary detachment in support of God-centered attachment.

John Woolman imagined his way into his own vocational lifestyle as a self-employed tailor. Living with this reciprocating principle during the mid-18th century, he came to the conclusion that he ought to keep his life free of as many commitments as possible in order to be free to respond to the leading of the Holy Spirit. As a corollary of this principle, he decided that he would only make enough clothing to earn a modest income to satisfy the reasonable needs of his family. Operating on this proposition he then had enough time to consult with Pennsylvania Quakers and the Indians during a period of severe Indian uprisings; and to journey at his own expense to England to lay upon the hearts of English Quaker slave traders his own God-given "scruple" that trading in slaves and the whole institution of slavery were wrong.

It is possible to practice voluntary detachment. I have known and counselled with any number of friends for whom such detachment was essential in terms of release from a debilitating, unproductive job. Others have imagined their way through those detachments, which left them lonely and despairing, into new and creative attachment. Where can we begin today?

Remember that any single step and all of this together leads us to the losing of life in order that we find it in its ultimate and intimate relationship with God and Christ. Take into those zones of silence and recollection the final series of quotations under this heading.

It is possible to move back and forth in developing the art of attachment and detachment. From members of various seminars over the past ten years has come the clear affirmation that to live under the discipline of this reciprocating principle is to live with a green and growing inescapable idea which is now integral to their living. This can be our experience from here on out if you are ready to accept the challenge.

An Exercise in Detachment

One of the seminar participants told of an exercise he used with a youth group in preparation for their visiting elderly persons in a retirement home. This experiment is valid for use personally or as an exercise to be used at the conclusion of a seminar discussion of this chapter.

Each young person was asked to write on ten separate pieces of paper the ten most important things in his or her life. The ten slips were then spread out in front of each young person. Since they were sitting next each other, each individual was asked to reach over to the person next right and take away at random six of the ten slips. Then each person was asked to reflect upon their feeling and attitudes about the four remaining items. How important were these which were left? Were the six which were gone more important? What would life be like with only these four left?

This is a very helpful way of placing oneself in tune with senior citizens living in retirement. It can be a very sure way in which by imaginative forethought we come to an understanding of what would happen to us if any or many of the most important things of ours were taken from us irrevocably.

Selections from the "Family Documents"

. . . How different is the experience of Life . . . when the Eternal Presence suffuses it! Suddenly, unexpectedly, the

Divine Presence is upon us. Secretly, astonishingly, we are lifted in a plateau of peace. The dinning clamour of daily events--so real, so urgent they have been!--is framed in a new frame, is seen from a new perspective. The former things are passed away; behold, they have become new. This world, our world, and its problems, does not disappear nor lose its value. It reappears in a new light, upheld in a new and amazingly *quiet* power. Calm replaces strain, peace replaces anxiety. Assurance, relaxation, and integration of life set in. With hushed breath we do our tasks. Reverently we live in the presence of the Holy . . . Life itself becomes a sacrament wherein sin is blasphemy. A deep longing for personal righteousness and purity sets in. Old tempting weaknesses no longer appeal as they did before. In patience we smile in loving concern for those who rush about with excited desperation. Oh, why can they not see the ocean of light and love which flows completely over the ocean of darkness and death! But all things [are] in ***God's*** Providence. A little taste of Cosmic Patience, which ***God*** must have for a wayward world, becomes ours. The world's work is to be done. But it doesn't have to be *finished* by us. We have taken ourselves too seriously. The life of God overarches *all* lifetimes . . . .

[9]*Thomas Kelly*

Let me tell an anecdote about someone who greatly desired something of our Lord. I told her that she was not ready for it and that if God gave it to her, while still she was not ready, it would hurt her. You ask: "Why was she not ready? Hadn't she goodwill? You say that given the will, everything is possible and that everything, perfection included, depends on the will."

That is correct; but "will" must be understood in two senses. There is first the contingent and nonessential will and then there is the providential will, creative and habitual. The truth is that it is not enough that ***our hearts*** . . . shall have . . . ***detached*** moments, in which to seek union with God; but there must be a disciplined detachment which precedes and follows [the moment of union] and only in that way may ***we*** receive the great things of God and God . . . in them. If, however, one is not ready for the gifts, they do harm and God in them. That is why God cannot always give us the things we ask for. The fault is not ***with God***;

God is a thousand times more ready to give than we are to receive. It is we who do violence and wrong ***God*** by hindering ***God's*** natural action with our unreadiness.

We ought to learn through God's gifts to get away from selfishness, to care no more for what we have a right to, to seek nothing for our own, neither instrument, pleasure, spirituality, delight, reward, the Kingdom of Heaven, nor that our wills be done . . . . Therefore it is not enough to surrender self and all that goes with it once. We have to renew the surrender often, for thus we shall be free and unfettered in all we do.

[10]*Meister Eckhart*

In later years we look back upon our spiritual history and give . . . thanks for the long process by which ***God*** loosed us from all these persons and possessions to which in our blindness and selfishness we had become so firmly tied. At the time we did not detect in this work of detachment the hidden, mysterious, powerful, persistent action of God . . . ***God*** works in us in myriad, hidden, and mysterious ways; in times of sickness, in the breaking of our earthly friendships, in the betrayals which have left us lonely and hurt, in the many disappointments, in the countless experiences of restlessness, in the death of those dear to us.

[11]*Charles Whiston*

As we give ourselves more and more fully and deeply to adoration of God, we find that adoration develops imperceptibly into self-giving. When we adore, we want to give. What we want to give is not simply external gifts, but ourselves. Self-giving is inseparable from truly Christian adoration. Self-giving is our progression from self-ownership and self-will unto the full sovereignty of God. It involves the renunciation of self-centeredness and self-seeking; and also our being born of the spirit into new selfhood, organized about God's will.

[12]*Charles Whiston*

We know that we have become so deeply attached to things and to persons and to ourselves that we have no longer power to detach ourselves. We gradually learn that not we ourselves, but God, is the main factor and agent in the long, progressive work of detachment. For it is God alone who sees and knows fully the nature and danger of our earthly attachments, to which we are so often blind. ***God*** sees, as we cannot see, the danger of inordinate and possessive attachment of husband and wife, of parent and child, of friend and friend.

When we awaken to the incomparableness of the fellowship that God offers us to that which we now have with ***other persons***, we shall realize that only as we cease to cling possessively and inordinately to the human friendships can we begin to enter into the wondrous and joyful spiritual fellowship with God, which will then bestow upon us a new spiritual ***relationship*** with ***others***, far deeper and richer than we ever had before with them. Then we shall accept the deep truth of our Lord's own words: "He that loseth his life shall find it; he that keepeth his life shall lose it." There is then a major place and emphasis in our life of praying for this detaching action of God and for our response of giving full consent to God.

[13]*Charles Whiston*

Through the death of friends and loved ones; through sufferings permitted or sent to us in God's providence; through the failure of our schemes, plans, and hopes for self-aggrandizement; through our experiences of boredom, loneliness, and restlessness; through sickness and accidents: through all these experiences we center our whole attention on the effect not upon others but upon ourselves, and we are so far from being God-centered that God acts to detach us from ourselves.

[14]*Charles Whiston*

Those who wish to help others to grow don't aim at making the growing person become a dependent--they aim at helping ***her or*** him to be able to live with reciprocal peers in a creative field-relationship. Those who wish to help others in order to assuage their own inadequacy really wish to arrest those they ostensibly would help, and keep them as clients.

[15]*Gerald Heard*

Reflection and Action

- Reread Selection #11. Draw a line on a large blank sheet of paper. Mark one end Birth and the other your present age. Looking back on your spiritual history, record the ages and a few notes about events that reflect "this work of detachment" as it has been present in your life.

- What would be included in a discipline that would have the goal of increasing your attachment with God?

- After reading and reflecting on Selection #9 (See Chapter XI, "More Selections from the Family Documents," for Chapter VIII), consider these questions:

- If the rhythm of detachment and attachment involves death, decision and rebirth, where could you begin making this cycle operative in your life?

- After reading #15, as you reflect upon its meaning, translate this into an application to your close relationships with one or two persons. Can you bring those relationships into a "creative field-relationship" of reciprocal peers? How does this relate to Henri Nouwen's concept of granting persons "free space?"

Selection Footnotes

1. *The Eternal Promise*, p. 16.
2. Adrian vanKaam, *On Being Involved: The Rhythm of Involvement and Detachment in Human Life*, (Denville, NJ: Dimension Books, 1970), p. 50.
3. *The Valley of the Shadow*, p. 88.
4. *Approaching the Sacred*, p. 86.
5. *A Place for You*. The page numbers appear in these seven at the end of each quotation.
6. Paul Tournier, *A Place for You*, translated by Edwin Hudson. (New York and Evanston: Harper and Row Publishers, 1968), p. 145.
7. *The Valley of the Shadow*, pp. 70-71.
8. *On Beginning From Within*, the next eight quotations are from pp. 132-135
9. *The Eternal Promise*, pp. 20-21.
10. *Meister Echkart*, pp. 32-33.
11. *Teach Us to Pray*, p. 77.
12. *Teach Us to Pray*, p. 95.
13. *Teach Us to Pray*, pp. 98-99.
14. *Teach Us to Pray*, p. 100.
15. *Training for a Life of Growth*, p. 34.

CHAPTER

IX

SPIRITUAL DISCIPLINES FOR EVERYDAY LIVING

John Bowen Coburn

1914--

Courtesy: John B. Coburn, Photograph by Fabian Bachrach

Bishop of the Diocese of Massachusetts, John Coburn has taught English and Biology at Robert College, Istanbul, Turkey, and was Dean of the Episcopal Theological School, Cambridge, Massachusetts 1957-69. He has also served as Rector of Grace Church, Amherst, Massachusetts, Chaplain at Amherst College and coach of the Amherst College Lacrosse Team, 1946-53. In addition to serving as Dean of Trinity Cathedral, Newark, New Jersey and Rector of St. James Church, New York, John Coburn has written ten books between 1957 and 1980. In the category of "family documents" are: Prayer and Personal Religion; Twentieth Century Spiritual Letters; A Life to Live; A Way to Pray: A Diary of Prayers; Personal and Private; The Hope of Glory. In these writings relating to what it means for an individual to "hasten unto God," John Coburn's full life as minister, educator and administrator illustrates what it means then to "hasten into the world."

Chapter IX

JOY AND THE LIFTED HEART

We experience joy as a result of the disciplined spiritual life. It is an inner sense of well-being centered in our experience of God.

TOWARD A DEFINITION OF JOY

Every time we are in God's presence we find our fragmented lives reordered, our over-zealous urgent driving quieted and often redirected; and we have opened before us insights of all that is permanent, enduring and trustworthy. Susan Muto directs us to this permanence when she writes,

> "Behind the tempest is the cloudless night, beneath the turbulence of the sea is the calm of the ocean's floor."

Anker Larsen reflects more than once upon the essential rightness, goodness and beauty of reality and the world around us. After reflecting about and living our way into these deeper levels of reality, we may well be overwhelmed by a deep sense of gratitude and joy for being allowed to exist in such a world (see selection #4).

As each of us progresses on his or her own spiritual pilgrimage, we will come upon a variety of descriptions, by the saints of all ages, of ecstasy and rapture resulting from the deep and abiding experience of the presence of God. Although we may not experience the rapture of the saints, the experience of joy is possible for all of us when we reflect upon these experiences of others.

There can be no final, categorical, precise,intellectually stated definition of joy. Experienced joy resulting from God's illumination and presence can never be fully defined to the satisfaction of our finite minds; such joy can only be experienced by each of us in our own way. It can neither be taught or finally discussed into fullness; it can only be caught, and then practiced by each of us as we will; especially as we translate this joy into new and creative relationships with relatives, friends, neighbors and colleagues.

Selections from the "Family Documents"

What is the source of your joy? There are some who are dependent upon the mood of others for their happiness. They seem bound in mood one to another like Siamese twins. If the other person is happy, the happiness is immediately contagious. If the other person is sad, there is no insulation against that mood. There are some whose joy is dependent upon circumstances. When things do not go well, a deep gloom settles upon them, and all who touch their lives are caught in the fog of their despair. There are some whose joy is a matter of disposition and temperament. They cannot be sad because their glands will not let them. Their joy is not a matter for congratulations or praise; it is a gift of life, a talent, a gratuitous offering placed in their organism. There are some who must win their joy against high odds, squeeze it out of the arid ground of their living or wrest it from the stubborn sadness of circumstance. It is a determined joy, sharpened by the zest of triumph. There are still others who find their joy deep in the heart of their religious experience. It is not related to, dependent upon, or derived from, any circumstances or conditions in the midst of which they must live. It is a joy independent of all vicissitudes. There is a strange quality of awe in their joy, that is but a reflection of the deep calm water of the spirit out of which it comes. It is primarily a discovery of the soul, when God's . . . presence is found, where there are no words, no outward song, only the Divine Movement. This is the joy that the world cannot give. This is the joy that keeps watch against all the emissaries of sadness of mind and weariness of soul. This is the joy that comforts and is the companion, as we walk even through the valley of the shadow of death.

[1]*Howard Thurman*

Only a few people, and those few but infrequently, know ecstasy. It is a big word; it means a state of being outside oneself and outside time, caught up in an overwhelming emotion; it implies a high occasion and a greatness of response to it. Mystics have used the word to express the ineffable joy of union with Reality, the flight, in Plotinus' phrase of the alone to the Alone; it applies to the selfless raptures of human love and parenthood, to what artists feel when what they create seems to be coming through them from something beyond.

[2]*Elizabeth Gray Vining*

There is a wholesome, a strengthening *zest* attached to all action which is right and appropriate for the agent; and there is unhealthily weakening *excitement*, which accompanies or follows all activity that is wrong or inappropriate. Hence one great end, and one sure test of right living and right disposition, is the degree to which such living and dispositions make zest to prevail in our lives and make excitement to disappear from them. Now there is no zest comparable to the zest, the expansion, the joy brought to the soul by God and the soul's close union with Him.

[3]*Baron von Hügel*

Anker Larsen and a friend who had long discussed the difference between being a closed or open person shared this experience:

One day when we were again together, and were discussing all sorts of trivialities, she happened to look out of the window. There stood a beech tree with its top bathed in the evening sunlight. As her glance fell upon the tree, she was moved by a profound gladness that *the tree was growing there*, and by a deep gratitude for *being allowed to see it*. Overwhelmed, she turned to me and told me this. Then she looked again at the tree. It was still there, with the sunlight still upon it--it was the same tree and yet quite different. The tree which she now saw was beautiful, and evoked a feeling of aesthetic satisfaction. Besides, it belonged to her, she could do with it what she liked. She could chop it down or leave it, she could be good and give the wood to the poor--a very ethical way of using a tree. In that short, happy moment, however, the tree had not belonged to her, and it was neither beautiful nor ugly; it was just a tree which stood there and grew and filled her with thankfulness that she was present--present without ulterior motives. In that moment she had caught a glimpse of Reality.

[4]*Johannes Anker Larsen*

Reflection and Action

- In the midst of your diversified and sometimes highly fragmented life have you ever been aware of "the cloudless night above the tempest, or the calm of the ocean floor beneath the surface tempest?"

- If so, write about such an experience in your personal journal. If not how do you imagine you might discover such reality?

- Each day during the coming week, reflect on present or past experiences of joy in your life. Record the emotions of these experiences in whatever way you wish--poetry, prose, reflective writing, art, or representative music or songs.

THE MEANING OF JOY

DISCOVERED IN ITS PRACTICE

To have the joy of a lifted heart is to cultivate a lifestyle in which our directed attention is sensitive to all that is good and true and beautiful. Then we begin to expand our awareness of joy in our actual living experience; we become free, open, warm-hearted, and radiant.

This is a call to discover all in the world around us that gives joy. Too frequently "realism" has been thought of only in terms of honest facing of the tough, unpleasant, and difficult aspects of our lives and our world. And in such a view, any attempt to put the spotlight on things of joy and beauty has been regarded as escapism. What we recognize here is the genuine reality of living our way into joy, beauty and truth just as surely as we can elect to live our way into gloom, despair and disillusionment by an overdose of negative realism.

How then may we experience the joy of a lifted heart? Consider the concept of "minor ecstasies" as Elizabeth Gray Vining describes them (see quotations #5 and 6). What have been the minor ecstasies we experienced recently? As we think back across the days and weeks, we may become aware that there were minor ecstasies, but we had been too overwhelmed with other matters, too overburdened with problems to solve, too emotionally upset either to recognize or enjoy them.

Such reflection can lead us to discover the discipline of the joyed life and the lifted heart. From here on, then, we resolve to live sensitively and unhurriedly so that we will be prepared to receive and appreciate these minor ecstasies as they enter our lives. And once we have entered into this discipline, it is truly remarkable how many of them break in upon us in the course of a routine week.

Dare we live with this concept until it becomes our lifestyle, and we can share our joy and insights with others? All of these quotations from the "family documents" provide some of the sources of insight into this spiritual discipline of joy. Read these devotionally, reflect, meditate, pray, and then practice the joy of the lifted heart.

Another way of practicing joy is to think of ourselves in a different way. Selection #16 in Chapter IV introduced us to this different way. If we think of ourselves and each one of us as feeling, and character as a collection of feelings, then we can say that a good person is a trust feeling. But if we are a *fear* feeling, then we each become a vortex which creates obstacles, tension, anxiety, anger, and immediate resistance. If, however, we are a confidence, then we are sources of courage and quiet calmness. Now consider how this relates to joy.

If we are a joy, then we are centers of hope, resilience; and we lift hearts, we give others the motivation to turn around and begin to see their own lives from the perspectives of the lifted heart. How do we become a joy? First by recognizing the splendor and graciousness of God's presence in our lives, however incomplete our "practice of the presence" may be.

Another way to experience joy is to live Meister Eckhart's assurance that God comes to those who have eyes to see--

evenly; and therefore God is evenly on all paths that lead to *the presence of God*. Can we experience Eckhart's joy and security by matching our evenness with the evenness of God?

Finally, the practice of living with the joy of a lifted heart provides a much more solid and sound basis for dealing with everything that negative realism rightly identifies and forces upon us. How many of us know the joy which grows out of living in and through negative experiences of tension, opposition and confrontation? More often than not there is more opportunity for learning and growth by individuals in these situations, than when everything is on even keel.

There can be joy in welcoming such situations of trial, tribulation and stress with their potential opportunities for growth and learning, for reconciliation and creative living. Here is a very concrete illustration of how joy is found at the very center of decision-making even in the midst of radical dissolution.

At Crozer Seminary over an eight-year period, 1962-70, our eighteen faculty and administrative staff moved from being a diffuse, distracted and nearly disillusioned collection of highly trained individuals, to becoming a genuinely free, committed, disciplined and joyful community of persons each living more surely up to capacity, each finding satisfaction in his or her own achievements as well as in the growth and success of our entire enterprise.

Early in our eighth year it became evident that we ought to seek a merger with another strong Protestant and ecumenical graduate theological seminary. After eight months of exploration, the decision was made to join the Colgate-Rochester, Bexley Hall complex at Rochester, New York.

Then we came to the final days of decision and separation. After the policy decision to merge was completed, we faced the far more difficult experience of deciding which seven among the eighteen of us were to go to Rochester and which eleven of us were to be free to seek other vocational assignments.

In a four-hour meeting all eighteen of us made the decision and named the seven persons who would go to Rochester, thus leaving the rest of us, including myself, free to seek other employment. There was a deep and abiding joy that emerged from that experience; a joy which was rooted and grounded in the reality of a genuine community that could make such a radical decision out of love and respect without being torn asunder by jealousy, hard feelings or bitterness. The remaining eleven discovered new dimensions of courage as we learned to live with the fact that our freedom to seek new work had no implicit guarantees of any future employment whatsoever.

Then came the final baccalaureate service which became a "celebration of separation" and a final faculty-administration farewell dinner. In both of these was a pervading sense of deep and abiding joy. We were aware of the truly remarkable community we had developed together and we rejoiced in our privilege for having been allowed to participate in its emergence. While we were saddened by the realities of separation, there was an underlying joy pervading all our celebration for we knew that in our lives there was the permanent reality of all that had been and that wherever we went, the "Crozer process" would be forever a permanent source of strength and its remembrance would provide joy to all of us who had been involved. And so it has been to this very hour!

Selections from the "Family Documents"

I am thinking of what I have learned to call minor ecstasies, bits of star dust which are for all of us, however monotonous our days and cramped our lives, however limited our opportunities.

Everyone has these moments, more or less often, according as they are recognized and cherished. Something seen, something heard, something felt, flashes upon one with a bright freshness, and the heart, tired or sick or sad or merely indifferent, stirs and lifts in answer. Different things do it for different people, but the result is the same: that fleeting instant when we lose ourselves in joy and wonder. It is minor because it is slight and so soon gone; it is an ecstasy because there is an impersonal quality in the vivid thrust of happiness we feel, and because the stir lingers in the memory. Fragments of beauty and truth lie in every path; they need only the seeing eye and the receptive spirit to become the stuff of authentic minor ecstasies.

[5]*Elizabeth Gray Vining*

I well remember the first one that I recognized and consciously put away in my mind as a child hoards the birthday pearl to make a necklace. I was fifteen, and it was August in Cape May. Because the land comes down in a point between the ocean on the east and the wide and apparently shoreless bay on the west, the sun there sets over the water. We liked for that reason to walk on the boardwalk after dinner. The western sky one evening was filled with flame and molten gold, and gold and flame shone in all the moving facets of the water. Behind us the eastern sky was pearly; into it the moon rose, spilling pale silver over the gray-blue sea. Even as I caught my breath at the lovely drama of the contrast, an airplane, a great silver bird more rare and wonderful then than now, came suddenly out of the heart of the sunset, sailed above the long, lonely beach, and flew deep into the moonlight. My young heart bounded against my ribs like a bird in a cage, and memory has held that scene for me in colors as bright and soft as those in which I first saw it. Ever since, that memory has been for me a sort of yardstick; if what I see or hear makes me feel at all as that made me feel, then it is a minor ecstasy.

There have been countless others down the years: crape myrtle flashing through the slanting silver of a sudden southern downpour; the flute passages in Beethoven's Fourth Symphony; the cold curve of the river in winter where it turns between purple wooded banks; shared laughter over nothing more than fundamental understanding; the call of a cuckoo above the peat bogs in Skye; the whistle of a cardinal in the dark of a suburban February morning; the smell of wet wood and seaweed at a ferry wharf; the fragrance of sunwarmed honeysuckle on stone walls.

Once when for long months sorrow had clamped tight my heart, it was a minor ecstasy that showed me that life might again hold joy for me. I woke in the morning to the sound, I thought, of rain on the porch roof, but when I opened my eyes I saw that it was not raindrops making that soft and playful patter but locust blossoms falling from the tree above. For a fleeting second my cramped and stiff heart knew again the happiness that is of the universe and not of itself and its possessions, and like Sara Teasdale, when in similar circumstances she heard the wood thrush through the dusk, "I snatched life back against my breast, and kissed it, scars and all."

[6]*Elizabeth Gray Vining*

There is a divine illumination from earthly things that will bring great joy and heavenly release to you if seen through the pure eyes of the Spirit; when you bathe, when you eat, when you walk, when you sleep--these are great symbols and are holy . . . . Have more joy in your daily life . . . . The idea of renouncing joy is destructive; have greater joy, but be sure the source of it is within rather than without--and, lest you be misled, that simply means to be more aware of ***God whom*** you worship while you play, for ***God*** abides in the lifted heart.

[7]*Letters of the Scattered Brotherhood*

Spring is really coming now . . . . Here in the prison yard there is a thrush which sings beautifully in the morning, and now in the evening too. One is grateful for little things, and that is surely a gain.

[8]*Dietrich Bonhoeffer*

Now, some people despise the little things of life. It is their mistake, for they thus prevent themselves from getting God's greatness out of these little things. God is every way, evenly in all ways, to him who has the eyes to see . . . .

Some people want to recognize God only in some pleasant enlightenment--and then they get pleasure and enlightenment but not God. Somewhere it is written that God shines in the darkness where every now and then we get a glimpse of ***the Presence***. More often, God is where ***the divine*** light is least apparent. Therefore we ought to expect God in all manners and all things evenly . . . .

All paths lead to God ***who*** is on them all evenly, to ***each one*** who knows. I am well aware that a person may get more out of one technique than another but it is not best so. God responds to all techniques evenly to a knowing ***person*** . . . .

Whatever that way that leads you most frequently to awareness of God, follow that way; and if another way appears, different from the first, and you quit the first and take the second, and the second works, it is all right. It would be nobler and better, however, to achieve rest and security through evenness, by which one might . . . enjoy ***God*** in any manner, in anything, and not have to delay and hunt around for your special way: *that has been my joy*! To this end all kinds of activities may contribute and any work may be a help; but if it does not, let it go!

[9]*Meister Eckhart*

Give us grace and strength to persevere. Give us courage and gayety and the quiet mind. Spare to us our friends and soften to us our enemies. Give us the strength to encounter that which is to come, that we may be brave in peril, constant in tribulation, temperate in wrath, and in all changes of fortune, and down to the gates of death, loyal and loving to one another . . . . "To be a joy-bearer and a joy-giver says everything," Mother Janet Stuart wrote, ". . . and if one gives joy to others one is doing God's work."

[10]*Elizabeth Gray Vining*

Lift yourselves again, lift your spirits high! It is so true that it is not a question of fighting but rather a need of lifting, offering a gay and happy spirit in worship. There is discipline required in a stand against appetites for they are subtle and return, when you are unaware, for the onslaught; and as I have said so many times, it is not only the physical appetites which tempt, but there is a greed of the tongue for those idle words of which he spoke. There are destructive satisfactions in words which fly from the tongue tinged with malice; there are appetites for self-justification and enjoyment in resentment and hot storms of anger. When we realize that there is a mental gluttony for such emotional reactions and a dark pleasure in such indulgence--then we can begin to deal with them. The next time you are tempted by any greed of body or mind, by humanly justifiable anger, or quick resentment, repeat to yourself as quietly as you can his words, "I am the way!"--or just the great word, "Omniscience!"--and see how the boiling cauldron of heavy poison can be transmuted to light steam which will evaporate in the blue. You will be freed, your mind cleared, your body will feel lighter because your spirit has been lifted. I can promise you a great joy from such obedience, for that is true discipline, that is dominion. Will you succeed the first time? I do not know. Does that matter! Lift your spirit and you will hear the guiding voice and know the joy that is fulfilling.

[11]*Letters from the Scattered Brotherhood*

I eat and drink in remembrance of him eternally alive in me; it is a profound communion and a great practical help. As you eat the bread of life spiritually with the bread materially, your inspiration will strengthen you for the day. As I have told you, this is a primer lesson, for what is needful for you is to keep in contact with the Spirit, to make the habit of doing so. And you yourselves will change by forming the habit of tenderness toward common things, the habit of communing and bringing down into everyday actions the heavenly grace. Everything you touch, feeling the warmth of an open fire, is an outward and visible witness of the spiritual law. Bathe in water as you would in spirit. Water is the source of life, it is a spiritual symbol. Let the shock of it on your flesh be a reminder of your contact with the invisible faith within you. Use your imaginations and be like that humble friar, Brother Lawrence, or the great artists of all time, who took the humble simple things close to them and transfigured them and themselves. For spiritual awakening allies you to the great poets and artists. Such is the wonder and the grandeur of the spirit, its transforming and glamorous beauty . . . . Illumine the common things and you will fill your skies with stars. Go, seeking goodness and you will find it; seeking beauty and it will be upon your face. Thus will you walk the glorious way, using the common elements of daily life as rods and staffs. Nothing is too small for your consideration and for your use.

". . . Do this in remembrance of me." Do all things in remembrance of him--*remember your way out*! . . . . Remember always with joy and never with strain or boredom, for love only can find the way.

[12]*Letters of the Scattered Brotherhood*

Reflection and Action

- Try thinking of yourself as a feeling of joy. Carry with you throughout each day this idea--today I am joyous, and there is joy to be discovered. Observe how your behaviour as a joy feeling influences your own life and the lives of those around you.

- Think about the minor ecstasies you have had over the past two years. Put them in your personal journal and describe what difference they made to you in your daily routine.

- Reread selection #5. How closed or open are you to these images. How do color and music contribute to your joy?

THE CONSEQUENCES OF JOY

Begin by noticing how many of these writings relate joy with courage and fearlessness. When we study, reflect and pray for true understanding of this, we may then begin to discover courage through joy. There is no greater or truer example of this than our Lord's teaching about joy and his courage on the Cross.

Then consider what it means to form the habit of tenderness in approaching all common things. Tenderness, empathy, sensitivity for persons, all of these qualities emerge more surely from those of us who live with the joy of the lifted heart.

Joy which results from our living with the abiding presence of God provides a sure ground of trust, assurance, and freedom to be fearless in every aspect and experience of our lives. Here as in the case of all other of these spiritual disciplines we are equipped and strengthened to live more creatively with those very same people, issues, responsibilities, demands and conflicts that confront us everyday.

Joy can and does have consequences even when it comes to our experiences of suffering. Our understanding and practice of joy will be more complete if we are willing to grapple with the most difficult of all insights and disciplines, namely the discovery of joy in the midst of suffering.

It is a long and sure testimony that at the heart of the Christian life, joy and suffering are inextricably bound together. After we have done all we can to alleviate suffering, to eradicate suffering, there is a residue of suffering that may well come to any of us at any time. Such suffering cannot be explained away as punishment for sin, nor can it be successfully transmuted by a stoical attitude of "grin and bear it."

Sin, suffering, disease and death are very realistic portions of the total life which is given to us. Yet while we must work diligently to eradicate sin, suffering and disease we must at the same time ask what is the creative response to *all* life that is given to us.

It is important to be constantly at the task of unmasking the true nature of evil within ourselves and within our world. However, our limited success in this effort should never hinder us from concentrating on the process of transformation and redemption which was forever made possible by the death and resurrection of our Lord. What is possible has been shown to us in quotation #17 by Baron von Hügel. His words spring out of experience and his disciplined life shows that suffering can be transformed though not dispelled. Our expectations are not that suffering be eliminated, only that it be transformed and become an instrument of redemption.

Selections from the "Family Documents"

At the heart of the Christian life there lies a great mystery; suffering and joy are inextricably bound together. The absence of suffering does not bring joy. Indeed, there is no abiding joy except as it rises out of suffering. The path to joy is discovered as sufferings are accepted for the love of God. The greatest joy of all. . . Christians is to know that as ***we*** gladly embrace ***our*** sufferings for the love of God ***we*** offer ***our*** most potent prayer to release the power of God in the world.

[13]*John Coburn*

Joy does have consequences even for suffering.

The secret is for us to accept such sufferings joyfully for the love of God. This is quite a different thing from gritting our teeth to endure them in a spirit of resignation. For us to accept suffering willingly and gladly is to help Christ to release God's power in the world to fight against the power of evil and sin and suffering. This is to share in a measure the same joy that was set before him, for which he endured the cross.

[14]*John Coburn*

. . . Every act of joyful acceptance of our sufferings for the love of God releases a power in the world that helps all ***persons*** to carry their crosses. Each such act sets free one more channel for the power of God in the lives of ***people,*** so that there is released an access of strength for every person who is carrying on ***a*** battle against temptation or sin or suffering. In this way we help to marshall more of the resources of God in ***the*** continuing struggle against all that is evil and wrong in the world. Our individual response to ***God,*** by embracing our suffering for love of ***God,*** makes ***God's*** Spirit more available for all ***persons*** in their own individual struggles against evil in their own lives.

There is an interrelatedness of the Spirit in and through all human relationships. Perhaps, when all is said and done, the greatest help we can be to one another is to accept our own suffering joyfully for the love of God and thus release as much of God's power into the world as we can, in order that all ***people*** may be strengthened by ***God's*** Spirit to embrace and carry well their own crosses.

[15]*John Coburn*

The reason that suffering joyfully for the love of God is so powerful is very simply that this is the way of the cross. This is the way Christ did his work. It was not only in his living and teaching and healing, but finally in his dying on the cross, that he was able to accomplish that which he was meant to do in redeeming the world. The world is a different place because he accepted joyfully his sufferings for the love of God.

And it is not too much to say that the world can be a different place as we accept joyfully our sufferings for the love of God. This is to have some part--a small part, but our part--in Christ's great act of redemption. It is to make available for all people our share in ***God's*** Spirit. There is, therefore, no such thing as "useless" suffering. On the contrary, suffering for God, in the spirit of Christ, is the most "useful" act a person can do. People who are sufferers permanently are potentially the most useful citizens in God's Kingdom. Every ounce of suffering accepted in this way is transformed by God into power to be released to ***God's*** glory and for the good of ***all people.***

This is the path to joy, for there is no joy greater than knowing that we are partakers with Christ in the work God intended for him and for all the members of his body. This is to serve on earth ***the One*** from whom we came, to whom we belong, and with whom we shall live forever. It is for this that we were born.

[16]*John Coburn*

To a friend in his last illness (1916)

I need hardly assure you that your illness--the weakness and pain you are suffering, in their various degrees and kinds of tryingness--that all these things are now very much in my mind and heart. Indeed they remain constantly present before me, even when they have to be in the background of my consciousness.

With our dearest Gertrud we were able, for a considerable time, to hope that God would still give her many a year of life. And you yourself are not yet sixty, or barely that. May God give you yet many a year of life! But quite distinct from the question of the length of her life, was that of the *quality* of it--of the suffering and limitations mingling with, and imposed upon, pretty well all her activities. All these things were a present, indeed a pressing question.

And, looking back now, I am grateful for nothing so much as for this--that, given the suffering and trials which God then sent or permitted, He also soon gave her a light, far more vivid and continuous than it used to be, and an evergrowing acceptance and active utilization of it, as to the place, meaning and unique fruitfulness of such suffering, thus met (as it were) halfway, in the mysterious, but most certain, most real scheme of the deepest life and of God . . . .

I put all this to yourself, as I do to myself, because I have long felt that it is *the apparent sterility of suffering* which adds the final touch of trial to our pains; and that this appearance is *most truly* only an appearance. Not, of course, that suffering, simply of itself, is good or operates good; but that God is more living and real than all suffering and all sin; and that He can, and will, and does give concomitant opportunities and graces and growths to the sufferer, if and when the latter is humble, watchful and prayerful in such utilizations.

[17]*Baron von Hügel*

Baron von Hügel to his niece:

"Grasp the nettle, my little old thing! Religion has never made me comfy. I have been in the deserts ten years. All deepened life is deepened suffering, deepened dreariness, deepened joy. Suffering and joy. The final note of religion is joy."

[18]*Baron von Hügel*

A master skater was in conversation with a group of boys. "How is it done?" they asked, "how do you go about it?" He tried to explain it to them, and then they went to the lake and buckled on their skates. They had hardly stepped on the ice when the first one fell down. "You did not start the right way," said one of them, "the words of the master were clear, he said so-and-so." "No," said another, "the master's words were clear, he said so-and-so." They quarreled, they beat each other; in the end they lay on the ice with bleeding noses, and none of them had got any further. That is the history of all theology.

A few boys, however, had been standing watchfully on both feet. Suddenly, whether due to a movement in themselves or a gust of wind without, they glided a little distance over the ice. Carefully they yielded to an inner feeling of how it should be done, slowly they got their balance, and began gradually to skate. They looked at each other in happy surprise and exclaimed: "Yes, that is how the master explained it." With every step of freedom which they gained in this way they confirmed the master's words, they actually *experienced* them.

When they finally moved freely and rapidly across the ice, they loved him all the more, because he had shown them that it could be done. Without his example they would never have dared to believe it. The more like him they became, the less they had to ponder over his teaching, and the deeper they learned to love him. Such is the path of those who experience Eternity.

[19]*Johannes Anker Larsen*

Reflection and Action

- Have you experienced anything like "joy in suffering" in your life? Have you observed it in the lives of others? Can you think of an example of "suffering transformed?"

- What are your feelings and concerns when you are present to the suffering of another person?

- "The more like him they became the less they had to ponder over his teaching and the deeper they learned to love him." What does this part of this quotation say to you and your living?

Selection Footnotes

1. *Deep is the Hunger*, pp. 160-161.
2. Elizabeth Gray Vining, *The World in Tune* (New York: Harper and Brothers, Publishers, 1954), pp. 27-28.
3. *Spiritual Counsel and Letters of Baron Friedrich von Hügel*, p. 120.
4. *With the Door Open*, pp. 95-96.
5. *The World in Tune*, p. 28.
6. *The World in Tune*, pp. 29-31.
7. *Letters of the Scattered Brotherhood*, pp. 32-33.
8. *Letters and Papers from Prison*, p. 22.
9. *Meister Eckhart*, pp. 249-250.
10. *The World in Tune*, pp. 79-80. A Prayer by Robert Louis Stevenson.
11. *Letters of the Scattered Brotherhood*, pp. 90-91.
12. *Letters of the Scattered Brotherhood*, pp. 106-107.
13. John B. Coburn, *Prayer and Personal Religion* (Philadelphia: Westminster Press, 1957), p. 90.
14. *Prayer and Personal Religion*, p. 92.
15. *Prayer and Personal Religion*, pp. 93-94.
16. *Prayer and Personal Religion*, pp. 95-96.
17. *Spiritual Counsel and Letters of Baron Friedrich von Hügel*, pp. 67-68.
18. *Letters from Baron Friedrich von Hügel to a Niece*, edited with an introduction by Gwendolen Greene (London and Toronto: J. M. Dent and Sons, Ltd., 1932), p. xvi.
19. *With the Door Open*, p. 110-112.

CHAPTER X

SPIRITUAL DISCIPLINES FOR EVERYDAY LIVING

Evelyn Underhill
1875 - 1941

Courtesy: Tessa Sayle from the Mowbray edition of *Anthology of the Love of God*

Born into a wealthy English family, the daughter of a lawyer and married to Hubert Stuart Moore, a barrister-at-law, Evelyn Underhill was a writer of novels and poetry, and a widely known lecturer, and author of some of the most definitive books on Mysticism, Worship and the Life of the Spirit. Evelyn Underhill considered herself as one "not brought up to religion." Yet on her own she pursued a growing interest in the life of faith, and particularly the spiritual and mystical elements. That interest blossomed into a life deeply in tune with a profound sense of the love of God. Evelyn Underhill's faith was evident in her social service and involvement, as she worked among the poor in the slums of North Kensington. Her mysticism thus had an intrinsically ethical thrust.

Through her numerous "family document" writings on devotional life and the inner life and the inner experience of faith, Evelyn Underhill has left an indelible mark upon the literature of the life of the spirit.

Chapter X

THE INDISSOLUBLE TIE: "HASTEN UNTO GOD HASTEN INTO THE WORLD"

If we have begun to understand through prayer and reflection what it means to live interrelatedly and at the same time with creative solitude; if we have begun to discover the presence of God; if we have made the first real moves into genuine humility and love and entered into new dimensions of joy; and if we have found freedom in living with the principle of attachment and detachment; we discover we have lived our way right into the midst of loving God with all our mind, heart, soul and strength and our neighbors as ourselves.

With such living comes the awareness of the indissoluble tie between discovering God and service and justice to all people everywhere.

THE INDISSOLUBLE TIE: DEFINITION AND DESCRIPTION

"Hasten unto God and hasten into the world" is the way Thomas Kelly describes this indissoluble tie. Douglas Steere states it clearly when he says that "work without contemplation is bitter and blind, but that contemplation without work . . . is callow and empty."[1]

[1]Douglas V. Steere, *Work and Contemplation* (New York: Harper and Brothers, Publishers, 1957), p. 22. This entire book is important for a full understanding of the indissoluble tie. Another classic statement of this principle is found in Elizabeth O'Connor's *Journey Inward, Journey Outward*.

Whatever our finite insights and beliefs about human relations, social justice and freedom, unless they have been refined in the fire of God's wisdom, justice and love, they will prove too limited, too superficial, too inept and inadequate to finally confront and overcome the evils we seek to replace with good. Equally, if we become so enamored with discovering God, so selfishly involved in our own soul's salvation, and forget that we are called to be the "agents of the eternal charity," we are trapped into self-righteous arrogance, superiority and disdain for others. Loving God means the "centering down" into God's will, love, justice, mercy and grace in order that we may deal with all of life; family, friendship, work, social action, every facet from this new and permanent perspective.

Read the gospel accounts of Christ's forty days in the wilderness and the transfiguration, then read beyond each account to discover how he returned with renewed strength, insight, and courage to teach and heal people. Indeed his whole ministry was undergirded by this deep sense of vital relationship to God--the model for everyone of us to "hasten unto God" in order to "hasten into the world."

Selections from the "Family Documents"

The times are severe, the need is great and we must *hasten*: we all agree. But whither shall we hasten? . . . We must *hasten unto God*; and we must *hasten into the world* . . . . We must first *hasten unto God* . . . . The center of religion is in a living, vital, unspeakably intimate fellowship of the soul with God, wherein we sing and dance and leap for joy in ***God's*** Presence. And some of us have found that life, that overturning, realigning experience of ***God's*** immediacy, and we walk in joy and power.

[1]*Thomas Kelly*

The straightest road to social gospel runs through profound mystical experience. The paradox of true mysticism is that individual experience leads to social passion, that the nonuseful engenders the greatest utility. If we seek a social gospel, we must find it most deeply rooted in the mystic way. Love of God and love of neighbor are not two commandments, but one. It is the highest experience of the mystic, when ***our souls are*** known to be one with God . . . , that utility drops off and flutters away, useless, to earth, that world-shaking consciousness of ***all persons*** in need arises in one and ***one*** knows ***oneself*** to be the channel of Divine Life. The birth of true mysticism brings with it the birthday of the widest social gospel. "American" Christianity is in need of this deeper strain of expression of direct contact with God, as the source, not of world-flight, but of the most intensely "practical" Christianity that has yet been known.

[2]*Thomas Kelly*

Utter dependence on God must be balanced by courageous initiative.

[3]*Evelyn Underhill*

Living with an intensity which entails . . . the extremes of suffering and of joy, the saint is always, at . . . full development, both active and contemplative . . . for the Christian saint, union with God means union with One who is both Here and There, both humble and Almighty, self-given and transcendent. Therefore it cannot mean mere flight from this world and its needs, or any other private satisfaction however spiritual and exalted. The very genius of Christianity is generosity, *Agape*; and the saint stands out as the self-emptied channel of that supernatural Love. The rich, active and life-giving character of Christian holiness depends directly on the Christian doctrine of the Nature of God. By that constant re-immersion in the atmosphere of Eternity which is the essence of ***personal*** Prayer, the Christian saint becomes able in . . . turn to radiate Eternity: and the more profound ***the*** contemplation, the more he ***or she*** loves the world and tries to serve it as the tool of the Divine creative love.

[4]*Evelyn Underhill*

. . . the stretching out as it were of one hand towards ***God's*** perfection, the limit where Divine and human meet, and of the other, in complete friendliness and generosity, towards the sins and imperfections of ***individuals***. Neither action is particularly easy in a practical way; but unless we try to manage this, we need not regard ourselves as genuine friends of Christ. It is the double, simultaneous outstretching that matters; this only can open the heart wide enough to let in God, and so make of each ***person*** who achieves it a mediator of ***God's*** reality to other ***people***. The nonreligious socialist seems to stretch out one hand, and the non-social pietist the other. But one without the other is useless. Both at once: that is where the difficulty comes in. It sometimes seems a demand which we can hardly meet.

[5]*Evelyn Underhill*

Yet the vision may be clouded over, and for lack of that vision the people perish. Vision and clear insight are the fruits of contemplation, and they are vital. At heart, the contemplative is one who clearly sees with the eyes of God, the clear light which shines in the emptiness of the human spirit. It is clear vision which enables the truly spiritual ***person*** to see beneath the surface of events, to see through the illusion and the phoney claims of human systems, to see beyond the immediate and the transient to the reality. Consequently the contemplative is more of a threat to injustice than the social activist who merely sees the piecemeal need. For contemplative vision is revolutionary vision, and it is the achievement of this vision which is the fruit of true spiritual direction.

A spirituality of clear vision goes hand in hand with love. To see with the eyes of God is to see truthfully and lovingly. Such a love is not sentimental or naive: it is a love which undermines oppression and burns away illusion and falsehood, a love which has been through the fire, a love which has been purified through struggle. It is a love which has known solitude and despair. No spiritual direction can be seen as adequate in Christian terms unless it is preparing men and women for the struggle of love against spiritual wickedness in the structures of the fallen world and in the depths of the heart. Contemplation is an entering into this struggle because it is a way of looking at reality which cuts through the facades and the bogus claims. Because of this, contemplation is the vital prerequisite for human liberation.

[6]*Kenneth Leech*

Reflection and Action

- Consider the word from Selection #4, "the saint is always, at . . . full development, both active and contemplative." As you think of your life at the present time list the "active" components. List the "contemplative" components. How are these components interrelated for you?

- Do you think "hastening unto God" can prevent "burnout" in a person who is "hastening into the world"? How? Why?

- Do you see the importance of "hastening into the world" to prevent our becoming self-righteous and self-satisfied in "hastening unto God"?

- Imagine yourself explaining to a class of young children the principle of the *indissoluble tie*. How do you think this principle of spiritual discipline should be taught and experienced?

THE PRACTICE OF HASTENING

UNTO GOD AND INTO THE WORLD

The practice begins with prayer and contemplation which means daily recourse to the peace and power of God. Turn to God in many silent intervals, some momentarily, others of longer duration; upon waking up or just before going to sleep, or riding the bus, subway or streetcar to work, in waiting that minute or two for the red light to change, and occasionally those choice longer periods of time of one-half hour or more. In all of this we are to be still and know God. For when we are within the divine perspective it is possible to experience the expulsive power of God's love which redeems and redirects our lives. Such expulsive love was the divine perspective which motivated Albert Schweitzer to leave his highly successful medical and musical careers in Europe to live a life of enduring service in ministering to the peoples of Africa.

It is what John Woolman refers to when he speaks about having a "scruple," concerning certain practices that created injustice and cruelty. In similar fashion Quakers keep identifying "concerns" which must be addressed in creative and loving fashion. Such specific concerns particularize their more generalized concern for cosmic suffering and cosmic responsibility which otherwise might evaporate into a "vague yearning for a golden Paradise." Try living with a good scruple or two--have a lasting and genuine concern about one or two of the deep and radical issues of our time (peace, hunger, justice, and freedom for people) and begin to discover God as you hasten into the world.

Selections from the "Family Documents"

The ***saints do*** not arrive at . . . ethical insight from a study of the power ethics of mass-groups. ***They*** arrive at it from a firsthand knowledge of the power of the *I*, the *Me* and, the *Mine* in the hearts of ***all persons*** and of the expulsive power of God's love to melt them down and to allow ***the beloved community*** to emerge. Group egotism, group pride, and group sin are all intense realities for the ***saints***, and ***they know*** them as a lump that is hard to reduce. But ***they*** would not let the lump-like nature of group sin intimidate ***them*** into accepting it as an ultimate and irreducible surd. God has faced lumps of corporate sin before, even lumps that were in their surroundings more coherent and more defiant than those of our day, and ***God*** has softened them up and often dissolved them. The ***saints know*** that ***they do*** not work alone.

[7]*Douglas Steere*

Now if it is true that real contemplation, real worship, must confess as Katherine Mansfield does in her *Journals*, "I went upstairs and tried to pray but I could not, for I had done no work;" if contemplation dare not come empty-handed to the Source of Grace; if it must mingle and involve itself with work, then the sharp line of separation that the alternation principle places between the activity of work and the activity of contemplation begins to vanish.

If a band of eighteenth-century Alsatian villagers in the course of a Sunday's worship under their pastor, John Frederick Oberlin, resolve to build a road to safeguard their village from the perils of the dangerous mountain path; if they carry out this resolve the next Saturday, their pastor among them; and if on Saturday night before returning to their homes they take the Lord's supper together, there begins to be a flowing together of work and contemplation that makes it more and more difficult to discover where the one leaves off and where the other begins.

If early in his life John Woolman is brought by contemplation to feel the incongruity of loving God and holding a fellow human being in slavery, and if his life is put in order, step by step, so that his witness to this insight can be shared with Quaker slave-owners in distant places, and if as he travels Woolman becomes more and more aware of his dependence upon the operativeness of what he has found in worship in the midst of the interviews he has with those whose hearts he would reach, it is once again apparent that it is not alternation but the simultaneous operation of work and worship, of work and contemplation, that has taken place and that in fact always takes place as a condition of sanctity emerges. Here, with the barriers down, we may glimpse the real order of creation, the power to do what Meister Eckhart triumphantly pronounces is higher than work, and higher than contemplation, namely, the power to "work collectedly."

[8]*Douglas Steere*

Far more should we believe in training for spiritual service, for participation in the building of the City of God; and this has not much in common with what commonly passes for religious education. It means in practice the effort to live some sort of inner life harmonious with the great principles of Christian spirituality; penitence, renunciation, self-surrender, and daily recourse to the peace and power of God.

[9]*Evelyn Underhill*

This double action--interior and ever-deepening communion with God, and because of it ever-widening, outgoing towards the world as tools and channels of God, the balanced life of faith and works, surrender and activity--must always involve a certain tension between the two movements.

[10]*Evelyn Underhill*

. . . the general function of ***the saint's*** charity in social evolution is vital and essential. If things are ever to move upward, someone must be ready to take the first step, and assume the risk of it. No one who is not willing to try charity, to try non-resistance as the saint is always willing, can tell whether these methods will or will not succeed. When they do succeed, they are far more powerfully successful than force or worldly prudence. Force destroys enemies; and the best that can be said of prudence is that it keeps what we already have in safety. But non-resistance, when successful turns enemies into friends; and charity regenerates its objects. These saintly methods are . . . creative energies; and genuine saints find in the elevated excitement with which their faith endows them an authority and impressiveness which makes them irresistible in situations where men of shallower nature cannot get on at all without the use of wordly prudence . . . ***The saint*** is an effective ferment of goodness, a slow transmuter of the earthly into a more heavenly order.

[11]*William James*

Attend to the Eternal that He may recreate you and sow you deep into the furrows of the world's suffering . . . . Only those who go into the travail of today, *bearing a seed within them*, a seed of awareness of the heavenly dimensions of humanity, can return in joy. Where this seed of divine awareness is quickened and grows, there Calvary is enacted again in joy. And Calvary is still the hope of the world. Each one of us has the seed of Christ within . . . . In each of us the amazing and the dangerous seed of Christ is present. It is only a seed. It is very small, like the grain of mustard seed. The Christ that is formed in us is small indeed but He is great with eternity. But if we dare to take this awakened seed of Christ into the midst of the world's suffering, it will grow. That's why the Quaker work camps are important. Take a young man or young woman in whom Christ is only dimly formed, but one in whom the seed of Christ is alive. Put him ***or her*** into a distressed area, into a refugee camp, into a poverty region. Let ***them*** go into the world's suffering bearing this seed with ***them***, and in suffering it will grow, and Christ will be more and more fully formed in ***them***. As the grain of mustard seed grew so large that the birds found shelter in it, so the ***person*** who bears an awakened seed into the world's suffering will grow until ***that individual*** becomes a refuge for many.

[12]*Thomas Kelly*

Evelyn Underhill refers to a book on town planning by Professor Lethaby. In his work, Lethaby shows how we could practice loving God and loving others when he

appealed for the fostering in men and women--and specially in children--of the sense of the sacredness of their town: of its comeliness, dignity, beauty, as the outward expressions of the corporate soul, something which all could love and seek to further and preserve. Did we have this, we should come to feel that hideous buildings, vulgar advertisements, and still more bad and degraded housing conditions, were actual insults offered to the Spirit of God; and we should try perhaps instead to do honour to ***God's*** holy power in our constructive work, considering all its problems in that Universal Spirit, to which George Fox was always inviting us to have recourse. But this means a firm grasp of the fact of God's Presence, a perpetual keeping of the Pattern in focus; and this is not to be had unless we pay attention to it.

[13]*Evelyn Underhill*

"I have felt," said John Woolman the Quaker, "a longing in my mind that people might come into cleanness of spirit, cleanness of person, cleanness about their houses and gardens; and I think even the minds of people are in some degree hindered from the pure operation of the Holy Spirit, when they breathe much of the bad air of towns."

[14]*John Woolman*

John Donne's poem on the resurrection describes Christ's death and resurrection: "He was all gold when he lay down, but rose all tincture." The alchemists of Donne's time had as their ultimate goal the making of a "tincture" that would transmute all base metals into gold. Evelyn Underhill uses Donne's poetic analogy to describe the consequences of the incarnation for us.

. . . the living Christ is a tincture, not added to life but transmuting life wherever He enters it; and therefore that we must seek to bring under that influence, not only the souls of individuals, but the corporate soul too, and so effect its transmutation. It is this change, not the imposition of a new moral code, which we should mean by Christianization of society; for Christian law can only be understood and practised by Christian souls. Such a Christianization of society involves, ultimately, the complete interpenetration of God and human life; the drenching of life, on all its levels, with the Divine Charity--its complete irradiation by the spirit of goodness, beauty and love.

[15]*Evelyn Underhill*

. . . there develops that full and massive type of prayer in which spiritual power is developed, and human creatures become fellow workers with the Spirit, tools and channels through which God's creative work is done. That is the life of Charity: the life of friendship with God, for which we were made. Growth in spiritual personality means growth in charity. And charity--energetic love of God, and of all ***persons*** in God, operating in the world of prayer, is the live wire along which the Power of God, indwelling our finite spirits, can and does act on other souls and other things; rescuing, healing, giving support and light. That, of course, is real intercession; . . . Such secret intercessory prayer ought to penetrate and accompany all our active work, if it is really to be turned to the purposes of God . . . . Thus prayer . . . is and must be present in all disinterested striving for Perfection, for Goodness, for Truth and Beauty, or for the betterment of the children of God.

[16]*Evelyn Underhill*

Reflection and Action

- Do you have now or have you had a "concern" to which you could apply the practice of hastening unto God and and into the world? Describe this concern to another person, telling them how you came to be in touch with it and why it is important to you.

- How have you or how could you hasten into the world with this concern? How could you hasten unto God with it?

- After reading selection #13, ask yourself, "do I have any sense of the sacredness of the town or city in which I live?" What will it take from you and other citizens to preserve and enrich those sacred elements?

THE CONSEQUENCES OF ALL THIS

How does it work? What really can be done in living out a balanced life of faith and works? Suppose we were to take the first steps in living in charity, within the discipline of non-violence; suppose we stand up for freedom and justice against some gross form of enslavement or injustice. What would happen, does happen? Take a look at our "beliefs" under which we have been fulfilling our commitments to work for social righteousness and justice. When we bring them under the divine perspective, all of our beliefs and methodologies are informed, refined, and can be significantly improved. Equally, we may discover that some of these beliefs, when seen in this new way, do have more permanence and universal validity than we have previously seen or understood.

Let's consider in depth the "belief" in non-violence as a central principle and method for social change. When I am centered down into God's presence, when I have experienced the fact of God's support in all of my life including my failures as well as my successes, when I have experienced such Divine assurance, then there is never any need for violence on my part. No matter what the conflict or confrontation, living within

God's presence and will enables me to move almost immediately from the superficial surface issues, which all too often call for violent response, to the more central and genuine issues about which both the confronter and the confronted really share basic concerns.

Having hastened unto God, I need never be afraid of anything any human being can do to me. Yes, the violent person may hurt, wreck, and kill but in no way can such actions ultimately prevail against that which is essentially right. Study carefully and reflect upon the non-violent methods used by Martin Luther King, Jr. by which racial justice was achieved in certain areas of the struggle. The fact that the total victory has not been won--and in some instances, there may even be setbacks in some of these initial victories--in no way invalidates the principle nor the methodology. It simply makes clear the fact that there are not enough disciplined practitioners to provide the continuing, constant application and improvement of non-violence as a way of life in the application of the Christian gospel of reconciliation, justice, and freedom.

Only as the practice of the presence of God informs the principle and method of non-violence--and I am convinced through personal experience that it does--only then can any one of us discover this as a genuine lifestyle. Here is an illustration of how it works.

In the midst of the second World War, I became deeply involved in helping to relocate Japanese Americans. Under the scare pressures which suggested espionage and sabotage by Japanese Americans living mostly on the West Coast, the government forced the evacuation of thousands of Japanese Americans from their homes and lands. These families were herded into detention camps where they remained until new government regulations came through allowing individuals and families to relocate in other sections of the United States with the exception of a 200-mile strip on each coast.

When I was invited to take an active part in the relocation process, I accepted with enthusiasm based on the firm conviction that we had to preserve democracy and protect the freedom of all peoples in our land at the very time when we were engaged in fighting dictatorship and fascist totalitarianism in Germany, Italy, and Japan.

One of my first assignments was to organize a citizens' committee in Cleveland, Ohio, to relocate Japanese Americans. My first call early one morning was upon the layman who was one of the leaders of the Cleveland Council of Churches. This man had more than one personal involvement in the war effort. He believed wholeheartedly and without reservation in the inherent rightness of our position and the total wrongness and diabolical nature of our enemies.

His reaction to my invitation to take leadership in organizing for and relocating Japanese Americans was as nearly violent as anything I have experienced. While he did not throw me bodily out of his office, he did so verbally and made it clear that he would take steps to see that my church recalled me from participation in this scandalous, traitorous endeavor.

When his anger and emotion subsided, with as much calmness as I could muster and in a quiet and simple yet direct way, I expressed my sorrow that I had caused him pain, but then restated as briefly as I could my reasons for being led of God to undertake this mission and expressed regret that a person of his stature in the ecumenical movement could not join in this important endeavor. He dismissed me summarily and with continued upbraiding. Never in all my life have I been in such a negative situation. On my first call where of all places I expected to get encouragement and help, I had instead received anger, total rejection, and hostility. Where to go next, if at all, was my next question when I regained my emotional equilibrium.

Cleveland did organize, as a result of my week of work, and did relocate over five hundred families; and I learned later that while my violent antagonist did not take the lead, the Council of Churches became one of the leading agencies in relocation. Furthermore, six to eight weeks after my disastrous visit, this very man was one who voted to hire a Japanese American secretary to work in the Council of Churches' office.

When we hasten into the world, it is important to remember that achievement of any goal requires sustained follow-through. The following story illustrates this point. In a particularly long and bitter strike situation in our town, our ministers' association was pressured by the unions to become aggressive advocates for raising strike relief funds for unemployed strikers. We went to work through a subcommittee--not to raise money, but first of all to find out what if any relief was available from all sources. This brought the wrath of the union officials down upon our heads for daring to question their word for the fact that there was desperate need. We did our homework thoroughly and found to our surprise that there were adequate funds available under legitimate and appropriate conditions so that no striker's family needed to suffer unduly.

In the course of our investigation, we decided to invite both labor and management to a series of dinner and evening meetings to probe for the real issues and seek creative and positive answers to the real sources of tension. In the six months we met together, we began to make some real headway after we got beyond the initial fears, hostilities, and anxieties with which we began. The role of our subcommittee was that of a non-violent catalyst seeking quietly and confidently to elicit truth and have it accepted by both parties.

Then in the summer, four of the five of us on the subcommittee were called to serve other churches in other communities, and our exciting and creative experiment came to a halt. So much is lost and so little gained because of our lack of follow-through for whatever reason--in this instance, mobility of the clergy, or it might be due to loss of interest, poor planning, or fatigue!

Two quotations in the section on consequences will challenge each one of us to ask the question "Where do I begin?" and then motivate us to follow through.

In all of this, keep in mind that we are not expected to be burdened equally with the totality of wrongs to be righted. God places a few central tasks as our specific responsibilities. "For each of us these special undertakings are our share in the joyous burdens of love."

If, indeed, spiritual disciplines for everyday living result in our setting out on a life-long pilgrimage, we will find, once we are on our way, that *discipline* is of the essence. Any pilgrimage with God is for life! By now one fact stands out above all we have encountered in this book--with each discipline, we have only just begun! In living our way into each of these there must be time to try to practice new insights gained, to reflect on the consequences of our actions, and to return joyfully again and again with deeper understanding and more effective practice. The fine tuning and interplay between all of these is the added dimension that gives not only continuity but integration to our emerging lifestyle of "hastening unto God and hastening into the world."

Selections from the "Family Documents"

And the whole of the spiritual life can be regarded as a progressive realization of this truth, as we expand into fuller personal being; deeper, humbler and more loving awareness of God. From one point of view all real human progress means such spiritualization--in technical language, a growth in and a yielding to grace . . . [Christians] can never accept the Utopia of the kind-hearted materialist; or give comfort, safety, even political freedom, the rank of a Christian ideal. Civilization and spiritualization are not the same thing; and for the Christian, spiritualization must always come first. On the other hand we are bound to work for the elimination, here and now of all conditions hostile to that spiritualization; all checks on the soul's healthy life. Thus the many things which are plainly hostile--drink, prostitution, bad housing, tyranny, reduced moral standards, embittered class or race relationships--become of intense importance . . . to the most thorough-going supernaturalist; and are all matters with which religion ought to deal.

[17]*Evelyn Underhill*

Every civilization that increases in secularity sows the seeds of its own self-destruction . . . . But if God so lives in us that ***God's*** imperative beauty and holiness shine through us upon others, God *penetrates* and pierces the mask, the sham, the hollowness, and ***we*** become exposed, naked, defenseless before God. And this self-confident, earth-contented culture needs to be stripped of its self-sufficiency and know itself in the light of *God's Life* and holiness.

[18]*Thomas Kelly*

But we tend to forget that we were also "created in the Image of God," and are therefore *responsible persons*, whose acts and decisions are fraught with a terrible significance. It is our relation with *God* which invests our lives with this strange dignity, a dignity which demands "that every human being should be treated as a responsible human person, with rights and duties, an inner sacrosanct life, as well as a community life."

[19]*Olive Wyon*

As the souls of the saints grow, and their real spiritual Personality begins to appear; so on one hand we find that their loving identity with all other souls grows too, and on the other hand that loving union with God which makes them in a special degree the friends and agents of the Eternal Charity, becomes ever deeper, more delicate, more selfless, more complete. They are possessed and devoured by the longing to help, to heal, to save. Thus the deep joy which persists through their darkest hours and utmost weariness, has nothing in common with the placid happiness of the devotee. Feeling and bearing the mysterious burden of the sins and sufferings of the world, their growth in sanctity is always a growth in meekness and in penance . . . . The attitude of the redeeming saint, in . . . simplicity and self-abasement, remains to the end the attitude of the Publican. ***The saint's*** many reasons for thanksgiving never include his ***or her*** own superior state. We notice too in the best of them a certain sweetness, easiness and lack of rigorism which comes from dying to self and its limitations . . . .

[20]*Evelyn Underhill*

Catherine of Siena's loyalty to the Church Triumphant was never in question, but her denunciations and prophetic warnings against the corruptions in the church of her day never ceased until her death. To the pope's shallow efforts at reform she bluntly insists, "If you want to rebuild, you must destroy right down to the foundation." Theresa of Avila and John of the Cross spent the latter part of their lives travelling in a lumber wagon all over Spain, establishing and nursing through infancy a severely reformed Discalced Order of Carmelites against every known kind of opposition from the Church's hierarchy. To name a few from the Protestant group, Boehme, Fox, Woolman, Oberlin and Matilda Wrede all denounced wrong in high places and busied themselves with constructive reform.

The great Christian saints might well have had chiseled on their tombstones, if we could find them, the emblem that is borne by Ibsen's black obelisk in Oslo, a hammer. For they, too, used a hammer against the lump with great power. But beside the hammer would have to be placed the figure of a trowel. For the great Christian saints have been builders. The saint has softened the lump in more than one institution, ***and*** has also presided over the building of a creative solution on its site. Space does not permit of the enumeration of the details of Benedict's Rule that has given a creative structure to fourteen hundred years of communistic living in Christian monasticism; of Bernard of Clairvaux's spiritual power as an arbitrator that could bring stiff-necked dukes, like Aquitaine, literally to their knees in penance, or a rival pope to a secret midnight abdication in Bernard's chambers; of Francis of Assisi's reconciliation of warring municipal factions in central Italy or of the profound stroke for good upon the social and economic life of southern Europe in the thirteenth and fourteenth centuries which his inauguration of the Franciscan Third Order effected; of Groote's holy educational mission in the creation of the Brethren of the Common Life, out of which came the pious guild of teaching brothers; or of the spiritually-grounded social innovations of Vincent de Paul, Fox, Woolman or Oberlin. Striking at the heart of these established institutional lumps, often with creative institutional innovations, these men and women were mightily feared by the selfish vested interests of their day, even though long after their death those who quaked may have participated in their canonization.

[21]*Douglas Steere*

It demands two things: "the perfection of ***our*** work and a little touch of contemplation." That means the union of skill and vision both consecrated. One without the other is no good; we shall not get the measurement of the city right. Accept then this conception of the Kingdom of God on earth, as built up by ***our*** very best work, directed by ***our*** very best prayer; and see what it must mean in efficiency and beauty, industry and joy. Take that measurement into slums, factories, schools, committee rooms, labour exchanges and building-estates--the perfection of ***our*** work and a little touch of contemplation--and then, measure against this scale ourselves and our average performances. The first result will probably be profound humiliation.

[22]*Evelyn Underhill*

. . . in the words of John Woolman--"To labour for a perfect redemption from the spirit of oppression is the great business of the whole family of Jesus Christ in this world." We are called to pray, and to work, for a new social and international order, informed by a spiritual purpose, in which every human being shall have full freedom to use all his gifts and faculties in the service of God.

[23]*Olive Wyon*

There is among Christian men and women, a growing sense of the need of making the social order in which we live less inconsistent with the Spirit of Christ than it is at the present time: solving some of its most acute problems, and our own daily and hourly problems too, not in a spirit of compromise, but as Christian logic requires them to be solved . . . for it means nothing less than the carrying through of the implicits of the spiritual world into every detail of the common life, bringing to bear on that recalcitrant common life the power and love given to us by our faith.

[24]*Evelyn Underhill*

Surrender to the promptings of the Eternal Now may involve the absurd courage of faith in the face of insuperable obstacles. But it does not release us from all intelligent and rational and co-ordinated behavior, all reasoning and consistency. Speaking of his openings Fox said he found that "they answered one another and answered the scriptures." There is a unity and coherence and rational continuity in the out-cropping guidances of Spirit-led ***persons***.

[25]*Thomas Kelly*

. . . in the experience of Divine Presence that which flows over the ocean of darkness is an infinite ocean of light and *love*. In the Eternal Now all ***people*** become seen in a new way. We enfold them in our love, and we and they are enfolded together within the great Love of God as we know it in Christ. Once walk in the Now and ***we*** are changed, in our sight, as we see them from the plateau heights. They aren't just masses of struggling beings, furthering or thwarting our ambitions, or, in far larger numbers, utterly alien to and insulated from us. We become identified with them and suffer when they suffer and rejoice when they rejoice. One might almost say we become cosmic mothers, tenderly caring for all. But that, I believe, is experienced only in the acutest stages of mystic ecstasy, ... In such a sense of Presence there is a vast background of cosmic Love and tender care for all things . . . but in the foreground arise special objects of love and concern and tender responsibility. The people we know best, see oftenest, have most to do with, these are *reloved* in a new and deeper way.

[26]*Thomas Kelly*

Not only does all creation have a new smell, as Fox found, but it has a new value, as enwrapped in the infinite Love of God, wherein not a sparrow falls to the ground without ***God***. Have you *experienced* this concern for the sparrow's fall? This is not just Jesus' experience. Nor is it His *inference about God's* tender love; it is the *record of His experience in God*. There is a tendering of the soul, toward *everything* in creation, from the sparrow's fall to the slave under the lash. The hard-lined face of a money-bitten financier is as deeply touching to the *tendered* soul as are the burned-out eyes of miners' children, remote and unseen victims of his so-called success. There is a sense in which, in this terrible tenderness, we become one with God and bear in our quivering souls the sins and burdens, the benightedness and the tragedy of the creatures of the whole world, and suffer in their suffering, and die in their death.

[27]*Thomas Kelly*

In reference to Kagawa's poem, "To Tears," Kelly writes,

This then is the voice of an *authentic*, who knows the tendering of the Presence, a tendering which issues in the burden-bearing, cross-carrying, Calvary re-enacting life.

[28]*Thomas Kelly*

But it is a particularization of *my* responsibility also, in a world too vast and a lifetime too short for me to carry all responsibilities. My cosmic love, or the Divine Lover loving within me, cannot accomplish its full intent, *which is universal saviorhood*, within the limits of three score years and ten. But the Loving Presence does not burden us equally with all things, but considerately puts upon each of us just a few central tasks, as emphatic responsibilities. For each of us these special undertakings are our share in the joyous burdens of love.

Thus the state of having a concern has a foreground and a background. In the foreground is the special task, uniquely illuminated, toward which we feel a special yearning and care . . . . But in the background is a second level, or layer, of universal concern for all the multitude of good things that need doing. Toward them all we feel kindly, but we are dismissed from active service in most of them. And we have an easy mind in the presence of desperately real needs which are not our direct responsibility. We cannot die on *every* cross, nor are we expected to.

[29]*Thomas Kelly*

It is our frightened selfish resistance, or worse than our resistance, our disgusting pious apathy, our dull certainty that social regeneration won't happen, which stops it from happening. Our frightful lack of the dynamic virtues--Faith, Hope, and Charity . . . . A genuine Christian ought to be alive all over, with a depth and vitality of soul that makes shallow judgements and prejudices impossible. A Christian social order should be permeated in every part of this life: controlled by a supernatural aim.

[30]*Evelyn Underhill*

Social concern is the dynamic Life of God at work in the world, made special and emphatic and unique, particularized in each individual or group who is sensitive and tender in the leading-strings of love.

[31]*Thomas Kelly*

We in this epoch of social-mindedness are in danger of a twenty-four-hour-day application of the cup-of-cold-water program. [What is needed are] bands of men and women and of serious youths, [who will understand that it is] . . . not with *social techniques* but with God-motivations born out of deep immersion in the ocean of the Love of God . . . their *skills* in techniques should be gotten in secular places. But down at the base of life, for all such people, would be a fellowship in a common Life which is the Light within every ***one*** who is kindled and enflamed by God.

[32]*Thomas Kelly*

Reflection and Action

- Consider what are the barriers to your own hastening unto God and into the world. Using imaginative forethought, imagine those barriers being removed.

- Ask yourself the question "Where do I begin?" List all the conerns you can think of that need action. Choose the three concerns that are most important to you. Ask yourself "Where do I begin?" with these. Then begin--hastening unto God and into the world!

Selection Footnotes

1. *The Eternal Promise*, p. 111.
2. *The Eternal Promise*, p. 15.
3. Evelyn Underhill, *Mixed Pasture*. (Freeport, NY: Librarian Press, 1968), p. 50.
4. *Mixed Pasture*, pp. 35-36.
5. *Mixed Pasture*, pp. 73-74.
6. Kenneth Leech, *Soul Friend: The Practice of Christian Spirituality*. (San Francisco: Harper and Row, Publishers, 1977), p. 191.
7. *On Beginning From Within*, p. 23.
8. *Work and Contemplation*, pp. 142-143.
9. *Mixed Pasture*, pp. 75-76.
10. *Mixed Pasture*, pp. 51-52.
11. William James, *The Varieties of Religious Experience*. (New York: The New American Library of World Literature, Inc., Mentor Books, 1958), pp. 277-279.
12. *The Eternal Promise*, pp. 41-43.
13. *Mixed Pasture*, pp. 69-70.
14. *Mixed Pasture*, p. 106: quotation from John Woolman.
15. *Mixed Pasture*, p. 65.
16. *Mixed Pasture*, pp. 56-57.
17. *Mixed Pasture*, pp. 100-101.
18. *The Eternal Promise*, pp. 112-113.
19. *The School of Prayer*, p. 144.
20. *Mixed Pasture*, pp. 30-31.
21. *On Beginning From Within*, pp. 24-26.
22. *Mixed Pasture*, p. 78.
23. *The School of Prayer*, pp. 155-156.
24. *Mixed Pasture*, p. 63.
25. *A Testament of Devotion*, p. 104.
26. *A Testament of Devotion*, pp. 99-100.
27. *A Testament of Devotion*, pp. 106-107.
28. *A Testament of Devotion*, p. 108.

29. *A Testament of Devotion*, pp. 108-109.

30. *Mixed Pasture*, p. 87.

31. *A Testament of Devotion*, p. 111.

32. *The Eternal Promise*, p. 117.

CHAPTER XI

SPIRITUAL DISCIPLINES FOR EVERYDAY LIVING

Chapter XI

More Selections from the "Family Documents" for Meditation, Reflection and Action

(These selections relate, beginning with Chapter III, to the sections of each chapter)

INTERRELATEDNESS
More Selections for Chapter III

OUR ESSENTIAL UNITY

Walter Kaufman in the prologue of his new translation of Buber's *I and Thou* speaks about the main emphasis of the book as follows:

The central stress falls on You--not Thou. God is present when I confront You. But if I look away from You, I ignore him. As long as I merely experience or use you, I deny God. But when I encounter You I encounter him.

[1]*Martin Buber*

. . . This dynamic love, once purged of self-interest, is ours to use on spiritual levels; it is an engine for working with God on other souls. The saints so used it, often at tremendous cost to themselves, and with tremendous effect. As their personality grew in strength and expanded in adoration, so they were drawn on to desperate and heroic wrestling for souls; to those exhausting and creative activities, that steady and generous giving of support, that redeeming prayer by which human spirits are called to work with God. Especially in its most mysterious reaches, in its redemptive, self-immolating action on suffering and sin, their intercession dimly reproduces and continues the supernatural work of Christ. Real saints do feel and bear the weight of the sins and pains of the world. It is the human soul's greatest privilege that we can thus accept redemptive suffering for one another--and they do.

St. Theresa says that if anyone claiming to be united to God is always in a state of peaceful beatitude, she simply does not believe in their union with God. Such a union, to her mind, involves great sorrow for the sin and pain of the world; a sense of identity not only with God but also with all other souls, and a great longing to redeem and heal. That is real supernatural charity. It is a call to love and save not the nice but the nasty; not the lovable but the unlovely, the hard, the narrow, and the embittered, and the tiresome, who are so much worse. To love irrespective of merit or opinion or personal preference; to love even those who offend our taste. If you are to love your people thus, translating your love, as you must, into unremitting intercessory work, and avoid being swamped by the great ocean of suffering, sin and need to which you are sent; once again this will only be done by maintaining and feeding the temper of adoration and trustful adherence. This is the heart of the life of prayer; and only in so far as we work from this centre can we safely dare to touch other souls and seek to affect them. For such intercession is a sacrificial job; and sacrificial jobs need the support of a strong inner life if they are to be carried through. They are rooted and grounded in love.

[2]*Evelyn Underhill*

PRACTICE REQUIRES CREATIVE, WHOLESOME, RESILIENT INDIVIDUALS

We are in eros [love] not only when we experience our biological, lustful energies but also when we are able to open ourselves and participate, via imagination and emotional and spiritual sensitivity, in forms and meanings beyond ourselves in the interpersonal world and the world of nature around us.

[3]*Rollo May*

For eros is the power which *attracts* us. The essence of eros is that it draws us from ahead, whereas sex pushes us from behind . . . . Eros is the drive toward union with what we belong to--union with our own possibilities, union with significant other persons in our world in relation to whom we discover our own self-fulfillment.

[4]*Rollo May*

Our feelings not only take into consideration the other person but are in a real sense partially *formed by the feelings of the other persons present.* We *feel* in a magnetic field. A sensitive person learns, often without being conscious of doing so, to pick up the feelings of the persons around ***one*** as a violin string resonates to the vibration of every other musical string in the room, although in such infinitesimally small degrees that it may not be detectable to the ear.

[5]*Rollo May*

Lawrence LeShan in discussing the validity of psychic healing speaks of loving and caring in the following manner.

What we have here began to become clear. The healer views the healee in the Clairvoyant Reality at a level close to that in which All is One. However, he ***or she*** is focused by love, by caring, by *caritas*, on the healee: this is an essential factor. In Agnes Sanford's words, "Only love can generate the healing fire." Ambrose and Olga Worral have said, "We must care. We must care for others deeply and urgently, wholly and immediately; our minds, our spirits must reach out to them." Sanford wrote: "When we pray in accordance with the law of love, we pray in accordance with the will of God."

It is essential that there be a deeply intense caring and a viewing of the healee and oneself as one, as being united in a universe--the Clairvoyant Reality--in which this unity is possible.

[6]*Lawrence Le Shan*

THE CONSEQUENCES OF INTERRELATEDNESS

"When fully conceived, the care-structure includes the phenomenon of Selfhood," writes Heidegger. When we do not care, we lose our being; and care is the way back to being. If I care about being, I will shepherd it with some attention paid to its welfare, whereas if I do not care, my being disintegrates . . . . The constancy of the self is guaranteed by care.

[7]*Rollo May*

The common, original meaning of "intentionality" and "care" lies in the little term "tend," which is both the root of intentionality and meaning of care. Tend means a tendency, an inclination, a throwing of one's weight on a given side, a movement; and also to mind, to attend, to await, to show solicitude for. In this sense, it is the source of both love and will.

[8]*Rollo May*

Two people, three people, ten people may be in living touch with one another through ***God*** who underlies their separate lives. This is an astounding experience, which I can only describe but cannot explain in the language of science. But in vivid experience of divine Fellowship it is there. We know that these souls are with us, lifting their lives and ours continuously to God and opening themselves, with us, in steady and humble obedience to ***God***. It is as if the boundaries of our self were enlarged, as if we were within them and as if they were within us. Their strength, given to them by God, becomes our strength, and our joy, given to us by God, becomes their joy. In confidence and love we live together in ***God***. On the borders of the experience lie amazing events, at which reputable psychologists scoff, and for which I would not try any accounting. But the solid kernel of community of life in God is in the center of the experience, renewing our life and courage and commitment and love. For daily and hourly the cosmic Sacrament is enacted, the Bread and the Wine are divided amongst us by a heavenly Ministrant, and the substance of His body becomes our life and the substance of His blood flows in our veins. Holy is the Fellowship, wondrous is the Ministrant, marvelous is the Grail.

[9]*Thomas Kelly*

. . . In worship we have our neighbors to right and left, before and behind, yet the Eternal Presence is over all and beneath all. Worship does not consist in achieving a mental state of concentrated isolation from one's fellows. But in depth of common worship it is as if we found our separate lives were all one life, within whom we live and move and have our being. Communication seems to take place sometimes without words having been spoken. In the silence we received an unexpected commission to bear in loving intentness [sic] the spiritual need of another person sitting nearby. And that person goes away, uplifted and refreshed. Sometimes in that beautiful experience of living worship which the Friends have called "the gathered meeting," it is as if we joined hands and hearts, and lifted them together toward the unspeakable glory. Or it is as if that light and warmth dissolved us together into one . . . . And we go forth, with hushed voices, and with power and peace and joy . . . .

[10]*Thomas Kelly*

Selection Footnotes

1. *I and Thou*, p. 28.
2. *Concerning the Inner Life with The House of the Soul* pp. 50-51.
3. *Love and Will*, p. 79.
4. *Love and Will*, p. 74.
5. *Love and Will*, p. 91.
6. *The Medium, the Mystic, and the Physicist*, pp. 106-107.
7. *Love and Will*, p. 290.
8. *Love and Will*, pp. 292-293.
9. *A Testament of Devotion*, pp. 86-87.
10. *The Eternal Promise*, p. 31.

ON BEING ALONE: FROM LONELINESS TO SOLITUDE

More Selections for Chapter IV

OUR OWN ENDURING CENTER

Each ***person*** at some time goes into the awful vault of ***self***; there alone ***to be*** silenced. It is here *you are before you became*; it is here you remain in the advance of inevitable progression. You may wonder how this thing you cannot see is yourself and you begin to be aware of how much of you is asleep. Also your whole record is here.

[1]*Letters of the Scattered Brotherhood*

Betty Stewart, a contemporary woman of rare sensitivity and a splendid spiritual maturity, puts it all together for us when she describes what it means to move from the strength of one's own Self to meet others of similar, if not greater strength, and in such meeting to discover God.

I am sort of contained in a general heart-expansion . . . . I am doing something quite astonishing. There are influences around me radiating the warmth of human affection, only with so much greater power. I dissolve to their love; I surround them as they surround me . . . . It's so transforming, breath-taking . . . . Now, the strange thing is, I reach out and spread the atmosphere around each one I care for. And it enlarges and grows stronger and becomes firm, like a continent in surrounding ocean . . . . I'm so puzzled because it's still an individuality. I am that firm body and yet it is composed of many people.

. . . by means of the heart expansion people call love, the sensation of super-sympathy--this outflowing and inflowing, this most thrilling and exquisite life--we come the nearest we can to apprehending the conception of God . . . . I know now what that phrase means: God is Love. It always sounded so straining and affected. I don't like it yet; but that is my stupidity . . . . "Only by collecting a group of your dearest, going forth with your heart among them, cementing, as it were, a collective entity, and continually enlarging it, can you start toward comprehension of the Universal Consciousness."

[2]*Betty Stewart*

THE PRACTICE OF CREATIVE SOLITUDE

By day I was much amongst people, and had many trials to go through; but in the evenings I was mostly alone, and I may with thankfulness acknowledge, that in those times the spirit of supplication was often poured upon me; under which I was frequently exercised, and felt my strength renewed.

[3]*John Woolman*

Frederick B. Tolles, in his introduction to the *Journal*, in commenting upon Woolman's 1763 visit to the warring Indians of the Pennsylvania frontier says:

He had no "peace plan" to offer--only himself and his understanding heart. Early in the course of his ministry he had decided that it was the source and motive of his actions that mattered most, that he should be "looking less at the effects of [his] labors than at the pure motion and reality of the concern, as it arises from heavenly love."

[4]*Frederick B. Tolles about John Woolman*

Come back, come back and in holy stillness be lifted high above all this! Your dominion over yourself and the circumstances of your life can be glorious if you will keep your center clean, illumined and still in immortal silence. Here is selflessness, here is revealed true knowledge, wisdom, power and courage; the dignity of courage which is loyal to that which is not your human self. You will be given divine strategy in dealing with seemingly hopeless difficulties. The hates, criticisms, annoyances, the instinctive dislikes . . . keep them in the outer circumference. Turn your face away, turn it within toward that which is shining there. This is the kingdom of heaven. This is the task most needed now for yourself, for your loved ones, for your time. Each one anchored in this omnipotent stillness strengthens the soul of your nation.

[5]*Letters of the Scattered Brotherhood*

THE CONSEQUENCES OF BEING ALONE

Life from the Center is a life of unhurried peace and power. It is simple. It is serene. It is amazing. It is triumphant. It is radiant. It takes no time, but it occupies all our time. And it makes our life programs new and overcoming. We need not get frantic. ***God*** is at the helm. And when our little day is done we lie down quietly in peace, for all is well.

[6]*Thomas Kelly*

There is within us a power that could lift the world out of its ignorance and misery if we only knew how to use it, if we would seek and find. When you meditate open not only your listening mind, but the other door of your mind as well, so that the spirit streams out as fast as it comes in. Store nothing . . . . A tree grows not by the pulling of the sun only, but by the richness of the soil . . . . Go into the calm and luminous silence to renew, but stay in the soil of your life. No, there is nothing to fear. Do not waste time wishing for peace; there is no peace in a world, there is only peace in one's own soul. Get more fearless peace into your souls and then you will be some good!

[7]*Letters of the Scattered Brotherhood*

Your release lies in taking these moments, both the star moments and the nettles and in holding them in each hand while you consider them. By this act of the free will you become a master, for at last you take your appointed place in your own unfoldment.

This dwelling upon your own states is not a dangerous knitting of the brows in introspection, for there is no self-love in the process, neither is there pride nor self-pity. To know yourself you must become impersonal and selfless; then with that calm, impersonal knowledge which is given to you in cooling draughts, you will free and cleanse yourself of the states and events which made them so very real and ungovernable.

[8]*Letters of the Scattered Brotherhood*

Selection Footnotes

1. *Letters of the Scattered Brotherhood*, p. 144.
2. "*A Way of Individuation*," pp. 24-25.
3. *The Journal of John Woolman*, p. 10.
4. *The Journal of John Woolman*, Introduction by Frederick B. Tolles, p. xi.
5. *Letters of the Scattered Brotherhood*, pp. 181-182.
6. *A Testament of Devotion*, p. 124.
7. *Letters of the Scattered Brotherhood*, Letter from J.P.M., p. 121.
8. *Letters of the Scattered Brotherhood*, p. 175.

THE PRACTICE OF THE PRESENCE OF GOD

More Selections for Chapter V

THE EXPERIENCE OF GOD'S PRESENCE

One day when he was feeling more wretched than usual he made his way to the choir after the midday meal and settled himself in one of the lower stalls on the right-hand side. It was January 21, the feast of Saint Agnes. As he stood there alone, a perfect specimen of melancholia, his soul was mysteriously transported, either in the body or out of the body. Human words fail when it comes to describing what he saw and heard in this ecstasy; it was a vision without form or mode but containing in itself the form and mode of every pleasurable sensation. His heart was simultaneously hungry and appeased; his wishes were stilled and every desire found its fulfillment. He did nothing but stare into the brilliant reflection, oblivious of himself and all creatures, forgetful of the passage of time. It was a sweet foretaste of heaven's unending bliss.

After about an hour he returned to his senses and said to himself: "If that was not a foretaste of heaven, then I do not know what heaven is. Now I am fully convinced that every suffering that can possibly come my way is a cheap price to pay for such a gain. Alas, dear God, where was I and where am I now? Oh that the memory of this hour may always stay fresh in my mind."

[1]*Henry Suso*

THE PRACTICE ITSELF

Besides, consider that God does not so much seek our deeds as the motive of love which makes us do them, and the pliancy which ***God*** exacts in our will. ***People*** hardly judge our actions except from without. God counts as nothing everything in our actions which seems most brilliant in the eyes of the world. What ***God*** wants, is a pure intention. It is a will ready for everything, and yielding in ***God's*** hands. It is a sincere detachment from ourselves.

[2]*François Fénelon*

Do not give up then, but work away at it till you have this longing. When you first begin, you find only darkness, and as it were a cloud of unknowing. You don't know what this means except that in your will you feel a simple steadfast intention reaching out towards God. Do what you will, this darkness and this cloud remain between you and God, and stop you both from seeing ***God*** in the clear light of rational understanding, and from experiencing ***God's*** loving sweetness in your affection. Reconcile yourself to wait in this darkness as long as is necessary, but still go on longing after ***God*** whom you love. For if you are to feel . . . or to see ***God*** in this life, it must always be in this cloud, in this darkness. And if you will work hard at what I tell you, I believe that through God's mercy you will achieve this very thing.

[3]*The Cloud of Unknowing*

So when you feel by . . . grace . . . that God . . . is calling you to this work, and you intend to respond, lift your heart to God with humble love. And really mean God . . . who created you, and bought you, and graciously called you to this state of life.

And think no other thought of ***God***. It all depends on your desire. A naked intention directed to God, . . . alone, is wholly sufficient.

[4]*The Cloud of Unknowing*

That all bodily mortifications and other exercises are useless, but as they serve to arrive at the union with GOD by love: that he had well considered this, and found it the shortest way, to go straight to ***God*** by a continual practice of love, and doing all things for ***God's*** sake.

[5]*Brother Lawrence*

That he had no qualms; for said he, when I *fail* in my duty, I readily acknowledge it, saying, "*I am used to do so: I shall never do otherwise, if I am left to myself.*" If I fail not, then I give GOD thanks, acknowledging that it comes from ***God***.

[6]*Brother Lawrence*

That he expected hereafter some great pain of body or mind; that the worst that could happen to him would be to lose that sense of GOD, which he had enjoyed so long; but that the goodness of GOD assured him that ***God*** would not forsake him utterly, and that ***God*** would give to him strength to bear whatever evil ***God*** permitted to befall him: and that he therefore feared nothing, and had no occasion to take counsel with anybody about his soul. That when he had attempted to do it, he had always come away more perplexed; and that as he was conscious of his readiness to lay down his life for the love of GOD, he had no apprehension of danger. That perfect abandonment to GOD was the sure way to heaven, a way on which we had always sufficient light for our conduct.

[7]*Brother Lawrence*

That there was need neither of art nor science for going to GOD, but only a heart resolutely determined to apply itself to nothing but ***God***, or for ***God's*** sake, and to love ***God*** only.

[8]*Brother Lawrence*

THE CONSEQUENCES OF PRACTICING THE PRESENCE OF GOD

Yet it is primarily through history that God speaks to ***us*** because history is none other than the concrete significance of this time, this place, this situation. In this time, place, and situation, in this concrete context, revelation comes not as some universal, which is always there for me to apprehend at each moment but does not itself move to meet me, but as the Eternal entering into time, as ***persons*** meeting the Eternal in a moment of time, in a moment of history, whether it is the personal history of the individual or the history of a group of people.

[9]*Maurice Friedman*

No purpose intervenes between I and You, no greed and no anticipation; and longing itself is changed as it plunges from the dream into appearance. Every means is an obstacle. Only where all means have disintegrated encounters occur.

[10]*Martin Buber*

I feel more and more convinced that only a spirituality which thus puts the whole emphasis on the Reality of God, perpetually turning to ***God***, losing itself in ***God***, refusing to allow even the most pressing work or practical problems, even sin and failure, to distract from God--only this is a safe foundation for spiritual work. This alone is able to keep alive the awed, adoring sense of the mysteries among which we move, and of the tiny bit which at the best we ourselves can apprehend of them--and yet, considering that immensity and our tininess, the marvel of what we do know and feel . . . .

The inner life means an ever-deepening awareness of all this: the slowly growing and concrete realization of a Life and a Spirit within us immeasurably exceeding our own, and absorbing, transmuting, supernaturalizing our lives by all ways and at all times. It means the loving sense of God, as so immeasurably beyond us as to keep us in a constant attitude of humblest awe--and yet so deeply and closely with us, as to invite our clinging trust and loyal love. This, it seems to me, is what theological terms like Transcendence and Immanence can come to mean to us when re-interpreted in the life of prayer.

[11]*Evelyn Underhill*

Selection Footnotes

1. Henry Suso, *The Exemplar*, Vol. I, p. 7.
2. *Christian Perfection*, p. 34.
3. *The Cloud of Unknowing*, pp. 53-54.
4. *The Cloud of Unknowing*, p. 61.
5. *The Practice of the Presence of God*, p. 15.
6. *The Practice of the Presence of God*, p. 16.
7. *The Practice of the Presence of God*, pp. 18-19.
8. *The Practice of the Presence of God*, p. 19.
9. Maurice Friedman, *Touchstones of Reality* (New York: E. P. Dutton, 1972), p. 130.
10. *I and Thou*, pp. 62-63.
11. *Concerning the Inner Life*, pp. 12-13.

GENUINE HUMILITY

More Selections for Chapter VI

GOD THE CENTER AND SOURCE OF GENUINE HUMILITY

Their lives grounded in and sustained by God, they are incapable of any kind of pride; because they give back to God all the benefits He has bestowed on them, they do not glorify each other, but do all things to the Glory of God alone.

[1]*Dag Hammarskjöld*

In perfect humility all selfishness disappears and your soul no longer lives for itself or in itself for God; and it is lost, . . . submerged, . . . and transformed into ***God*** . . . . The joy of the mystical love of God springs from a liberation from all self-hood by the annihilation of every trace of pride . . . . The only way to possess ***God's*** greatness is to pass through the needle's eye of your own absolute insufficiency.

[2]*Thomas Merton*

The fruits of holy obedience are many. But two are so closely linked together that they can scarcely be treated separately. They are the passion for personal holiness and the sense of utter humility. God inflames the soul with a craving for absolute purity, . . . and empties us of ourselves in order that ***God*** may become all.

[3]*Thomas Kelly*

THE PRACTICE OF GENUINE HUMILITY

But in devotional reading we engage not simply our intellects, but our whole being. We become quiet, receptive, expectant, docile, and above all else, humble. Any attempt on our part to ferret out the hidden mysteries of God by our own abilities will result in total failure. What cleverness and pride cannot accomplish is accomplished by humility . . . .

We need therefore to sit receptive, open-minded, alert,

quiet, before it. Furthermore, no single inspection is sufficient. Many repeated visits to the same painting are required before we begin to grasp its significance. We know that we must wait patiently until, in its own way and time, it discloses its meanings. The truth in the painting must find and fit the need that is in us. We go then to the painting in many different moods.

So, too, it is with devotional reading. We narrow down our attention to a few very great books of devotion, or even to a single book. We read them humbly, in quietude, open-minded, alert, docile, and ponder them faithfully over many years. Slowly . . . through this reading saving truths concerning *God* and concerning us *are revealed by the Eternal Presence.*

[4]*Charles Whiston*

Living in envy means that I am not centered in my true self. My life becomes one of comparison. I am forever asking what others have and what I am missing. When I find out that I have less than they do, I may try to diminish my sense of lack by belittling what is theirs.

As long as I live outside myself in envious observation of others, I cannot be myself. I can only begin to become myself when I accept what I am. I should not be preoccupied with the ways in which others differ from me. These differences tell me what I am not. I need to come to an awareness of who I am in relation to my Divine Origin.

God originates me continually. Were ***God*** to turn . . . from me for a fraction of a second, I would no longer be. Each moment ***God*** makes me be in my uniqueness, ***and*** gives me my own hidden name which I will fully know only in eternity, a name nobody else has received or will receive.

[5]*Adrian van Kaam*

The Christian believes that ***we originate*** from God as . . . unique ***persons***. The Eternal . . . calls ***us*** in Christ to be ***ourselves*** out of love for God and ***each other***. To be sure, Christian spirituality speaks about giving up myself, forgetting myself, dying to the old ***self***. This does not mean, however, that a Christian should lose his ***or her*** identity or fuse with the Godhead. It means that as a Christian, I should distance myself from false self-images. I should not strive after an isolated God-like self. I must give up self-centered plans and projects. I must find my original self as hidden in God. The original life of a Christian, as St. Paul says, is hidden in Christ.

Each person is called to become his ***or her*** own self and yet to become at-one with God. I must become the unique person I am meant to be. The more I become what my Creator called me to be originally, the more I will be united with my Divine Origin. This union with my Origin deepens my originality. Mine is an originality that God wills from eternity. ***God*** originated me as precisely this person and nobody else.

[6]*Adrian van Kaam*

CONSEQUENCES AND ACTION

[Strengthened by the presence of God] Humility which lives joyfully from the Thou of creative love is the true courage to seize one's own existence in selfless identification with the Thou of the neighbor, in the service of self-evident love.

[7]*Bernard Härirg*

When he had finished, he examined himself how he had discharged his duty: if he found *well*, he returned thanks to GOD; if otherwise, he asked pardon; and without being discouraged he set his mind right again and continued his exercise of the *Presence of* GOD as if he had never deviated from it.

[8]*Brother Lawrence*

. . . Through God's grace, suffering can be made meaningful and useful. It can become a means of expiation, a way of showing our love for God by joining Christ in the work of redemption. It is this love in the midst of affliction's fire that urged the saints to even seek or request suffering from God.

Those who have suffered and can reflect quietly on their

experience, who with great courage have managed to overcome the poison of bitterness, tell us that suffering can be a blessing in disguise because of the purifying effect it has on the human soul. Poets, saints, and spiritual masters feel compassion for the suffering of ***humanity*** but conclude that there is hardly a better way to begin the process of inner purification. Suffering reminds us of our creaturehood. It awakens us from the illusion of ego control and teaches the central spiritual attitude of humility.

At times in the spiritual life, I may be an active agent in this purification process. For instance, I may try to discipline my vital desires through fasting. I may set aside more time for prayer and meditation. I try to overcome sinful ***self***-centered attitudes and to detach myself from whatever binds my attention to the exclusion of God. I may try also to quell the rumblings of my imagination and emotions. In such efforts I cooperate actively with the purifying action of God's grace.

At other times the agent of suffering is outside of me. I do not choose to be afflicted; I am afflicted. Suffering may come in the form of an unreasonable person, a cantankerous neighbor, a nagging wife, a domineering husband, an unjust boss who cheats me out of a promotion. Such passive suffering is often more acute than the active form. What matters now is my attitude toward it. Do I become bitter and lie in wait for revenge, or can I receive such suffering from God's hand and use it as an occasion for spiritual deepening?

[9]*Susan Muto*

The humble lover is high-minded. Because ***one*** loves, ***one*** discovers everywhere the beautiful, the good, and the lovable in order to serve and to emulate it in admiration. This high-minded disposition springs from humility especially in the presence of God. Loving worship is the basic attitude and ultimate root of humility.

[10]*Bernard Häring*

But humility gives an unprejudiced view of one's own and others' worth and unworths.

[11]*Bernard Häring*

However, it would be untrue to confess oneself as a poor sinner before God if there were not also united with this admittance the will to accept lovingly and confidingly the dispensation of God, even in the very place where God cuts and cauterizes like a good surgeon. The proud man rebels in misfortune: "How have I deserved this?" But the humble man recognizes even in his affliction that God deals kindly with him. He speaks a grateful confiding yes even to the difficult things that God may demand of him. In the measure that he is a lover he comes in his fulfillment of God's will to the decisive truth, to the vital recognition that *love is the heart of all things*.

[12]*Bernard Häring*

Selection Footnotes

1. *Markings*, p. 91.
2. *New Seeds of Contemplation*, pp. 181-182.
3. *A Testament of Devotion*, pp. 61-62.
4. *Teach Us to Pray*, pp. 151-152.
5. *On Being Yourself*, p. 91.
6. *On Being Yourself*, pp. 7-8.
7. *Christian Maturity*, p. 91.
8. *The Practice of the Presence of God*, p. 25.
9. *Steps Along the Way*, pp. 52-53.
10. *Christian Maturity*, p. 95.
11. *Christian Maturity*, p. 96.
12. *Christian Maturity*, p. 97.

"THE GREATEST OF THESE IS LOVE"

More Selections for Chapter VII

OUR LOVE OF GOD AND GOD'S LOVE FOR US

To you whom I love I say, let us go on loving one another, for love comes from God. Every man who truly loves is God's son and has some knowledge of him. But the man who does not love cannot know him at all, for God is love.

[1]*New Testament in Modern English*

It is true that no human being has ever had a direct vision of God. Yet if we love one another God does actually live within us, and his love grows in us toward perfection. And, as I wrote above, the guarantee of our living in him and his living in us is the share of his own Spirit which he gives us.

[2]*New Testament in Modern English*

The mystics, to give them their short familiar name, are men and women who insist that they know for certain the presence and activity of that which they call the Love of God.

[3]*Evelyn Underhill*

LOVE: that over-worked and ill-used word, often confused on the one hand with passion and on the other with amiability. If we ask the most fashionable . . . psychologists what love is, ***they say*** that it is the impulse urging us towards that end which is the fulfillment of any series of deeds or "behavior-cycle;" the psychic thread on which all the apparently separate actions making up that cycle are strung and united. In this sense love need not be fully conscious, to reach the level of feeling; but it *must* be an imperative, inward urge. And if we ask those who have known and taught the life of the Spirit, they too say that love is a passionate tendency, an inward vital urge of the soul towards its Source; which impels every living thing to pursue the most profound trend of its being, reaches consciousness in the form of self-giving and of desire, and its only satisfying goal in God. Love is for them much more than its emotional manifestations. It is "the ultimate cause of the true activities of all active things"--no less.

[4]*Evelyn Underhill*

Pure Love or Charity--utter self-giving which is our reply to the Love of God--is the same as sanctity. What is pure love? That which gives and gives and never demands. In the words of Gertrude More: *Courageous, humble, constant; not worn out with labours, not daunted by difficulties*--bravely sticking it out when tired, disheartened, worried. And to do this, we look beyond it all, trying to respond to the Love of God, seeking and serving Christ in ***everyone***.

[5]*Evelyn Underhill*

THE PRACTICE OF LOVING GOD

He told me, that *the foundation of the spiritual life* in *him*, had been a high notion and esteem of GOD in faith . . . *that he might perform all his actions for the love of GOD.*

[6]*Brother Lawrence*

Love means the going out of our lonely being to what is other. Love for God is a homecoming. It is return to the source, a regaining of the lost core of our lives. All human life is a seeking for that mysterious other, that lost home, that forgotten source, that hidden core.

[7]*Adrian van Kaam*

. . . God does not look at what you do but only at your love and at the devotion and will behind your deeds. It matters little . . . what we do, but ***God*** does care a lot about the attitudes our deeds express.

[8]*Meister Eckhart*

The one who truly loves does not love once and for all. Nor does ***one*** use a part of ***one's*** love, and then again another part. For to change it into small coins is not to use it rightly. No, ***one*** loves with all of ***one's*** love. It is wholly present in each expression. ***One*** continues to give it away as a whole and yet . . . keeps it intact as a whole in ***one's*** heart.

[9]*Søren Kierkegaard*

. . . this precept [that thou shalt love the Lord thy God with all thy strength] means that I ought to consecrate to God all my plans, all my views, all my actions, having no other intention in them but that of pleasing ***God***; fulfilling all my duties only for love of ***God***; employing my talents, my goods, my possessions, my credit and my authority to make **God** loved better; to have an ardent zeal for ***God's*** Glory, and to further it as much as lies in my power . . . .

[10]*Nicholas Grou*

To serve God by love is the most simple way, since it reduces all to one single motive which dominates every other, or in which all others are comprised. If I love God, I fear **God** with the kind of fear that is most pleasing to **God** and most useful for me. If I love God, I hope in ***God's*** promises with the firmest confidence, and I ensure their fulfillment, as far as is possible in this world. If I love God, I have no need to think about the acquisition of each virtue in particular; the exercise of love includes each and all of them, and makes us practise them by the motive of love itself in a higher and more perfect way than if I were to exercise each one by the motive peculiar to that virtue. Love dispenses me from that crowd of methods and practices, which the greater number of people seek after so eagerly that they are continually changing; attaching themselves today to this and tomorrow to that, and in the end they embarrass themselves with so many, which serve to disturb their peace and retard their progress in the way of holiness. Love has only one method, and that is, to follow the instinct of grace which leads us to love; it has only one practice, which is, to love at all times, in all places, and in every situation; it has only one act, to which every other refers, only one motive, loving because it loves; it has only one end, loving in order to love. What can be more simple? But is there any means of perfection that this simplicity does not embrace? Is there any that it does not use and employ excellently, drawing from it more profit than if it stopped at that single means considered in itself? The simplicity of the way of love draws the soul near to the state of the Blessed, who see God *only* to love ***God***. If love adds hope to love, it is because the soul does not yet possess God as the Blessed do.

[11]*Nicholas Grou*

THE CONSEQUENCES OF LOVING

The sense of Presence! I have spoken of it as stealing on one unawares. It is recorded of John Wilhem Rowntree that as he left a great physician's office, where he had just been told that his advancing blindness could not be stayed, he stood by some railings for a few moments to collect himself when he "suddenly felt the love of God wrap him about as though a visible presence enfolded him and a joy filled him such as he had never known before." An amazing timeliness of the Invading Love, as the Everlasting stole about him in his sorrow.

[12]*Thomas Kelly*

Today we know that love in its three developing stages is the power which has made ***us*** so dominant a species that not only ***do we*** overrun the globe but all other species exist only at ***our*** pleasure. These three stages are: *eros*, the need to be loved and so to develop unprecedented power of affective-effective interest; *agape*, the irresistible cooperation of unlimited mutual trust and liability, responsibility and confidence; *charis*, the power to be interested and moved by every living thing.

[13]*Gerald Heard*

We must now recognize that the force which runs life is Love in its threefold levels of need for love, capacity to reciprocate love and power to give love. The fact that this is the sequence whereby we come to know this force indicates the stages whereby we may, and indeed alone can, build up our development until we become wholly free and creative, a constant channel of nonentropic, death-defeating, consciousness-expanding energy.

[14]*Gerald Heard*

Many people feel it is too painful so to investigate their basic motivation. They feel they must be liked. They therefore go out to perform good deeds so as to assure themselves that they are really givers. But in point of fact they are still only needy. Hence they are bound to look for gratitude. This seeking in the object of their charity for loving admiration makes their munificence merely money whereby they can purchase love. The object of such "affection" feels patronized. People who lie open to charitable assistance are themselves generally persons in great need of *eros*--requiring, as much as their patronizer, to be loved and not asked to return gratitude that might assuage another's lack of *eros*. The people who have begun to develop out of *eros* are reaching *agape* and once established in the reciprocal group love, they naturally do not stand in need of patronage.

[15]*Gerald Heard*

The person still at *eros* may refuse to go on to *agape* . . . while if, when *agape* is attained, *agape* in its turn does not develop into *charis*, then the mutual-admiration, ingrown group becomes the narrow, exclusive, excommunicative church of the elect who are saved from otherwise universal damnation. The group love turns into schizoid "party discipline," suspicion and guilt.

[16]*Gerald Heard*

But in point of fact ***we are*** so different from this picture of ***ourselves*** that for ***us*** to have real self-love, love for a complete self, a real ego, *is* a form of altruism and faith. For before we can discover that there is in ourselves any such person to love (let alone such a person who could be loved), we have to gain the power to control, and shape into a whole person, a swarm of divergent drives, pointless urges, dissoluting indulgences and aimless idlings. To really love yourself, we have been told, is our first duty. And most of us have made such a mess of it that we either rush out to get others to love us or, if we are even more ignorant, we rush out to love others. In either case something in us, deep-down, knows we have failed to find anything lovable, anything worth being wanted, in ourselves. And when, through the inevitable failure of these escapisms, we have to confront the fact that we possess no personality--and a nothing cannot be loved--we sink into the pessimism of addiction or the cynicism of nihilism.

[17]*Gerald Heard*

Only the ***people*** who ***are*** whole in ***themselves and are*** based in a group unit of wholeness can deliver . . . **individuals** from the ego-fissure, lead ***them*** where ***they*** may grow in the field of other freed persons and teach ***them*** to look on to a fulfillment which will more than validate and reward all ***their*** exertion. For the whole ***person*** of *charis* has this capacity to lead through the fact that he ***or she*** is fulfilling life; ***she or*** he is the emergence of the new species. Our chaos by its very destructiveness produced the vacuum that ***the charis person*** alone can fill. Our sense of futile frustration is the unspoken question ***she or*** he alone can answer.

[18]*Gerald Heard*

Selection Footnotes

1. *The New Testament in Modern English,* I John 4:7-8, p. 521.
2. *The New Testament in Modern English,* I John 4:12-13, pp. 521-522.
3. *An Anthology of the Love of God,* p. 3.
4. *An Anthology of the Love of God,* p. 29.
5. *An Anthology of the Love of God,* p. 29.
6. *The Practice of the Presence of God,* p. 17.
7. *Spirituality and the Gentle Life,* pp. 61-62.
8. *Meister Eckhart,* p. 22.
9. *Purity of Heart,* p. 33.
10. *Meditations on the Love of God,* p. 40.
11. *Meditations on the Love of God,* pp. 79-80.
12. *A Testament of Devotion,* pp. 94-95.

13. Gerald Heard, *Training for a Life of Growth* (Santa Monica, CA: The Wayfarer Press, 1959), p. 26.
14. *Training for a Life of Growth*, p. 29.
15. *Training for a Life of Growth*, p. 32.
16. *Training for a Life of Growth*, p. 36.
17. *Training for a Life of Growth*, pp. 54-55.
18. *Training for a Life of Growth*, p. 84.

THE ULTIMATE DISCIPLINE: ATTACHMENT WITH GOD

More Selections for Chapter VIII

THE BASIC CONCEPT

Professor Karlfried von Dürckheim has described the beginning attachment for the non-religious as:

. . . the spiritual events which unbelievers may experience with astonishment. Under heavy bombardment, for instance, or in the course of a serious illness, ***one*** suddenly feels that he ***or she*** has gone beyond fear, and that this feeling does not come from ***oneself***, but that it is something given. . . . Without . . . knowing why, ***one*** has penetrated a different world, the world of transcendence. ***One*** has achieved a break-through into that unknown world where he ***or she*** discovers . . . strange realities: a life which is lived beyond the natural phenomena of life and death, a meaning of things that is beyond the rational categories of sense and nonsense, a love that is beyond the emotional experiences of sympathy and antipathy and a "yes" which transcends the logical contradictions of "yes" and "no."

[1]*Karlfried von Dürckheim*

. . . an authentic abandonment can never be imposed from without, that has value only if it is spontaneous, if it comes from the heart, from an inner conviction, a free decision. This is what I call the power of God . . . a call from the Spirit, a spiritual movement, an intervention by God.

[2]*Paul Tournier*

What I must do therefore, is to go . . . quietly and ask ***God*** to speak to me and show me moment by moment what ***is expected*** of me. I know very well that ***God*** never asks of us more than one thing at a time and that it is this simplicity in what God wills that can deliver us from ***our*** ambiguity. If I really seek to do ***God's*** will I can cast on ***God*** all the cares I have about other things I cannot do.

[3]*Paul Tournier*

PRACTICING THE ULTIMATE DISCIPLINE

No, death means that I must go through the needle's eye, and that most, if not all, of what I have come to identify as my permanent possessions will be stripped from me.

[4]*Douglas Steere*

Detachment ought never to be practised for itself. I detach myself only in order to attach myself. I let go the evil or the less good in order to seize the better or the perfect. But I never let go in order to fall into a hole.

[5]*Baron von Hügel*

In all asceticism the principle of abstaining from things that are precious and good (from food, from speech, from physical comforts, from marriage) for the sake of accentuating something more good in itself is a sound principle and is sound practice, so long as it is done voluntarily and joyously and not grimly, and so long as it can be regarded as a matter of private vocation and is not universally pressed on others.

[6]*Douglas Steere*

THE CONSEQUENCES OF LIVING UNDER THIS ULTIMATE DISCIPLINE

Above all ***persons*** should take care to discipline ***themselves*** strictly and thoroughly. It would be fatal for . . . undisciplined and unskilled ***persons*** to try to do what an expert may do and, what is more, ***they*** would get nowhere by trying. Only when ***they have*** been thoroughly weaned away from things and things are alien to ***them***--only then may ***they*** do as ***they please*** with things, free to take them or leave them with impunity. The undisciplined ***persons***, however, cannot take pleasure or indulge in meat or drink or whatever ***they are*** fond of, without harm.

[7]*Meister Eckhart*

Then, too, there comes the insight that all such letting go may well be the ncessary preparation for new and more creative involvement. Adrian van Kaam's volume entitled *On Being Involved; The Rhythm of Involvement and Detachment in Human Life* provides an excellent and full expansion of this concept together with many specific insights about the nature of detachment and involvement. Here is his summary of the detachment-involvement rhythm:

Life is marked by these sequences of detachment and involvement.

They may be sudden or gradual, depending on my temperament and life history. Whether the experience is rapid or slow-moving, it will always entail a critical period in which the ultimate decision to stay where I am or to go forward must be made. Every major life decision implies the trauma of cutting myself loose from familiar feelings and habits in which I was safely embedded. I must risk the unknown. The decision to be reborn is my choice. No one can make it for me. To detach myself means to accept the consequences of my new stand, to risk failure as well as success.

The commitment which resolves the crisis of detachment should not be seen as stern willfulness; rather this "yes" is a gentle yielding to a new level of human and religious awareness, deeper than anything I have experienced in the past. Thus detachment becomes an occasion for a new act of self-surrender to the Sacred, which may be a vital turning point of my life. Once the crisis of detachment is overcome, restlessness may be transformed into serene certitude. I may now enter a period of regained equanimity and joyful fidelity to my new life style.

The rhythm of detachment and involvement thus evinces three phases: death, decision, rebirth. The death phase or that of detachment may bring with it initially a sense of frustration, anxiety, conflict. The phase of decision then binds death to rebirth, or detachment to new involvement, and marks the transition to a new way of life. The final phase, that of resurrection, is characterized by transcendence, transformation, and reintegration. These three phases are so profoundly intertwined that it is often difficult to perceive them as distinct in the actual time of crisis. Nonetheless, my willingness to renounce past views and feelings when these are obviously blocking my spiritual growth is a condition for my resurrection as a new person.

For the Christian, this grace of rebirth brings with it an added dimension: I live the mystery of the Risen Christ who is with me, here and now, and who communicates to me what each new mode of religious awareness may mean in terms of my involvement in the world. The teaching of the Lord reminds me that no way of life is ever entirely free of the inclination to self-centeredness. The purity of my religious involvement is constantly threatened. Thus I have to die constantly with Christ in order to purify my intentions. In light of His grace, I can rest in the assurance that I am never alone or without hope in my quest for the life of the spirit.

[8]*Adrian van Kaam*

On Pentecost the Spirit of the Lord spoke through ***the*** apostles in such a way that each one heard them speak in his own tongue. Pentecost is a reminder that the Spirit of the Lord is one of loving accommodation to each original person.

Collegiality enlightened by this Spirit can never mean the

suppression of someone's personal calling by a vocal majority. The unique eternal call of each person . . . and what the Holy Spirit wants ***that individual*** to do, cannot be at odds with one another. Both came from God.

Collegiality, mellowed and illumined by the Spirit, shows concern for what the call of each member of a social or charitable organization may be. It fears to impose on the person anything that could collide with God's Will for ***that individual***. Such sensitivity demands detachment that only grace can give. A detachment from the plans of the organization when the Spirit clearly wants to use a member for something else. A detachment from envy when the individual thus called happens to obtain benefits unavailable to others. A detachment from my limited judgment when I realize that by background and education I am not capable of understanding why some members must do what ***they do*** the way ***they do*** it.

Collegiality of spiritual ***persons*** who are humble and detached is a blessing. Collegiality without humility can be hell on earth.

[9]*Adrian von Kaam*

Selection Footnotes

1. *A Place for You*, quotation from Karlfried von Dürckheim, p. 203.
2. *A Place for You*, p. 151.
3. *A Place for You*, p. 167.
4. *On Beginning From Within*, p. 124.
5. *Spiritual Counsel and Letters of Baron Friedrich von Hügel*, p. 175.
6. *On Beginning From Within*, p. 66-67.
7. *Meister Eckhart*, p. 32.
8. *On Being Involved*, pp. 98-100.
9. *On Being Yourself*, pp. 102-103.

JOY AND THE LIFTED HEART

More Selections for Chapter IX

TOWARD A DEFINITION OF JOY

Joy is the emotional experience which our kind ***God*** in heaven has attached to the discharge of the most fundamental of all the higher activities--namely, those of inner growth and outer creativeness. Joy is the triumph of life; it is the sign that we are living our true life as spiritual beings. We are sent into the world to become something and to make something. The two are in practice so closely connected as to be almost inseparable. Our personality expands by creativeness, and creates spontaneously as it expands. Joy is the signal that we are spiritually alive and active. Wherever joy is, creation has been; and the richer the creation, the deeper the joy.

[1]*W. R. Inge*

. . . the End and the Measure are the same--the love of God above all things and the love of our neighbour as ourselves. And this love of God, where uninhibited and full, brings joy--it seeks God, Joy; and it finds Joy, God.

[2]*Baron von Hügel*

The wondrous in contrast to the resistant response is another sign of the self's blossoming. When my eye is illumined from within by the divine light, no longer do I see myself as a lonely soldier on a vast battlefield where my life counts for little. I see myself as held by the Holy, as loved into life, not as a separate entity, independent of ***humanity*** and God, but as part and parcel of ***God's*** whole wondrous cosmos, ***God's*** mysterious divine project and its inner coherence.

Where before I saw fragmentation and fight, I now see communion and reconciliation. I place myself in God's presence each time I realize that ***God*** is not only present in the place where I am but also in a special way in the depths of my soul, which ***God*** enlightens and sanctifies . . . since ***God*** is, as St. Francis says, the heart of my heart, the soul of my soul.

Such a view of self at one with nature, ***humanity*** and God may momentarily dim when pressures mount, but through prayer and nearness to Christ I can place myself once again in presence to God. Behind the tempest is the cloudless night. Beneath the turbulence of the sea is the calm of the ocean's floor. Here the illumined soul rests in God. The duration of my rest may be short, but the effects of such stillness remain to direct me back to God when the actual sense of ***God's*** presence recedes. Remembering this moment of nearness to the Beloved and living from within its light readies me to receive the gift of spiritual peace when and if ***God*** chooses to grant it.

[3]*Susan Muto*

THE MEANING OF JOY

DISCOVERED IN ITS PRACTICE

Life has always been dangerous and no one is spared the conflict within ***oneself***, though a joyful courage attracts a joyful life . . . . Again as an old soldier, I say, attack without effort the idea of happiness. Insist on it, demand it . . . for from the beauty of a lifted heart come the joyful issues of life. Now is the time to rise up and tambour your spirit with drumsticks of joy! . . . As for this idea of happiness do not misunderstand me; it is the joy of courage which brings the faith to win.

[4]*Letters of the Scattered Brotherhood*

On waking wake in joy and plunge yourself into great stillness. Dissolve your universe into thought. Then meet the news, meet the onslaught as if it were the barking of a pack of dogs far away outside of this still park of your estate. Carry this stillness of serene sky, quiet pools and transcendent beauty with you . . . . Wake . . . and stand released in this holy stillness . . . [the constant Presence].

[5]*Letters of the Scattered Brotherhood*

Accept your responsibilities gaily, happily. Take these disciplines that you set up for yourselves like a happy game, for it can be most joyful. Soon you will discover that when you are in it--this game--you are all right and when you are out of it you are all wrong. Therefore employ every method you can to be near the fountain and the reward will be your deeper enjoyment of life. That is the testimony that has come down from the saints.

[6]*Letters of the Scattered Brotherhood*

Pleasures *can* be provided and pain *can* be avoided, if we use or abuse other beings. But joy cannot be attained and sorrow cannot be overcome in this way. Joy is possible only when we are driven towards things and persons because of what they are and not because of what we can get from them . . . . Our joy about knowing truth and experiencing beauty is spoiled if we enjoy not the truth and the beauty but the fact that it is *I* who enjoys them.

Power can give joy only if it is free from the pleasure about having power and if it is a method of creating something worthwhile.

[7]*Paul Tillich*

THE CONSEQUENCES OF JOY

To seek pleasure for the sake of pleasure is to avoid reality, the reality of other beings and the reality of ourselves. But only the fulfillment of what we really are can give us joy. Joy is nothing else than the awareness of our being fulfilled in our true being, in our personal center. And this fulfillment is possible only if we unite ourselves with what others really are. It is reality that gives joy, and reality alone. The Bible speaks so often of joy because it is the most realistic of all books. "Rejoice!" That means: "Penetrate from what *seems* to be real to that which is *really* real." Mere pleasure, in yourselves and in all other beings, remains in the realm of illusion about reality. Joy is born out of union with reality itself.

[8]*Paul Tillich*

In the hope that we may be captivated by his deep sensitivity and abiding joy the following are quoted from

Anker Larsen. Throughout, he is describing the conditions of the spiritual life and its disciplines which make possible our experiences of reality and result in deep and abiding joy.

One day I was loitering in the garden with no particular object in view. I had been working hard, and had to stop to recover breath. I was tired of my work in my study, and so I strolled idly along the garden paths. I walked and walked, until I found myself standing in front of a dyke by the wood. As I glanced at it, there was a flash of lightning, and the puzzle picture was easy to read. It was a dyke by one of the fields belonging to the estate where I was born. I actually saw it. That is to say, at that moment I did not distinguish between this dyke and the old one, between my present ego and the one of the past. The two phenomena were *simultaneous and one* . . . .

No, the similarity did not lie outside of myself, in what I was looking at, but within myself, in the manner of my perception. I had succeeded in seeing this dyke *honestly and straightforwardly* with the eyes which were my birthright. The profound joy of reality filled me; my own inner condition opened out, and became one with all the homogeneous conditions. It was not a question of remembrance, but of a state of being. I did not miss the old dykes, for they were present.

[9]*Johannes Anker Larsen*

That something happened while the inner state "widened out" was beyond question. After its occurrence I was not the same as before, I was better . . . with this improvement was closely associated a feeling of modesty, I may even say of humility. But above all I sensed a happy release from something--only as yet I did not quite know from what. These moments were full of bliss, but, strange as it may seem, it required courage to be open to them, inasmuch as it appeared that their price was the surrender of everything I was accustomed to regard as valuable; knowledge, talent, self-confidence. I had to climb down to the level of some Jones or Brown. I had to face the phenomena of life unfettered by any preconceived ideas. I well remember my extreme reluctance to strip off the flimsy newspaper culture which was in vogue at that time. I was afraid to see myself as naked as good old Adam without his garb of fig leaves.

I took courage, however, and learned to tarry in the moment whenever it came to me. I had not the feeling of wasting time or of inactivity, as I felt sure that while it lasted something significant was going on. The feeling of joy which it brought was the deepest, purest, and most precious joy I had experienced. The outcome of abiding in these moments was invariably the same; the feeling of joy became so profound that I felt it quite impossible to disregard the consciousness thereof; then it developed into enjoyment, and the moment had passed.

[10]*Johannes Anker Larsen*

When God entered into my life, warm and powerful, it was from them [the cottagers who were the farm laborers in his community] that I learned my right relationship to ***God***. For at first, the heavenly joy brought temptation with it--the temptation which makes of "God's grace" a pleasure, and makes God . . . the last great dissipation of ***humanity***. The history of religions records sufficient instances of this heavenly vice. To feel joy in the spiritual breathing is as inevitable as a feeling of happiness over convalescence, but there is no need to regard it as an end in itself. One can be disinterested toward that which takes place within, and know that the object of convalescence is health and not pleasurable sensation. "Thy will be done" applies also to our apportionment of heavenly bliss; "No more thereof than thou wilt, and not for my sake, but for the sake of that which thou intendest for me." Otherwise, one is as much enslaved by the more refined appetites of the soul as by the coarser lusts of body, and the thin wall separates ***us*** from Eternity as sharply as the thick one. It has even occurred to me at times that it would be better not to believe in God, because we would thus avoid conceiving ***God*** after our image, and would not attempt to force ***God*** into the service of our own purposes.

In this I saw the crux of the situation. I resolved to renounce my personal aims; I tried to "sell all I possessed," and to enter the service of the Great Farmer, to report to him merrily in the morning with the question: "What orders have you got for me today?" Here I recognized again the wish of my childhood and saw it fulfilled. Now I understood the inexplicable charm surrounding the cottagers and laborers as they looked up from their work for a moment and allowed their hands to rest. They were *free.*

They labored honestly and truly, but when they put away their tools, they did not drag about with them the burden of the possible *result* of their work. They accepted sunshine with a smile and rain without a curse. There was something lovable in the peaceful tone with which they remarked; "Yes, it's shocking bad weather to-day." They did not take rain as a personal offense! Personal independence from the result of their work! Until my final rest from labor will they be an inspiration for my daily life. It is possible to be free in the midst of wage slavery. It depends upon ourselves whether we choose to be slaves to our possessions and aims. "Thy will be done"--no joy is so exuberant as that which lies within these words. I readily admit that it may be painful to *have* to say them but as soon as they are said, the one great freedom lies before us; we have cast off the heaviest fetters--our own. This does not prevent one from taking faithful care of ***a*** few goods and chattels, but ***one*** can no longer fear to lose them.

[11]*Johannes Anker Larsen*

A grateful joy that the things are there, not because of the aesthetic pleasure they arouse nor the uses they may serve, but because they exist--along with ourselves--that is the criterion of seeing Reality itself. When we forget that the things we own belong to us, when our joy in their ownership is drowned in the joy of *their existence*, our lungs will have begun to breathe Eternity. Then there arises in ***us*** a *disinterested tenderness* which radiates from ***our beings*** without respect of person. That is the sun of Eternity, which shines upon the just and the unjust.

[12]*Johannes Anker Larsen*

Selection Footnotes

1. W. R. Inge, *Personal Religion and the Life of Devotion*, (London, New York: Longmans Green, 1924), p. 64.
2. *Spiritual Counsel and Letters of Baron Friedrich von Hügel*, p. 122.
3. *Steps Along the Way*, pp. 64-65.
4. *Letters of the Scattered Brotherhood*, pp. 38-39.
5. *Letters of the Scattered Brotherhood*, pp. 58-59.
6. *Letters of the Scattered Brotherhood*, p. 37.
7. Paul Tillich, *The New Being* (New York: Charles Scribner's Sons, 1955), p. 145.
8. *The New Being*, p. 146.
9. *With the Door Open*, pp. 37-39.
10. *With the Door Open*, pp. 40-42.
11. *With the Door Open*, pp. 67-70.
12. *With the Door Open*, p. 97.

THE INDISSOLUBLE TIE: "HASTEN UNTO GOD HASTEN INTO THE WORLD"

More Selections for Chapter X

THE INDISSOLUBLE TIE:

DEFINITON AND DESCRIPTION

Jan van Ruysbroeck in his *Book of the Twelve Beguines* describes the life of individuals who have arrived at union with God through creative prayer as, "ministering to the world without, in love and in mercy; whilst inwardly abiding in simplicity, in stillness, and in utter peace."

[1]*Evelyn Underhill*

. . . sanctification and sacrifice are two faces of one fact . . . [The saint] "partakes of the Divine nature" in the degree in which he ***or she*** is self-given to it. Subdued to the pressures and the demands of that mysterious energy, Its loving and untiring friend and servant, ***the saint*** becomes in . . . turn and in . . . small measure a creative personality; takes up his ***or her*** part in the eternal process of bringing forth within the world the life and love of God.

[2]*Evelyn Underhill*

Social beliefs and the actions they evoke may help me to suffer with others, but do they really make me one with them in the deepest sense? Should there not be something more original in myself and others that goes deeper than social beliefs alone, something that does not exclude these beliefs but sustains and nourishes them? Deeper than social beliefs is faith and I have to be sure that my enthusiastic beliefs are not taking the place of faith.

[3]*Adrian van Kaam*

Some years ago a center was set up for schooling men and women in meditation and contemplation. It was located in an isolated place with few neighbors about, and with no towns that were within easy reach. Food was purchased and brought in, so that these needs were well provided for. The living quarters, refectory, library, and chapel were superbly constructed and furnished. The climate was moderate and gracious; the site beautiful. A spiritual guide or guru of great gifts and dedication was in residence. From three to five hours a day were given to prayer in the little chapel. Much of the rest of the time went into reading and conversation and into counseling with the teacher. There was a garden where some worked a little when it suited them. After four years the center broke up and the people dispersed and the leader's comment was that charity between those who lived there had disappeared.

There are many factors that led to the shattering of this promising venture. But one issue stands out with such clarity that it would be almost universally agreed to by those who have sought to understand why this experiment broke down. It is the fact that these worshipers did not match their contemplation, their worship of God, with a redemptive outlet that drew some corner of the yearning, toiling creation up with them. Since few of them were called to the very special vocation of pure contemplatives who lay hold of creation from within by their lives of intercessory prayer for others, they could not bear, nor could they absorb, this concentration of worship without being more deeply engaged in works of charity whether in hard work in garden or household, in hospital work, in teaching, or even in writing. Without this connection, the worship, the contemplation, seemed to be lacking in redemptive, tendering power. It became unconvincing, and charity declined.

[4]*Douglas Steere*

THE PRACTICE OF "HASTENING UNTO GOD AND HASTENING INTO THE WORLD"

I take it that, in the widest sense, we mean by Contemplation the human self's method of stretching out towards truth which lies beyond and above ***an individual's*** reason; ***and*** communion with a reality which is not given us by the senses, or reached by logical thought . . . its true object is that mysterious Something Other, the Holy and Unchanging, which gives meaning to life.

[5]*Evelyn Underhill*

. . . Angela of Foligno . . . walking alone through the vineyards between Spello and Assisi . . . heard the Holy Spirit saying to her . . . "Behold and see! this is My Creation." And, gazing on that exquisite landscape . . . she was filled with an ineffable sweetness and joy . . . and she was possessed by a humility such as she had never known before.

We can translate that scene for ourselves, thinking of such a spring as that which we had this year: the beauty of the untouched English country, snowy with hawthorn, the downs starred with tiny perfect flowers, the amazing emerald life of the young beechwoods, the exultant singing of the birds--and the Spirit of God saying still in our hearts "Behold and see! this is My Creation!" We too, seeing this living and intricate beauty, were surely filled with gratitude and delight.

But now, reverse this picture; and suppose that we are condemned to go with Christ to some of the places which we, in our corporate capacity--Christian citizens of a Christian country--have made, or allowed through stupidity and sloth to come into existence. Imagine any one of us walking through the East End of London, or up the staircase of a lodging-house in Notting Dale--and then through Piccadilly, and up some staircases which one could find near there--or down our prison corridors--or through a poison-gas factory--with that Companion at our side. And suppose that it is our turn to meet that glance and say "Behold and see! This is *our* creation!" We can each complete that episode; but none without shame. Even to think of the contrast is surely to be possessed in our turn by such a penitence as we have never known before.

If we dare to complete the episode, to turn from this monumental exhibition of our corporate failure in intelligence and love, our greed, apathy, stupidity, lack of energetic faith, and look at the face of Christ; then, we cannot feel any doubt about the nature of the command which is laid on us. We have to meet that vision, fair and square,--that infinite love and compassion which ought to be our love and compassion too--with the knowledge in our minds that there are places in all our great cities where it is not possible for a child to grow up in unsullied purity. This is our creation. We know what Jesus thinks about children; and He brings to us the mind of God. Again, complete classes of the population are kept in a state of economic insecurity, which thwarts for them all chance of spiritual development: and we must hold such spiritual development--by which I do not mean piety--to be God's will for all ***of us*** . . . .

Christ demands the surrender of acquisitiveness: and ultimately a social order in which we can say to all men and women without irony, in respect of their bodily necessities, "Your heavenly Father knoweth that ye have need of all these things: but seek ye first the kingdom of God and His righteousness and all these things shall be added unto you." That alone--the corporate security which comes from the practical application of neighbourly love--is Christian citizenship. I do not say that this means the triumph of any particular *ism*: but it does mean, plainly, a triumph of the love and generosity of God in the heart and mind and strength of every individual of which that social order is built. Energy and intelligence, as well as mere feeling, dedicated to the purposes of Christ; and then brought to bear on the desperate problems of our corporate life. We have got that corporate life into such a mess now by our persistent acquiescence in a policy of clutch, that its problems seem to present insuperable difficulties; but there are no insuperable difficulties to Divine Love. It is strange that any Christian should look upon such a notion as fantastic, since it is merely the corollary of our faith in the power and present work of the Holy Spirit within life. Because of this faith we do not look upon it as fantastic, and do look upon the social order which neglect of Christian realism has brought into being, as grotesque. Therefore we are bound to consider, in a spirit of prayer and with an entire willingness to pay the necessary price, how best to tackle some of the problems which have been brought into being by this triumph of acquisitiveness over love.

[6]*Evelyn Underhill*

Our materialism is the survival and accentuation of primitive ***people's*** necessary preoccupation with the material world; the immense importance for ***them***--if ***they*** were to survive at all--of food, shelter, possessions; the sense that they are valuable for their own sakes, and being won with difficulty, must be clutched tight as the very substance of ***their lives*** . . . .

These antique tendencies, immensely strong, are now so cunningly disguised and rationalized that very few of us realize the half-savage and half-childish nature of the impelling instinct which causes us to love a bargain, to collect things for collecting's sake, to judge rich and poor by different standards, to resent a trespass, blindly to support our own class or country, to enjoy combative games and destructive sports, to feel uplifted by a patriotic song. None of these impelling instincts are wrong in themselves; but they are now occasions of wrong, because we have failed to sublimate them. We let them go on, in altered conditions, giving us suggestions appropriate to the Stone Age; instead of harnessing these vigorous springs of the psychic energy to the chariot of Christ. To do this

(1) We must replace material by spiritual values--the respect for wealth by the respect for beauty, the desire for goods by the desire for good, the desire for luxury by the desire for justice; quantity by quality; must dissolve acquisitiveness in that spirit of poverty which enjoys everything because it desires nothing.

(2) We must replace the belief in achievement through conflict and the defeat of our adversary--whether in the international, the economic or the political field--by belief in achievement through love, united effort, and the winning of our adversary: "Loving the unlovely into loveableness."

(3) We must replace tyranny between class and race by love between class and race; fraternity, the true fulfillment of the herd-instinct, overflowing its first narrow boundaries till it embraces the world.

[7]*Evelyn Underhill*

If we want to produce it, we must first produce a corporate change of heart; bit by bit Christianizing the social body from within, so that it may become more and more incapable of acts that conflict with the principle of love, and of tolerating for others conditions which we would never allow to affect those individuals for whom we really care. Corporate regeneration must follow the same course as personal regeneration. Accepting, like the individual Christian, the Incarnation as the clue to life, the community must grow into conformity with this belief. It can only do this along the same lines as the individual; namely, by a balanced process of analysis and synthesis. It must first track down and realize the true springs of its conduct; press back into the racial past, and discover the humiliating facts about those impulses which really condition our behaviour in such matters as nationalism, property, employment, servitude, sex. It must acknowledge how many notions necessary to a primitive state of society have become imbedded in our view of life; and thanks to the conservative nature of the social mind, still govern our corporate view of existence. It must further realize that these relics of the past, however imposing the disguises they now wear in financial and political circles, represent something less than ***our*** best here and now possibility: and that therefore our wholesale capitulation to them, our quiet assumption that you cannot go against "human nature" in its most acquisitive, self-regarding, and combative mood, has the character of sin. Having reached this level of self-knowledge, it may perhaps be brought to something equivalent to social penitence: may feel as a direct reproach every life damaged by bad housing, every child maimed by economic conditions, every soul stifled by luxury or obsessed by unreal values, every man or woman embittered and made hopeless by unemployment and friendlessness. And then, turning in one way or another to God, to Reality, to the true values declared in Christ, the work of whose creative Spirit its mingled stupidity and selfishness retards, society may set in hand the complementary movement of synthesis: the real building-up of Jerusalem, by perfect work and steady prayer.

[8]*Evelyn Underhill*

Before we can mend our unreal confusions, we must have a clear vision of the Real: and the gaining and holding of such a vision in personal life is one of the main functions of prayer, as in corporate life its holding up is the chief business of institutional religion. Efforts to Christianize our social conduct are foredoomed, unless those who undertake them give themselves time to look steadily at Christ.

[9]*Evelyn Underhill*

THE CONSEQUENCES OF ALL THIS

We find at the birth of every great spiritual movement, an awestruck and surrendered personality, seized and used by a Power other than itself; subdued to a purpose which he or she does not understand, and imperatively called to a career or an action, which often seems to bear little relation to its vast religious or historic results.

[10]*Evelyn Underhill*

Evelyn Underhill follows this statement with examples--St. Paul, Jerome, Augustine, Benedict, Gregory, Bernard, Hildegarde of Bingen, Angela of Foligno, Julian of Norwich, Catherine of Siena, Theresa, Elizabeth Fry, Vincent de Paul, Francis Xavier, Jacob Boehme, William Law, Abbé Huvelin, Mary Slessor, Albert Schweitzer. St. Francis, John Woolman and others. All were of this order of double action and all were effective in reconciliation and redemption of persons individually and collectively.

. . . the modern world may be brought to realize that religion is not to be justified by the improvements it may effect in this world; but by the news that it gives of another world. It is true that when this news--this metaphysical reality--is brought into human life and becomes dominant, all our reactions to the physical are profoundly modified. The more Eternal Life permeates our mentality, the more deep and rich becomes our interpretation of the temporal life, and the higher our standard of responsibility rises. And were the fusion between contemplation and action complete, the Kingdom of

God--which is already within, in the ground of our personality--would be manifest in space and time.

[11]*Evelyn Underhill*

But at the moment when the soul passes from all works into complete devotion and composure, it achieves the real "inward work:" the one, whole, true, undivided and indivisible. Where this work is performed in the ground and the stillness of the soul, above space and time, it breaks forth in temporal works, without ceasing, "without wherefore," without compulsion, without seeking for reward, without secondary purpose, in the free-outpouring of a new and truly liberated will . . . .

[12]*Rudolph Otto*

Ascetic as regards ***our*** spiritual growth and purification; benevolent as regards ***our*** natural status and rights. Christian social reform is not merely the effort of a number of clever, kindhearted, well-intentioned animals to make things as pleasant and wholesome all round as they possibly can. So far as it is a genuine activity of the spirit, it is the response of our individual spirits to the pressure of God's creative love, our effort to let that love find ever fuller expression through our action--one of the ways in which the Eternal Wisdom uses human personality "as ***individuals use their own hands***." We do not bring to it a true sense of vocation until we feel this; and feel, too, that all in it which truly matters points beyond this world.

[13]*Evelyn Underhill*

. . . Am *I* down in the flaming center of God? Have *I* come into the deeps, where the soul meets with God and knows ***God's*** Love and power? Have I discovered God as a living Immediacy, a sweet Presence and, a stirring, life-renovating Power within me? Do I walk by ***God's*** guidance, feeding every day, like knights of the Grail, on the body and blood of Christ, knowing every day and every act to be a sacrament?

[14]*Thomas Kelly*

For the holy Now is not something which we, by our activity, . . . overtake or come upon. It is a now which itself is dynamic, which lays hold actively upon us, which breaks in actively upon us and re-energizes us from within a new center. We can count upon this as the only secure dynamic, an all-potent factor in world events. For the Eternal is urgently, actively breaking into time, working through those who are willing *to be laid hold upon,* to surrender *self*-confidence and *self*-centered effort, that is, self-originated effort, and let the Eternal be the dynamic guide in recreating, through us, our time-world.

This is the first fruit of the Spirit--a joy unspeakable and full of glory.

[15]*Thomas Kelly*

But in the sense of Presence some of the past nows of our time-now change their character entirely. Our old failures are so apt to paralyze us. The Eternal Now may counsel: "Undertake this." Our time-now says: "See what a weakling you proved yourself to be in an earlier case. Better not try it now." But the assurance of the Eternal Now is enough, as it should have been for Moses: "Surely I shall be with thee." Submit yourself to the Eternal Now and in peace serene, in the boldness of perfect faith, you can advance into miraculous living, or, in the opposite direction, our time-now may say: "Do this. You are well prepared for it. Your education and training fit you, perhaps to teach, to preach, to counsel, to guide an enterprise. And if you don't nobody will." But the Eternal Now in us may say: "Stay. Wait. Don't rely upon yourself. Don't think you can reason yourself into your obligation . . . ."

Thus in faith we go forward, with breathtaking boldness, and in faith we stand still, unshaken, with amazing confidence. For the time-nows are rooted in the Eternal Now, which is a steadfast Presence, an infinite ocean of light and love which is flowing over the ocean of darkness and death.

[16]*Thomas Kelly*

There is a fellowship among those who have been baptized, deep under rolling waters of God's love, a fellowship too rich and precious to be described adequately . . . there was a *Verbundenheit*, a condition of being knit together . . . this *Verbundenheit*, wasn't due to their common outer experiences. It was due to their common *inner* experience in God. They knew and loved one another because they all knew they had found the same life-center. They had all gone deep into God, or God had gone down deep into them. In companionship with Jesus they had found His Life-center and that center was in God . . . . It is the stuff of the *Kingdom of God.* Early Friends knew this fellowship among themselves. They saw that, behind all the differences of education and age and social status, there was a Common Life-center, a blazing Light within . . . all who knew this and lived by it were in the Fellowship. You can love such neighbors as yourself even if you haven't known them in outer years as long as you have many an old friend.

[17]*Thomas Kelly*

Selection Footnotes

1. *Concerning the Inner Life*, p. 43.
2. *Mixed Pasture*, p. 30.
3. *On Being Yourself*, p. 68.
4. *Work and Contemplation*, pp. 128-129.
5. *Mixed Pasture*, pp. 7-8.
6. *Mixed Pasture*, pp. 66-69.
7. *Mixed Pasture*, pp. 79-81.
8. *Mixed Pasture*, pp. 81-82.
9. *Mixed Pasture*, p. 71.
10. *Mixed Pasture*, p. 36.
11. *Mixed Pasture*, p. 25.
12. *Mysticism East and West*, pp. 193-194.
13. *Mixed Pasture*, p. 108.
14. *The Eternal Promise*, p. 48.
15. *A Testament of Devotion*, pp. 98-99.
16. *A Testament of Devotion*, pp. 104-105.
17. *The Eternal Promise*, p. 119.

Selected Bibliography

●● These are books recommended for the beginning of a personal collection of the "family documents."

Andrewes, Lancelot. *The Private Devotions*, translated by John Henry Newman, S.P.C.K. New York: Abingdon-Cokesbury Press, 1950.

Anonymous. *The Cloud of Unknowing*, translated with introduction by Clifton Wolters. New York: Penguin Books Ltd. 1st ed., 1961; reprinted 1965, 1967, 1970, 1971, 1973, 1974.

Augustine, St. *The Confessions*, translated by Edward Bouverie Pusey, Great Books of the Western World, Vol. 18. Chicago: Encyclopedia Britannica, 1955.

Baillie, John. *A Diary of Readings*. New York: Charles Scribner's Sons, 1955.

_______. *The Sense of the Presence of God*. New York: Charles Scribner's Sons, 1962.

Baker, F. Augustin. *Holy Wisdom* (Directions for the Prayer of Contemplation). London: Burns, Oates and Washbourne, Ltd.

Bayly, Lewis. *Practice of Piety*. New York and London: Harper and Row, 1976.

Boehme, Jacob. *The Way to Christ*, translated by Peter Erb. Paulist Press, 1978.

Bonhoeffer, Dietrich. *The Cost of Discipleship*, translated by R. H. Fuller. London: SCM Press, 1959.

●● _______. *Letters and Papers from Prison*, revised and enlarged edition. New York: Macmillan, 1971.

Bernard of Clairvaux. *The Steps of Humility*, translated by G. B. Burch. Cambridge, MA: Harvard University Press, 1950.

_______. *On the Love of God*, ed. by H. Martin. London: SCM Press, 1959.

Brinton, Howard H. *Creative Worship*. London: Allen and Unwin Ltd., 1932, Swarthmore Lecture.

_______. *Critique by Eternity*. Wallingford, PA: Pendle Hill, 1943.

_______. *Divine and Human Society*, 1938, Wm. Penn Lecture.

Brunner, Cornelia. "Betty, A Way of Individuation," *Inward Light* #37. Washington, DC: Friends Conference on Religion and Psychology, Fall, 1950.

●● Buber, Martin. *I and Thou*, translated by W. Kaufmann. New York: Charles Scribner's Sons, 1970.

_______. *Tales of the Hassidim*. New York: Schocken, fifth printing, 1970.

Bunyan, John. *Pilgrim's Progress*, ed. by J. B. Wharey. Oxford: Clarendon Press, 1960, 2nd edition.

Chapman, Dom John. *The Spiritual Letters*. London: Sheed and Ward, 2nd edition, 1944.

Chapman, Raymond. *The Loneliness of Man*. Philadelphia: Fortress Press, 1963.

Cheney, Sheldon. *Men Who Have Walked With God*. New York: Alfred A. Knopf, 1946.

Coburn, John Bowen. *Prayer and Personal Religion*. Philadelphia: Westminster Press, 1957.

_______. *Twentieth Century Spiritual Letters*. Philadelphia: Westminster Press, 1967.

_______. *A Life to Live--A Way to Pray*. New York: Seabury Press, 1973.

_______. *A Diary of Prayers: Personal and Private*. Philadelphia: Westminster Press, 1975.

_______. *The Hope of Glory*. New York: Seabury Press, 1978.

deSales, Francis. *Introduction to a Devout Life*, translated by John K. Ryan. Garden City, New York: Image Books, 1950 and 1955.

_______. *The Love of God*, translated by V. Kerns. London: Burns and Oates, 1962.

Delp, Alfred. *The Prison Meditations of Father Alfred Delp*. New York: Herder and Herder, 1963.

Donne, John. *Devotions upon Emergent Occasions*. Ann Arbor: Univ. of Michigan Press, 1959.

●● Dunnam, Maxie. *The Workbook of Intercessory Prayer*. Nashville: The Upper Room, 1979.

●● Eckhart, Meister, translated and Introduction by R. B. Blakney. New York: Harper and Brothers Publishers, 1941.

●● Edwards, Tilden. *Spiritual Friend*. New York: Paulist Press, 1950.

●● Fénelon, François. *The Royal Way of the Cross*, letters and spiritual counsels of François Fénelon, translated by H. Sidney Lear, edited by Hall McElwaine Helms. Orleans, MA: The Community of Jesus, Inc., 1980.

_______. *Christian Perfection*. New York: Harper and Brothers Publishers, 1947.

Fox, George. *The Journal of George Fox*, #754, Everyman's Library. New York: E. P. Dutton and Company, 1924.

Friedman, Maurice. *Touchstones of Reality*. New York: E. P. Dutton, first edition, 1972.

Francis of Assisi, St. *The Little Flowers of St. Francis*. New York: E. P. Dutton, 1950.

_______. *Little Plays of St. Francis*, a dramatic cycle from the life and legend of St. Francis of Assisi, by Laurence Housman with a preface by H. Granville-Barker. New York: Jonathan Cape and Harrison Smith, n.d.

_______. *The Writings of St. Francis of Assisi*, translated by Paschal Robinson. Philadelphia: The Dolphin Press, 1906.

Frost, Bede. *The Art of Mental Prayer*. Milwaukee: Morehouse, 1931.

Grou, Jean Nicholas. *Manual for Interior Souls*, edited by Donal O'Sullivan. Westminster, MD: Newman Press, 1955.

_______. *Meditations on the Love of God*. London: Burns, Oates and Washbourne, 1948.

Hammarskjöld, Dag. *Markings*, translated by L. Sjoberg and W. H. Auden. New York: Alfred A. Knopf, 1964.

Häring, Bernard. *Embattled Witness: Memories of a Time of War*. New York: Seabury Press, a Crossroad Book, 1976.

_______. *Christian Maturity*. New York: Herder and Herder, 1944.

Heard, Gerald. *A Preface to Prayer*. New York and London: Harper and Brothers Publishers, 1944.

_______. *Training for a Life of Growth*. Santa Monica, CA: The Wayfarer Press, 1959.

_______. *Training for the Life of the Spirit*, new edition, Vol. #1. Blauvelt, NY: Steiner Books, 1976.

_______. *Training for the Life of the Spirit*, Vol. #2. Blauvelt, NY: Steiner Books, 1978.

Herman, Emily. *Creative Prayer*. New York & London: Harper and Brothers Publishers, 1934.

Hilton, Walter. *The Scale of Perfection*, translated by Leo Sherley Price. St. Meinrad, IN: Abbey Press, 1975.

Hollander, Annette, M. D. *How to Help Your Child Have a Spiritual Life* (A Parent's Guide to Inner Development). New York: A & W Publishers, Inc., 1980.

Holy Scripture. *The New Testament in Modern English*, translated by J. B. Phillips. New York: Macmillan, 1959.

_______. *The New English Bible*. New York: Oxford University Press, 1961-1970.

Huxley, Aldous. *The Perennial Philosophy*. New York: Harper and Row, 1945.

Inge, W. R. *Personal Religion and the Life of Devotion*. London: Longmans Green and Company, 1924.

_______. *Light, Life and Love*. London: Methuen Company, 1904.

James, William. *The Varieties of Religious Experience*. Garden City, NY: Doubleday and Company, 1978.

Jones, Rufus. *The Luminous Trail*. New York: The Macmillan Company, 1947.

_______. *Spiritual Energies in Daily Life*, New and Revised Edition. New York: The Macmillan Company, 1936.

_______. *Social Law in the Spiritual World--Studies in Human and Divine Inter-Relations*. Darley, PA: Arden Library, 1978. Reprint of 1904.

_______. *The Testimony of the Soul*. New York: The Macmillan Company, 1936.

John of the Cross, St. *Complete Works*, translated by Padre Silverio, edited by E. A. Peers. Westminster, MD: Newman Press, 1964.

_______. *Dark Night of the Soul*, translated by Allison Peers. Garden City, NY: Image Books, Doubleday and Company, 1959.

Julian of Norwich. *Revelations of Divine Love*, edited by Grace Warrack. London: Methuen Company, 1973.

●● Kelly, Thomas R. *A Testament of Devotion*, with biographical memoirs by Douglas V. Steere. New York and London: Harper and Brothers Publishers, 1941.

_______. *The Eternal Promise*. New York: Harper and Row, 1966.

_______. *Realities of the Spiritual World*. Wallingford, PA: Pendle Hill, 1942.

●● Kelsey, Morton T. *The Other Side of Silence* (A Guide to Christian Meditation). New York: Paulist Press, 1976.

●● Kempis, Thomas. *The Imitation of Christ*. New York: E. P. Dutton, 1976.

●● Kierkegaard, Søren. *Purity of Heart*, translated by Douglas V. Steere. New York: Harper and Brothers Publishers, 1938.

_______. *For Self Examination*. New York and London: Oxford Univ. Press, 1941.

Larsen, Johannes Anker. *With the Door Open*. New York: The Macmillan Company, 1931.

Law, William. *A Serious Call to a Devout and Holy Life*. Philadelphia: Westminster Press, 1955.

●● Lawrence of the Resurrection, Br. *The Practice of the Presence of God*. London: SCM Press. Old Tappan, NJ: Fleming A. Revell, 1956.

Leech, Kenneth. *Soul Friend: The Practice of Christian Spirituality*. San Francisco: Harper and Row Publishers, 1977.

LeShan, Lawrence. *How to Meditate*. Boston: Little, Brown and Company, Bantam Books, 1974 and seven later printings.

_______. *The Medium, the Mystic and the Physicist*. New York: Ballantine Books, an Esalen Book, 1974.

Lewis, C. S. *The Screwtape Letters and Screwtape Proposes a Toast*. New York: The Macmillan Company, 1966.

Liberman, Francis. *Spiritual Letters*, translated by Walter van de Putte. Pittsburgh, PA: Duquesne University Press, 1962, 1963, 1964, 1966.

●● Lilje, Hanns. *The Valley of the Shadow*, translated by Olive Wyon. Philadelphia: Fortress Press, 1977.

Macleod, George. *We Shall Rebuild*. Philadelphia: Kirkridge Pub., 1945.

Merton, Thomas. *No Man is an Island*. New York: Dell Pub. Company, a Chapel Book, 1955.

_______. *Life and Holiness*. New York: Doubleday and Company, Image Books, 1964.

●● _______. *New Seeds of Contemplation*. New York: New Directions Publishing Corp., a New Direction Book, 1972.

_______. *Thoughts in Solitude*. London: Burns and Oates, 1958.

Moustakas, Clark E. *Loneliness*. Englewood Cliffs, NJ: Prentice Hall, Inc. A Spectrum Book, 1961.

●● Muto, Susan. *Approaching the Sacred: An Introduction to Spiritual Reading*. Denville, NJ: Dimension Books, 1973.

_______. *A Practical Guide to Spiritual Reading*. Denville, NJ: Dimension Books, 1976.

_______. *Renewed at Each Awakening* (the Formative Power of Sacred Words). Denville, NJ: Dimension Books, 1979.

●● _______. *Steps Along the Way: the Path of Spiritual Reading*. Denville, NJ: Dimension Books, 1975.

_______. *The Journey Homeward on the Road of Spiritual Reading*. Denville, NJ: Dimension Books, 1977.

_______. *Celebrating the Single Life: A Spirituality for Single Persons in Today's World*. Garden City, NY: Doubleday and Company, Inc., 1982.

_______. *Blessings that Make Us Be*. New York: Crossroad, 1982.

Nicholas of Cusa. *The Vision of God*, with an introduction by E. Underhill. New York: F. Ungar Pub. Co., 1960.

●● Nouwen, Henri J. M. *Out of Solitude: Three Meditations on the Christian Life*. South Bend, IN: Ave Maria Press, Notre Dame, 1974.

●● _______. *Reaching Out: The Three Movements of the Spiritual Life*. Garden City, NY: Doubleday and Company, 1975.

_______. *The Genesee Diary*. Garden City, NY: Doubleday and Company, 1976.

O'Connor, Elizabeth. *Journey Inward--Journey Outward.* New York and London: Harper and Row, 1968.

———. *Our Many Selves.* New York and London: Harper and Row, 1957.

Otto, Rudolph. *Mysticism East and West.* New York: The Macmillan Company, 1972.

Pascal, Blaise. *Pensées.* New York: Penguin Press, 1966.

Paulsell, William O. *Taste and See: A Personal Guide to the Spiritual Life.* Nashville: The Upper Room, 1976.

Penn, William. *No Cross, No Crown.* Philadelphia, PA: for sale at Friends Book Store, n.d.

Phillips, Dorothy. *The Choice is Always Ours* (an Anthology on the Religious Way). New York: Richard R. Smith, 1948.

Raines, Robert. *Creative Brooding,* edited by R. A. Raines. New York: The Macmillan Company, 1966.

Rhude, Beth E. *Live the Questions Now: The Interior Life.* Women's Division, Board of Global Ministries, The United Methodist Church, 1980.

Rolle, Richard. *The Fire of Love: Le Chant d'Amour,* in French. Paris: Cerf, 1971.

Scougal, Henry. *The Life of God in the Soul of Man.* Philadelphia: Westminster Press, 1948.

Smith, Bradford. *Meditation.* Philadelphia and New York: Lippincott, 1963.

●● ———. *Dear Gift of Life.* Lebanon, PA: Pendle Hill Pamphlet, Sowers Printing Company, 1965.

Steere, Douglas V. *Dimensions of Prayer.* New York: Women's Division of Christian Service, 1962.

●● ———. *On Beginning From Within.* New York and London: Harper and Brothers Publishers, 1943.

———. *Prayer and Worship.* Richmond, IN: Friends United Press, 1978.

●● ———. *Doors Into Life* (Through Five Devotional Classics). New York: Harper and Brothers Publishers, 1948. First printing of the Upper Room edition, 1981.

———. *Work and Contemplation.* New York: Harper and Brothers Publishers, 1957.

Stolpe, Sven. *Dag Hammarskjöld*: A Spiritual Portrait. New York: Charles Scribner's Sons, 1966.

●● Strong, Mary. *Letters of the Scattered Brotherhood,* edited by M. Strong. New York: Harper and Brothers Publishers, 1948.

Suso, Henry. *The Exemplar: Life and Writings of Blessed Henry Suso,* two volumes translated by Sister M. Ann Edward. Dubuque, Iowa: Priory Press, 1966.

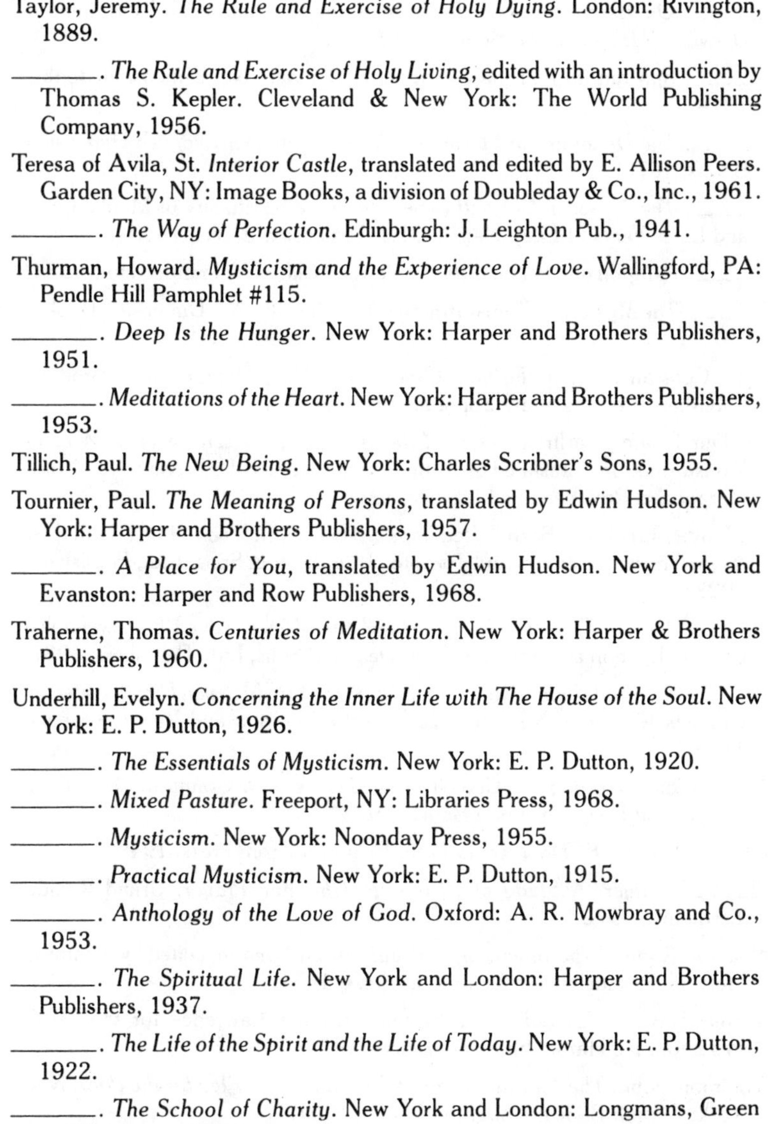

Taylor, Jeremy. *The Rule and Exercise of Holy Dying*. London: Rivington, 1889.

_______. *The Rule and Exercise of Holy Living*, edited with an introduction by Thomas S. Kepler. Cleveland & New York: The World Publishing Company, 1956.

Teresa of Avila, St. *Interior Castle*, translated and edited by E. Allison Peers. Garden City, NY: Image Books, a division of Doubleday & Co., Inc., 1961.

_______. *The Way of Perfection*. Edinburgh: J. Leighton Pub., 1941.

●● Thurman, Howard. *Mysticism and the Experience of Love*. Wallingford, PA: Pendle Hill Pamphlet #115.

●● _______. *Deep Is the Hunger*. New York: Harper and Brothers Publishers, 1951.

_______. *Meditations of the Heart*. New York: Harper and Brothers Publishers, 1953.

Tillich, Paul. *The New Being*. New York: Charles Scribner's Sons, 1955.

●● Tournier, Paul. *The Meaning of Persons*, translated by Edwin Hudson. New York: Harper and Brothers Publishers, 1957.

●● _______. *A Place for You*, translated by Edwin Hudson. New York and Evanston: Harper and Row Publishers, 1968.

Traherne, Thomas. *Centuries of Meditation*. New York: Harper & Brothers Publishers, 1960.

Underhill, Evelyn. *Concerning the Inner Life with The House of the Soul*. New York: E. P. Dutton, 1926.

_______. *The Essentials of Mysticism*. New York: E. P. Dutton, 1920.

_______. *Mixed Pasture*. Freeport, NY: Libraries Press, 1968.

_______. *Mysticism*. New York: Noonday Press, 1955.

_______. *Practical Mysticism*. New York: E. P. Dutton, 1915.

_______. *Anthology of the Love of God*. Oxford: A. R. Mowbray and Co., 1953.

_______. *The Spiritual Life*. New York and London: Harper and Brothers Publishers, 1937.

_______. *The Life of the Spirit and the Life of Today*. New York: E. P. Dutton, 1922.

_______. *The School of Charity*. New York and London: Longmans, Green and Company, 1956.

Van Kaam, Adrian. *Fulfillment in the Religious Life*. Denville, NJ: Dimension Books, 1969.

●● _______. *On Being Involved* (The Rhythm of Involvement and Detachment in Human Life). Denville, NJ: Dimension Books, 1970.

●● _______. *On Being Yourself: Reflections on Spirituality and Originality*. Denville, NJ: Dimension Books, 1972.

●● _______. *Spirituality and the Gentle Life*. Denville, NJ: Dimension Books, 1974.

_______. *The Dynamics of Spiritual Self-Direction*. Denville, NJ: Dimension Books, 1976.

_______. *The Transcendent Self* (The Formative Spirituality of Middle Early and Later Years of Life). Denville, NJ: Dimension Books, 1979.

_______. *Religion and Personality*. Englewood Cliffs, NJ: Prentice-Hall, 1964.

_______. *The Mystery of Transforming Love*. Denville, NJ: Dimension Books, 1972.

Vigil, Constancio. *The Fallow Land*. New York: Harper and Brothers Publishers. Permission by Editorial Atlantida, S.A., n.d.

von Dürckheim, Karlfried. *Daily Life as Spiritual Exercise: The Way of Transformation*, translated by Ruth Lewinneck and P. L. Travers. New York: Harper and Row Perennial Library, 1972.

von Hügel, Friedrich, Baron. *Readings from Friedrich von Hügel*, edited by Algar Thorold. London and Toronto: J. M. Dent & Sons, Ltd., Publishers, 1928.

_______. *Letters From Baron von Hügel* to a Niece, edited by Gwendolen Greene. London and Toronto: J. M. Dent and Sons, Ltd., Publishers, 1932.

●● _______. *Spiritual Counsel and Letters of Baron Friedrich von Hügel*, edited by Douglas V. Steere. New York & Evanston: Harper and Row Publishers, 1964.

Weil, Simone. *Waiting for God*, translated by Emma Craufurd. New York: Harper and Row, Colophon Books, 1973.

Whiston, Charles F. *Teach Us to Pray*. Boston: Pilgrim Press, 1949.

_______. *Prayer, A Study of Distinctive Christian Prayer*. Grand Rapids: Eerdmans, 1972.

Williams, Roger. *Experiments of Spiritual Life and Health*, edited by Winthrop Hudson. Philadelphia: Westminster Press, 1951.

Winter, David. *Closer Than a Brother* (Brother Lawrence for the 70's). Wheaton, IL: Harold Shaw Publishers, 1971.

Woolman, John. *The Journal of John Woolman and a Plea for the Poor*. New York: Corinth Books, Houghton Mifflin, 1961.

Wyon, Olive. *The School of Prayer*. Philadelphia: Westminster Press, 1944.

_______. *On the Way*. Philadelphia: Westminster Press, 1958.

_______. *Radiant Freedom: The Story of Emma Pieczynska*. London: Redhill, Lutterworth Press, 1942.

Spiritual Disciplines for Everyday Living

LEADER'S GUIDE

Suggestions for Directors of Seminars

Objectives

To acquaint individuals with those characteristics of the life of the spirit which, when understood and practiced, make for more creative, joyful living.

To assist persons to read reflectively and meditatively in depth.

To assist persons to become open and teachable in living with the great truths of their inherited faith, and with each other.

To provide insight and inspiration which will encourage individuals to become pilgrims in the life of the spirit.

Recruitment

Individuals should be invited on an informal basis. Generally there are a fair number of persons in churches and in graduate seminaries who are hungering for some solid nourishment in the things of the spirit, so that the offering of this seminar can be quietly promoted by word of mouth. A general announcement may be made but this should not be promoted with the idea that this seminar will be a sell-out success in an adult education series among other study groups.

Twenty persons constitute the maximum number to be enrolled. Twelve to sixteen is optimum, and six to eight the preferred minimum. If you find that there are more than twenty persons interested in joining the seminar, then schedule two parallel seminars. Or if the first seminar generates sufficient interest, then begin a second group whenever it is convenient.

There should emerge from the first seminar one or two persons who might become directors for similar seminars in succeeding years.

Prior to the first meeting of the seminar group, I have tried to talk with each person who has enrolled to be sure their expectations are in keeping with the aims and objectives we have in mind.

For example, I make it clear that this seminar is *not* a lecture-discussion class, nor is it an arena for theological or biblical argument. It is an exploration into the deeper meaning of the disciplined spiritual life, and this calls for open, seeking minds and hearts. I also indicate that while attendance will not be taken, it is expected that all who come will be there every week, barring illness or emergencies. To have people attend irregularly is to reduce seriously the quality of the group experience as well as impede its progress.

If people think to use this seminar as a means for advancing a particular biblical or theological point of view, then they would be well advised to find another forum.

If they are simply interested in another "course" in which they may, in a detached way, look at the content of the book with a critical and judgmental purpose in mind, then it will be a great disappointment to them and they should seek some other study group.

If individuals plan to come to this seminar in a window shopping mood then this seminar is certainly not for them.

Individuals who will find this an exciting, satisfying experience are those who will come caring enough to participate in all the sessions; who wish to enhance and enrich their faith, and who will be open to discovering from their reading and from other seminar members the broader dimensions of the truths they themselves hold. They will be willing to work at translating the insights gained into experiential reality at home, at work, and in all other aspects of their daily living.

Schedule

Within the seminaries, the seminar is offered on either a ten-week quarter plan, or a 13-14 week semester schedule for two and one-half hours, one day or evening each week.

Church groups usually meet for no more than two hours and for a ten-week period. In practice, however, these groups tend to go on beyond the two-hour limit, but never more than an extra half to three-quarters of an hour.

The ten to thirteen week format allows you to work through the entire ten chapters in a serious and relatively unhurried fashion. After this initial coverage, church groups often decide to continue meeting regularly. Several seminars have chosen to continue by returning for another nine or ten weeks to deal with each of these disciplines from the perspective: what additional insights have been discovered, what new ways have individuals begun the practice of each of these, and what next steps should be taken in this quest? Several seminars have continued from September through June, and after two months summer break have resumed again in the fall. The point is this: the seminar should go as long as there is the spirit and the initiative from within to continue it. But it must never be allowed to be frozen into some sort of dutifully perpetuated course.

It is hoped that the persons in such a seminar may decide to expand their knowledge of the life of the spirit through a study and practice of prayer, or they may decide to explore and integrate the serious task of journalling into their discipline. They may decide to undertake serious reading in depth of a number of the "family documents" of their own choosing.

This original seminar has proven to be the place of beginning and the means of inspiring persons to undertake any number of additional journeys into the vast resources of the spiritual life, individually or through the continuation of the seminar.

The Setting for the Seminar

The usual class-room set-up should be avoided at all costs. A large living room in someone's home is ideal, and preferably one that can be used regularly. The church parlor or lounge may be equally suitable. A variety of comfortable chairs in a circular arrangement provides an atmosphere conducive to openness. Seminaries generally have attractive lounges, seminar rooms or even board rooms which can be used.

Start on time, and break for ten minutes mid-way in the two and one-half hour stretch. Evening seminars have been successfully run either from 7-9:30 or from 7:30-10 P.M. The seminarians often prefer the earlier hour and lay persons like the extra half hour before beginning.

If the seminar is held in a home, it is best to agree that no refreshments are to be served; to do so introduces a whole new set of logistics which detract from the main purpose. Such socializing techniques are not at all necessary for the group will soon establish deeper and more lasting ties with one another that make the refreshment pattern unnecessary.

Requirements

For Church Groups

Here no graduate credit is involved. We concentrate on this source-text book, by reading, during the week, the chapter which will be under discussion at the next meeting of the group. I have found that many persons are interested in the bibliography and often want to know which books would be basic to building their own devotional libraries. Books starred in the bibliography are among those I have recommended which are in print, or may possibly be found in rare book stores and which do make a good initial collection.

In the two church groups in Pittsburgh, I took copies of many of these recommended books for those interested in buying some or all of them. Many persons bought most if not all of them. A good number of persons did reading on their own in these books simultaneously with the seminar reading and on a number of occasions would bring quotations and ideas from these volumes that were germane to the subject under consideration on a particular evening. However, there is no required additional reading for church groups.

For Seminary Credit

If the seminar is being given for graduate credit, then each director will have to work out a satisfactory set of requirements in addition to attendance and the reading of this source-text itself. I tried the term paper route and found that with every other professor requiring a term paper, one more for my seminar would further contribute to the superficiality of most such research simply because of the quantitative demands. Therefore, I have come more and more to ask for four book reviews in depth from these great devotional classics. Again, I offer these students the recommended books, asking them to select four of them for review and for possible purchase as the beginning of their own libraries in this field of spiritual discipline.

Since I'm not interested in the usual book review, I offer them some suggestions which are designed to help them read in depth and translate the insight of the book more surely into their understanding and their lives.

Final examinations in the seminar are singularly out of place. Each director will need to determine upon a method for discovering the degree of growth, insight and discernment experienced by each student, and that is no easy task. I'm still working at this, and cannot give any conclusive statement as to what is best.

Grades are another serious problem for such a graduate seminar. Frequently, where this is possible, students, at the outset, have elected to go the pass-fail route. It is important to talk through this question at the beginning of the seminar, and agree upon the expectations and standards for grading.

The Conduct of the Seminar

In the first meeting, work through the material in the Introduction and the first two chapters, so that there is some understanding of the radically different approach that is called for in this study.

As the seminar progresses you may have occasion to refer back to some of these essential directions if people are to be helped into a fuller experience of the content and resulting action offered.

Then take the chapters, beginning with Chapter III, one each week. There is no way you can cover everything, nor is it necessary to "get through" the material the way one does in a regular text-book course. What you are attempting to do each week is to demonstrate a method for enabling people to discover some of the insights in these writings quoted from the "family documents." In so doing, they may be challenged to live with all of the writing in each chapter over a period of years. At just this point, the Reflection and Action sections are designed to assist in this very process.

Right here it is important to emphasize the principle of "out and back," which is a strategic and integral element in the entire plan and program. All persons are encouraged to talk about the insights they have from their own experiences with, for example humility. They are also encouraged to live during the next week in open sensitivity to all evidences of genuine humility they see around them, as well as all experiences of pride which they find in themselves and others which is often destroying human relations in front of their very eyes. They are also encouraged to begin asking about the approaches they could take to help themselves as well as others to engage in the discipline of genuine humility.

People then come back to the seminar to add the experiential dimension to any further consideration of humility. Often after a week of this, people will return to the seminar with very helpful insights which they are eager to share with the group. If this happens, you ought to encourage the dialogue this will create. Do not worry about cutting into the time for considering the next discipline. You will find ways of allowing full time for the consideration of each discipline.

You too may have something to add from your own experience of living with humility the past week. Feel free to add your insight but *do it as one member of the group and not as director*.

And while we are talking about your contribution as director, here are several other important directions to keep in mind. Avoid doing a lot of talking yourself. That is difficult to do because, as director, people will ask a question which can easily be interpreted as being directed to you; or their comments may be made in such a way that it appears that a response from the director is expected. I find it very easy to fall into this trap. It takes a lot of quick and stern self-discipline to turn the question or the comment to the others in the seminar and ask for their insights.

This approach calls for your following very closely the comments to be sure everyone stays with the idea or insight under discussion. If some of the observations tend to be diluted or lead off into fuzzy or irrelevant ideas, then it is your responsibility to bring the exploration back to the issue at hand. Keep it all open and don't let people run away with it by riding a favorite subject, or by having to have a word to say on every point that is made.

Encourage participation but do not insist, as an indicator of success, that everyone must have talked each time. If you conduct the seminar with a high degree of openness, before it is finished everyone may well have spoken but only when it was appropriate and they genuinely felt led to do so.

The two guidelines discussed in full in Chapter II, are particularly helpful as guarantees for openness and at the same time curtailing the over-talkative persons and gently encouraging the quiet ones. If there is basic acceptance about being non-judgmental and in regarding any person's comments as "the truth as that person sees it," you have two guideposts which will quietly and effectively keep the seminar moving in creative channels of reflection.

Specific Ways of Approaching Each Chapter

Begin by exploring the meaning of the central theme under the first heading. What is being said--what do you understand this to mean for each individual--where does this particular writing touch your life?

Then consider the selections from the "family documents" which follow. Ask persons to talk about any one of the selections that gave them a new look or deeper insight. If someone says, for example, "Number 4 really got to me," ask that person to read the quotation aloud and then talk about what happened and why she or he was turned on. Then ask for other reactions to this same selection in the interest of amplifying the meaning of the concept involved. After that, you may want to ask about other quotations that "turned people on."

If no one comes up immediately with an insight growing out of their reading of the selections, you may need to use one that spoke to you. Read it and then show the group how you arrived at your new level of understanding. This generally "primes the pump."

After this has run its course (and don't force everyone to speak), relate all these insights to the central theme. For example, in the chapter on interrelatedness, you could gather all of the ideas which were put forth in learning about our essential unity, and then with a broader understanding move into the section on *Reflection and Action*.

In dealing with this, allow enough time for responses to one or two of these suggestions or questions, but don't feel you have to have complete answers and decisions for all. It is important for people to experience the process whereby through reflection we can prepare ourselves for action, and possibly decide upon the appropriate next step to be taken. Encourage people to use these in their own meditation.

In preparation for the next seminar, some self-starters may have already done some reflecting and acting and will have some interesting comments to make.

The same procedure can then be used with the second and third sections of each chapter.

There is no way, in two and a half hours, that the group can cover all the material. Be content to have considered seriously *some of the best of each subheading*. Here you, as director, will have to pace the progress and often in a quiet but decided way move the group from one section to another. For example, in moving to selections from the "family documents," I often ask "which one of these selections really spoke to your condition?" Then in moving to the Reflection and Action section you might ask "did anyone have an answer to this first question or did any of you try out one of these suggestions?" If no one responds to either of these, then be prepared to lead them into a consideration of either one question or one suggestion. As the seminar moves on, there is usually a high degree of spontaneity in reacting to much of the content in each chapter.

While these questions and suggestions may prove to be helpful to you and the individuals in the seminar, you should feel free to present questions and suggestions of your own design. Don't feel bound to these in the text; use your own creativity and imaginative forethought, and invite individuals to come up with other questions and suggestions which may well prove to be even more valid than those printed in these pages.

Be creative in conducting the seminar. All of this is a guide which may be helpful, but it need not be rigidly followed. There is only one essential, namely that you and the group stay with the book until you have completed one careful walk-through. You will find that there are many fascinating and important related themes and ideas which will present themselves for consideration almost every time you meet. Recognize their significance and relevance, but plan to take these in depth at a later time--possibly as subject matter for future seminars, or for individual study.

How to Use the Selections in Chapter XI

Originally all of these quotations were a part of the main body of the text. In rearranging the entire book, it was felt that fewer quotes under each sub-heading would make for more effective use in the seminar discussions. The remainder of these selections are to be used by individuals either at the time each chapter is under consideration, or for devotional reading and reflection by each person, long after the seminar is over.

In preparation for each week it is important for *you* to have read these additional selections in Chapter XI relating to the appropriate chapter. Occasionally it would be helpful for you to introduce one of these selections into the discussion by asking the group to look at the one you have chosen--read it aloud and discuss it briefly. This will help people discover the added treasury of insight to be found in these additional selections.

People may want to make these selections part of their reading during each week--at least this could be a kind of elective reading for those who wish to get the full flavor of the "family documents" during the seminar.

The Place of Prayer

Each seminar develops its own style of operation. Recently, one group found it essential to begin with ten to fifteen minutes of silent prayer as a means of getting themselves out of the hectic diversity in which everyone lives. Most groups prefer a period of prayer at the conclusion of the meeting. Here too, whatever corporate prayer is undertaken should always be in response to God's leading and in fulfillment of individual and group yearning, never as an automatic, dutiful way of opening or closing the seminar.

In a number of seminars the natural movement has been toward intercessory prayer relating to the individuals within the group, as well as to persons for whom each one of them may intercede. If this becomes a prime factor in any one of the seminars you are conducting, then here are three modest but effective devotional exercises which the group may wish to adopt.

1. The first of these is best used at the conclusion of the seminar dealing with Chapter III, Interrelatedness. This exercise involves the use of these ten adverbs:

Quietly	Trustfully
Easily	Serenely
Restfully	Joyously
Patiently	Courageously
Peacefully	Confidently

Invite each person to write down after each adverb what first comes to mind. This may be a word, a phrase, a sentence. *Do not* try for definition, or carefully thought out meditation.

All that is wanted is each person's first reaction. Do not insist that every adverb have a reaction--just as many as possible within ten to twelve minutes writing time.

Then provide an opportunity for people, as they wish, to read aloud what they have written. In the reading, as we listen with sensitivity, we discover persons are actually telling us a little more about themselves.

Remember that all through the previous sessions as individuals have felt free to state the truth as they understand it without being judged, such truth speaking often gives us deeper insight into the person speaking.

With such previous insight and out of the adverb exercise, we are then in a position to offer intercessory prayer for each other. It has been most creative, after people have spoken of their written responses to the adverbs, to ask that in prayerful silence we lift each person up to God by simply offering to God what insights we have concerning each individual. We make no demands nor special requests, just the offering of each other to be responsible to the leading of God's spirit.

Many years ago a friend of mine introduced me to these ten adverbs to be used as a Lenten exercise.

Here's where imaginative forethought may well come again into play. Try repeating and reflecting briefly on each of these adverbs just before you must participate in an adversary situation, where conflict resolution is required. People who have tried this discover attitudinal changes can take place as they try to work through the issue at hand. Try repeating as many of these as possible while waiting for the traffic light to change. Or try repeating them while shaving, drying or combing your hair, or while standing at the check-out counter at the super-market. Or if you ride the bus, train or subway to work, try this exercise during the trip. What would happen if this exercise were introduced for group reflection in your car pool? Why not try it?

Thus with the use of imaginative forethought there can be many more interesting ways in which individuals will discover the possibilities of this exercise for the enrichment of their spirits.

Actually such creative individual experiments could be reported back to the seminar.

2. *An Exercise with Music*: At the next or a subsequent seminar, the last thirty minutes can be taken with listening to a portion of a musical selection and then asking each person to describe his or her thoughts and reactions to what was heard. Any selection of symphonic or chamber music or other appropriate music will suffice. I like to use the last half of the third movement of Beethoven's Sixth Symphony, and the first

half of the fourth movement.

Again, in the spoken response, sensitive listening to what others are saying produces more understanding of each of the other persons present, thus broadening the base for the intercessory prayer that follows. After the talking is over, take time to lift each other into God's presence.

3. *An Exercise in Art*: Choose an art object--a small piece of sculpture, a carving, a painting, and use a concluding thirty minutes to invite everyone to respond in silence to this art work. Again ask people to share their spontaneous reactions as they considered this object.

By the time this third exercise is undertaken, the naturalness of personal disclosure will be quite genuinely given and accepted as persons continue to experience their way into what it means to offer intercessory prayer on behalf of each other.

After these three exercises, it remains for the seminar group to decide on next steps in providing the free space for intercession for others known and cared for by each individual.

From within the seminar participants there may come suggestions for additional devotional exercises which could be adopted by the group. The exercise in detachment found in Chapter VIII came from just such creative imagination. Several seminars have found that exercise to be a vivid way of thinking and feeling about detachment.

Conclusion

These suggestions are offered out of the experience of conducting twenty such seminars with seminarians, and with church groups. In all, many people have appreciated the openness of the whole approach and the freedom to explore as well as to react with a high degree of personal integrity to these disciplines of the spiritual life. However you amplify or modify all of this, do keep it open and free.

This very freedom, together with the earnest expectation of participating individuals, can be trusted to provide the climate in which God's spirit may illuminate and motivate people, in different ways, to discover the richness of the life of the spirit under these disciplines.

Notes

Notes

Notes

Notes